IN THE SHADE OF THE GIANT

California Slavic Studies, Vol. XIII

SERIES EDITORS

Nicholas V. Riasanovsky

Henrik Birnbaum

Thomas Eekman

Hugh McLean

IN THE
SHADE OF
THE GIANT

ESSAYS ON
TOLSTOY

EDITED BY
HUGH MCLEAN

University of California Press
Berkeley · Los Angeles · London

University of California Press
Berkeley and Los Angeles, California

University of California Press, Ltd.
London, England

© 1989 by
The Regents of the University of California

Library of Congress Cataloging-in-Publication Data
In the shade of the giant: essays on Tolstoy / edited by Hugh
McLean.
    p.   cm.—(California Slavic studies. 13)
    Bibliography: p.
    Includes index.
    ISBN 0-520-06405-4 (alk. paper)
    1. Tolstoy, Leo, graf, 1828-1910—Criticism and
interpretation. I. McLean, Hugh, 1925- . II. Series.
PG3410.I5   1989
891.73'3—dc19   88-20909
                                                CIP

Printed in the United States of America
1 2 3 4 5 6 7 8 9

In memory of
Gleb Struve
Co-founder and long-term editor of
California Slavic Studies

Contents

vii

Bibliographical Note

Unless otherwise indicated, all references to Tolstoy's works in this volume are cited from one of the following two editions: L. N. Tolstoj, *Polnoe sobranie sočinenij,* 90 vols. (Moscow, 1928–1958), the Jubilee Edition (hereafter referred to as *PSS,* followed by volume and page number); L. N. Tolstoj, *Sobranie sočinenij,* 20 vols. (Moscow, 1960–1965) (hereafter referred to as *SS,* followed by volume and page number).

Introduction

Hugh McLean

Tolstoy casts a long shadow. The only one of the nineteenth-century Russian giants to live on into our troubled century, he managed until his last breath to hold his grip on the world's attention. Even when he was an octogenarian, his domestic squabbles and his final pathetic decampment from ancestral home and wife of forty-eight years became a drama played on a world stage, just as thirty years earlier he had virtually obliged the world's clocks to stop while he wrestled with the "accursed questions": Why am I here? Why must I die? What should we do? Both these public dramas drew their emotional intensity from the conflict they embodied between two seemingly irreconcilable Tolstoyan personae, each seeking to negate the other: the husband, father, aristocratic landowner, and world-famous novelist on the one hand, and on the other the "humble" prophet of Christian anarchism, anticultural "simplification," and a love for others so undifferentiated that it could be bestowed equally on all fellow human beings.

These two Tolstoyan antagonists had already been masterfully adumbrated as literary characters. The first Tolstoy, lacking only his creator's literary talent, is Konstantin Levin, an efficient and enterprising farmer-manager, whose anguished philosophizing following upon his marriage and paternity seemed to have carried him through a typically Tolstoyan existential crisis to acceptance of himself both as fecund male and as a valid, contributing member of society. The second Tolstoy is Father Sergius, the guilt-ridden "saint" whose sanctity is repeatedly sullied by sexuality and pride and who finally seeks escape from himself and his ill-deserved fame into a dim obscurity in Siberia as "the hired man of a well-off peasant, working in the vegetable garden, teaching children, and attending to the sick."

Not even Tolstoy's death resolved the conflict. Succeeding generations have had to confront two seemingly incompatible Tolstoys and perhaps choose between them, sometimes working toward a sharper definition of the dualism. Isaiah Berlin's unforgettable application of the Archilochus metaphor of the hedgehog and the fox has become an indispensable part of the critical vocabulary of every student of Tolstoy, and more recently Richard Gustafson has offered an acutely perceived new version with his "resident" and "stranger."[1] The first, the Levinesque Tolstoy, seems to have had the greater staying power—Tolstoy as artist and "fox," inexhaustibly creative, uncannily perceptive, the exuberant celebrant of the life force; whereas after the terrible cataclysms and brutalities of the twentieth century "St. Leo" with his benignly utopian doctrines may seem hopelessly dated and naive. Yet, after all, it was precisely these doctrines that through Mohandas Gandhi inspired one of the great social metamorphoses of our time, the attainment of India's independence by nonviolent means, and, through Gandhi's impact on Martin Luther King, Jr., have left their mark on contemporary America.

Tolstoy's posthumous image of course looms largest in his homeland, though even there it is an image not devoid of anomalies. First of all, for Russians he is a figure justifying immense national pride, a preeminent literary master whose works are recognized the world over as belonging among the major classics of all time. With Tolstoy in their heritage Russians need experience no feelings of inferiority or backwardness. His claim to international homage is more widely accepted than that of any other Russian writer, even Pushkin (whose greatness is fully accessible only to those who can read him in Russian) or Dostoevsky (whom some still find too morbid, or too corrupted by ethnic hatreds, or—as Vladimir Nabokov professed to do—too slovenly an artist). All literate Russians read Tolstoy's novels as an integral part of growing up, and many read them again and again. Three places associated with Tolstoy have become national shrines: his ancestral estate at Yasnaya Polyana, his Moscow home at Khamovniki, and the railway station where he died, once called Astapovo, now rechristened Lev Tolstoy. Yet another Moscow building has been set aside as a Tolstoy museum, with a comprehensive library of Tolstoyana and a vast collection of Tolstoyan artifacts; in a nearby building the "steel room" where the millionaire A. I. Morozov once stored his stocks and bonds is now used to preserve Tolstoy's manuscripts.[2]

Beginning in 1928, the one-hundredth anniversary of Tolstoy's birth, the Soviet government gave full backing to a project to produce an impeccably scholarly edition of the complete works, the famous Jubilee Edition, that was to include not only published works but also diaries, letters, and drafts. The edition eventually ran to ninety volumes and was completed only in 1958. Since that date much new material has come to light, and an expanded edition may be undertaken soon. In the early phases of the Jubilee Edition the editor-in-chief was none other than Tolstoy's erstwhile disciple-in-chief, Vladimir Chertkov, who somehow managed to enforce a degree of piety toward the Tolstoyan texts not permitted in any other Soviet publication, including use of pre-Revolutionary orthography and capitalization of the word for God (Bog). (This dispensation, however, was summarily withdrawn after World War II, and Tolstoy's God, like everyone else's, was demoted to the lower case.) The Jubilee Edition dutifully included, though to be sure only in these expensive volumes with small press runs, all those Christian tracts and pacifist treatises that Tolstoy produced in his later years, works that make good Communists shudder with horror. There were, to be sure, some attempts in the 1930s to put a stop to such blasphemy, but in the end Tolstoyan piety prevailed. In the meantime, genuine followers of Tolstoy among the Russian peasantry were being energetically persecuted.[3]

From the official point of view it was—and is—important to protect the faithful against serious contamination by Tolstoyan heresy, and for mass consumption a "good" Tolstoy has therefore been selected and massively propagated. Mass editions are provided with insulating introductory articles presenting endless variations on themes derived from Communist scriptures, namely, the articles on Tolstoy penned by Lenin himself. From these sacred dicta comes the master formula that fits Tolstoy into the Marxist framework. Tolstoy, so the Leninist doctrine runs, at least in his later years became an ideologue of the "patriarchal peasantry." As such he stood in opposition both to his own class of aristocratic landowners and to the class of rapacious capitalists whose noxious ethos of greed and exploitation was beginning to pollute even sleepy rural Russia. Naturally, the patriarchal peasantry was too backward to understand either the advanced aspirations of the industrial working class or the realities of urban civilization; hence the limitations and dualism of Tolstoy's work, exhilaratingly right in its depiction of rural realities and of the degeneracy and corruption of the ruling classes, but naive and even reactionary in its proposed solutions. These sacred Leninist texts have been rehearsed, repeated, and explicated ad nauseam for generations now (in the Tolstoy Museum an entire drawer of the card catalogue is given over to works on the topic "Lenin and Tolstoy"). Still, one wonders whether the message has really been assimilated, for the Leninist filter appears to leak. In the reading room of the same museum, portraits of Lenin and Tolstoy face each other from opposite walls, and alongside each stands a glass case containing the complete edition of the man's works (for Tolstoy, the Jubilee Edition). The present writer spent six weeks in 1983 working daily in that reading room and observed that whereas the case with the Jubilee Edition was in constant and eager use, not one soul ever went near the Bolshevik leader's forlorn shelves.

Despite official constraints and taboos, however, Russian scholarship on Tolstoy has to its credit many brilliant and seminal achievements, beginning with the Jubilee Edition itself. From the early Soviet decades the outstanding contribution was undoubtedly the magnificent three volumes by Boris Eikhenbaum, to which he later added another; all but one of these have now been translated into English.[4] Eikhenbaum opened up whole new worlds, partly by the simple device of systematically reading all the books Tolstoy himself read and deducing the obvious linkages. Eikhenbaum's fellow formalist Viktor Shklovsky wrote a discerning book on *War and Peace* and, much later, an idiosyncratic but interesting biography.[5] The most important biographical study, however, is the monumental, though unfinished, work by Nikolai Gusev, subtitled modestly, in the Russian style, *Materials for a Biography*. After Gusev's death it was continued by Lidia Opulskaya.[6] Enormously meticulous and valuable textual studies have been carried out by Evelina Zaidenshnur and Vladimir Zhdanov.[7] Despite the dangerous proximity of religion, incisive studies of Tolstoy's intellectual development have been possible, camouflaged under the safer headings of "ethics" or "philosophy."[8] And there have been fruitful investigations of literary technique and style, both of individual novels and of Tolstoy's work as a whole.[9]

In the West until fairly recently most studies of Tolstoy were intended more for purposes of cultural intermediation than as original works of scholarship, but that qualification clearly no longer holds true. Western scholars have been able to venture into religious territory off limits to their Soviet colleagues, and they have also contributed many useful studies of Tolstoy's art.[10]

All post-Tolstoy writers, whether Russian or foreign, have had to contend with his image.[11] He and his books stand inescapably there, massive, majestic, seemingly impregnable. During his lifetime a few of his younger contemporaries, notably Chekhov and Gorky, managed to overcome their awe of the image and respond to the personality of the man. Chekhov, though first attracted by the moral force of Tolstoyanism, ultimately repudiated it as impracticable; and he could not stomach Tolstoy's cultural nihilism, his willful refusal to acknowledge the gigantic advances made in his lifetime by science and in particular by medicine. Nevertheless, Tolstoy always remained for Chekhov the supreme exemplar of literary excellence. As Chekhov once wrote to his friend Suvorin, "One thought of Tolstoy's Anna Karenina, and all Turgenev's ladies and their seductive shoulders collapse and disintegrate [*letjat k čortu*]."[12] And Gorky, though a reverent admirer of the writer, was also far from impressed by the pieties of "St. Leo." He has left us by far the most sensitive and revealing portrait we have of a complex, contradictory, and more human Tolstoy, the Tolstoy who kept escaping from behind the mask of "St. Leo," often mischievous, puckish, full of quirks and irreverences, the Tolstoy who said, "About women I'll tell the truth when I have one foot in the grave. I'll tell it, jump into my coffin, pull down the lid—and then [let them] try to get me!" [13]

Few Western writers had the opportunity for personal contact with Tolstoy, but they felt his spell nonetheless. Romain Rolland, who did have the good fortune to meet with Tolstoy, perhaps experienced the magic most profoundly. Though it was the art that first drew him to Tolstoy, in the end it was the moral grandeur of the old man that impressed him most: "In the gloomy twilight of the late nineteenth century [Tolstoy's light] shone as a star of consolation," as he wrote in his hagiographic *Vie de Tolstoi*.[14] The very bulk of Tolstoy's novels also perhaps inspired the creation of a whole library of giant literary works that proliferated in Europe in the decades after his death, including Rolland's own *Jean Christophe,* Roger Martin du Gard's *Thibaults,* and the greatest of them, *A la recherche du temps perdu.* Proust himself, incidentally, commented on the elephantine dimensions of Tolstoy, using them for a scatological put-down of Balzac. "Balzac," he wrote, "succeeds in giving the impression of greatness; in Tolstoi everything is great by nature—the droppings of an elephant beside those of a goat." [15]

It is hard to imagine two writers more diverse in style and temperament than G. B. Shaw and Tolstoy—the one irreverent, flashy, ready to sacrifice anything for the sake of a clever phrase; the other, at least in old age and in his public persona, earnest and serious, bearing on his shoulders the whole moral burden of mankind. Tolstoy had read some Shaw in 1908, probably *John Bull's Other Island* or *Major Barbara,* and judged him harshly: "I read Schaw [*sic*]," he wrote in his diary. "He is striking in his vulgarity. He not only has not a single idea of his own that rises above the vulgarity of the urban mob, but he does not understand a single great idea of the thinkers of the past." [16] Yet there were points of congruence too, among them shared skepticism about the world's idolatry of Shakespeare.[17] And in 1910 Shaw sent Tolstoy a copy of *The Showing-up of Blanco Posnet* with an accompanying letter in which, with characteristic Shavian wit, he defended himself against Tolstoy's charge of frivolousness: "You said that my manner in that book [*Man and Superman*] was not serious enough—that I make people laugh in my most earnest moments. But why should I not? Why should humour and laughter be excommunicated? Suppose the world were only one of God's jokes, would you work any the less to make it a good joke instead of a bad one?"[18] That wicked final sentence confirmed Tolstoy's low opinion of Shaw. On the envelope he wrote, "From Shaw clever stupidities," and in his formal reply, somewhat more tactfully, confessed that he had "received a very painful impression from the concluding words of your letter," reiterating what he had said earlier about *Man and Superman*, "The problem about God and evil is too important to be spoken of in jest."[19]

Shaw's fellow countryman James Joyce, author of the only twentieth-century novels, with the exception of Proust's masterpiece, that stand much chance of ranking alongside Tolstoy's in both dimensions and quality, had by the age of twenty-three already arrived at a balanced assessment of Tolstoy's place in Russian literature. Unlike Turgenev, Lermontov, Korolenko, and Gorky, each of whom has his limitations, "Tolstoy is a magnificent writer," Joyce wrote his brother. "He is never dull, never stupid, never tired, never pedantic, never theatrical! He is head and shoulders over the others." Joyce was also unimpressed by "St. Leo": "I don't take him very seriously as a Christian saint. I think he has a very genuine spiritual nature, but I suspect that he speaks the very best Russian with a St. Petersburg accent [technically wrong, but symbolically correct] and remembers the Christian name of his great-great grandfather."[20] Thirty years later, however, Joyce sent his daughter Lucia a volume of stories by Tolstoy including one very much the product of the would-be Christian saint, "How Much Land Does a Man Need?", and Joyce labeled it "the greatest short story to be found in world literature."[21]

The young Ernest Hemingway was more drawn to Turgenev, perhaps as fellow hunter and nature lover, than to Tolstoy, but he still thought Tolstoy had written the greatest book. "Turgenieff to me is the greatest writer there ever was," he wrote Archibald MacLeish in 1925. "Didn't write the greatest books, but was the greatest writer. . . . *War and Peace* is the best book I know, but imagine what a book it would have been if Turgenieff had written it."[22] Later on, however, Tolstoy seemed to have overtaken Turgenev in Hemingway's hierarchy of models or, rather, targets, for Hemingway, with that fatal instinct for self-parody that beset his later years, insisted on imagining himself in pugilistic combat with his great forebears:

> Am a man without any ambition, except to be champion of the world. I wouldn't fight Dr. Tolstoi in a 20 round bout because I know he would knock my ears off. The Dr. had terrific wind and could go forever and then some. But I would take him on for six and he would never hit me and I would knock the shit out of him and maybe knock him out. He is easy to hit. But boy how he can hit. If I can live to 60 I can beat him (MAYBE).[23]

Of all living writers, it would seem, it is Aleksandr Solzhenitsyn over whom Tolstoy casts the deepest shadow.[24] For Solzhenitsyn, Tolstoy is a constant presence, one who haunts him in all possible avatars: the beloved and benevolent forebear, the admired teacher and model, the overbearing antagonist to be wrestled with and perhaps defeated. The force of Tolstoy-as-model is immediately apparent to readers of Solzhenitsyn's novels, especially *The Red Wheel* (including its initial section, *August 1914*), which bids fair to emulate *War and Peace* both in its elephantine dimensions and in its effort to transform the novel into epic, making that private and personal genre encompass the theme of the destiny of nations. Solzhenitsyn seems to be the only writer bold enough to introduce Tolstoy as an actual literary character (in the second chapter of *August 1914*), an oracular old man timidly accosted by Sanya Lazhenitsyn (clearly modeled on Solzhenitsyn's father) in the gardens of Yasnaya Polyana. There Solzhenitsyn allows Sanya, despite his abashed inarticulateness, to get rather the best of the Master: "Lev Nikolaevich, are you sure that you are not exaggerating the power of love embedded in man? But what if love is not so strong, not so obligatory in everyone and does not prevail—why then won't your teaching prove fruitless? Or very, very premature?" To this Tolstoy can only repeat dogmatically, "Only with love." Nevertheless, Sanya's awe and reverence before the great sage remain overwhelming. And later, in *October 1916*, the same ex-Tolstoyan Sanya

Lazhenitsyn, who enlisted in the army in 1914 because he was "sorry for Russia," in a discussion with the chaplain, Father Severyan, is shown gravitating back toward the Orthodoxy of his childhood, despite a few rearguard Tolstoyan salvos concerning the church's indifference to the teachings of Jesus:

> Tolstoy is so sweeping in the way he repudiates everything, everything. The faith of simple folk, yes, of my parents, of our village, of everyone. Icons, candles, incense, holy water, wafers—all of that he sweeps away, leaving nothing. And the singing that rises to the cupola where the sun's rays mingle with the smoke of the incense. And these little candles—they come from the heart, and they point straight to heaven. And I love all that, simply from childhood. (chap. 5)

It is hoped that the present collection of essays will add some further illuminations to the world's quest for understanding and appreciation of the great Russian master.

NOTES

1. Isaiah Berlin, *The Hedgehog and the Fox: An Essay on Tolstoy's View of History* (New York, 1953). Richard F. Gustafson, *Leo Tolstoy, Resident and Stranger: A Study in Fiction and Theology* (Princeton, 1986).

2. E. S. Serebrovskaja, "Stal'naja komnata," in *Jasnopoljanskij sbornik* (Tula, 1968), pp. 89–99; V. F. Bulgakov, "Iz istorii muzeev L. N. Tolstogo v Moskve," in *Jasnopoljanskij sbornik*, pp. 22–44.

3. Mark Popovskij, *Russkie mužiki rasskazyvajut: Posledovateli L. N. Tolstogo v Sovetskom Sojuze, 1918–1977; dokumental'nyj rasskaz o krest'janakh-tolstovcakh v SSSR po materialam vyvezennogo na Zapad krest'janskogo arkhiva* (London, 1983).

4. Boris Ejkhenbaum, *Molodoj Tolstoj* (Petrograd, 1922); *Lev Tolstoj*, 2 vols. (Moscow, 1928–1931); *Lev Tolstoj v semidesjatye gody* (Leningrad, 1960); *The Young Tolstoy*, trans. Gary Kern (Ann Arbor, 1972); *Tolstoi in the Sixties*, trans. Duffield White (Ann Abor, 1982); *Tolstoi in the Seventies*, trans. Albert Kaspin (Ann Arbor, 1982).

5. Viktor Šklovskij, *Mater'jal i stil' v romane L'va Tolstogo "Vojna i mir"* (Moscow, 1929); *Lev Tolstoj* (Moscow, 1967).

6. Nikolaj Gusev, *Lev Nikolaevič Tolstoj*, 4 vols. (Moscow, 1954–1970); each volume is subtitled *Materialy k biografii*. Gusev's *Letopis' žizni i tvorčestva L. N. Tolstogo* (3d ed. Moscow, 1960) is also very valuable. Lidija Opul'skaja, *Lev Nikolaevič Tolstoj: Materialy k biografii s 1886 po 1892 god* (Moscow, 1979).

7. Evelina Zajdenšnur, *"Vojna i mir"* L. N. Tolstogo: Sozdanie velikoj knigi (Moscow, 1966); Vladimir Ždanov, Tvorčeskaja istorija *"Anny Kareninoj"*: Materialy i issledovanija (Moscow, 1957); Ot *"Anny Kareninoj"* k *"Voskreseniju"* (Moscow, 1967); Poslednie knigi L. N. Tolstogo (Moscow, 1971).
8. Boris Bursov, *Lev Tolstoj: Idejnye iskanija i tvorčeskij metod* (Moscow, 1960); Galina Galagan, L. N. Tolstoj: Khudožestvenno-ètičeskie iskanija (Leningrad, 1981); Elizaveta Kuprejanova, Èstetika L. N. Tolstogo (Moscow, 1966); Konstantin Lomunov, Èstetika L'va Tolstogo (Moscow, 1972).
9. Iakov Bilinkis, O tvorčestve L. N. Tolstogo: Očerki (Leningrad, 1959); Boris Bursov, *Lev Tolstoj i russkij roman* (Leningrad, 1963); Nikolaj Fortunatov, Tvorčeskaja laboratorija L. Tolstogo (Moscow, 1983); Pavel Gromov, O stile L'va Tolstogo (Leningrad, 1977); V. Kamjanov, Poètičeskij mir èposa: O romane L. Tolstogo *"Vojna i mir"* (Moscow, 1978); B. I. Kandiev, Roman-èpopeja L. N. Tolstogo *"Vojna i mir"* (Moscow, 1967); V. A. Kovalev, O stile khudožestvennoj prozy L. N. Tolstogo (Moscow, 1960); I. A. Potapov, Roman L. N. Tolstogo *"Vojna i mir"* (Moscow, 1979).
10. On religion: Gustafson, *Leo Tolstoy;* Nicolas Weisbein, L'évolution religieuse de Tolstoi (Paris, 1960). On Tolstoy's art: John Bayley, Tolstoy and the Novel (London, 1966); Ruth Crego Benson, *Women in Tolstoy: The Ideal and the Erotic* (Urbana, Ill., 1973); Reginald Christian, Tolstoy: A Critical Introduction (London, 1969), and Tolstoy's *"War and Peace"*: A Study (London, 1962); Sydney Schultze, The Structure of *"Anna Karenina"* (Ann Arbor, 1982); George Steiner, Tolstoy or Dostoevsky: An Essay in the Old Criticism (New York, 1959); Elisabeth Stenbock-Fermor, The Architecture of *"Anna Karenina"* (Lisse, 1975); Edward Wasiolek, Tolstoy's Major Fiction (Chicago, 1978).
11. For some of the references in this cursory and highly selective survey of foreign writers' responses to Tolstoy I am indebted to Tamara Motyleva's article "Lev Tolstoj i sovremennye inostrannye pisateli," in her Inostrannaja literatura i sovremennost' (Moscow, 1961), pp. 99–211. Her interpretations, however, are severely marred by Communist dogmatism and tendentiousness.
12. Cited from N. I. Gitovič, comp., Letopis' žizni i tvorčestva A. P. Čekhova (Moscow, 1955), p. 339, with use of the translation in Simon Karlinsky, ed., Letters of Anton Chekhov, trans. Michael Henry Heim (New York, 1973), p. 251. On Tolstoy and Chekhov, see Vladimir Lakšin, Tolstoj i Čekhov (Moscow, 1963; 2d ed. 1975).
13. A. M. Gor'kij, "Vospominanija o L've Nikolaeviče Tolstom," Sobranie sočinenij, 14 (1951): 290.
14. Romain Rolland, Vie de Tolstoi (Paris, 1911); cited from English translation, Tolstoi, trans. Bernard Miall (New York, 1911), p. 1.

15. Cited from *Marcel Proust on Art and Literature, 1896–1919*, trans. Sylvia Townsend Warner (New York, 1958), p. 378.

16. *PSS* 56:97.

17. See George Gibian, *Tolstoy and Shakespeare* (The Hague, 1957); S. M. Brejtburg, "B. Šou v spore s Tolstym o Šekspire," *Literaturnoe nasledstvo* 37–38 (1939): 617–32.

18. George Bernard Shaw, *Collected Letters, 1898–1910*, ed. Dan H. Laurence (London, 1972), p. 902.

19. Tolstoy to Shaw, 9 May 1910. *PSS* 81:254–55. The letter was written in Russian by Tolstoy and translated into English by Chertkov.

20. James Joyce to Stanislaus Joyce, July 1905. *Selected Letters of James Joyce*, ed. Richard Ellmann (New York, 1975), p. 73.

21. James Joyce to Lucia Joyce, 27 April 1935. *Selected Letters*, p. 372. Original in Italian: "Secondo me *How Much Land Does a Man Need* è la più grande novella che la letteratura del mondo conosce."

22. Hemingway to MacLeish, 20 December 1925. Ernest Hemingway, *Selected Letters, 1917–1961*, ed. Carlos Baker (New York, 1982), p. 179.

23. Hemingway to Charles Scribner, 6–7 September 1949. *Selected Letters*, p. 673.

24. Particularly illuminating on the subject of Solzhenitsyn and Tolstoy are two articles by Kathryn B. Feuer, "Solzhenitsyn and the Legacy of Tolstoy" and "*August 1914*: Solzhenitsyn and Tolstoy," in John B. Dunlop et al., eds., *Aleksandr Solzhenitsyn: Critical Essays and Documentary Materials* (Belmont, Mass., 1973), pp. 129–46; 372–81. The same volume contains an interesting article by Mary McCarthy, "The Tolstoy Connection," pp. 332–50. More recently, Vladislav Krasnov has discerningly reexamined the Solzhenitsyn-Tolstoy relationship in the light of the revised and much expanded version of *August 1914*: "Wrestling with Lev Tolstoi: War, Peace, and Revolution in Aleksandr Solzhenitsyn's New *Avgust Chetyrnadtsatogo*," *Slavic Review* 45 (Winter 1986): 707–19.

Allegro Tumultuosissimamente
Beethoven in Tolstoy's Fiction

Ruth Rischin

Music never was merely a pastime with Tolstoy but was a way of experiencing the quandary of himself, of testing to the boiling point his own principles and aesthetic values under the emotional impact of art. Unlike some of his contemporaries who incorporated musical motifs into their fiction, Tolstoy's musical allusions emerged out of his own experience not only as a listener but as a musician. The classical and romantic piano repertoire, selections from which he mastered in his youth and which he played alone or four hands, equipped him with the practical knowledge of the performer. Throughout his life Tolstoy theorized and talked about music with the many artists who visited him at Yasnaya Polyana. In his diary, his letters, and his polemical tracts he relentlessly dwelt on what to him was the central question of art, and he filled the pages of his novels and stories with accounts of the effect of music on his fictional listeners and performers. He never ceased to be confounded as well by the nature of music and its function in human society.

Over Tolstoy's ethical vision loom the two Titans of nineteenth-century music, Beethoven and Wagner. Wagner, in Tolstoy's view, was actually an anti-Titan, like Shakespeare—a pretentious dwarf masquerading as a giant. But Beethoven was another matter. Tolstoy responded to Beethoven's music in terms of a dichotomy between artistic practice and ethics that he began to formulate as early as the 1850s and that late in life he argued in the moral tracts of the 1890s.

Tolstoy first assessed Beethoven's music when as a young man he was bringing interior monologue as a technique of psychological delineation to early refinement in his prose. A great deal of scholarly attention has been focused on the poetic and often symbolic devices that Tolstoy evolved for portraying the inner life of his characters. Yet the connection between Tolstoy's creation of psychological metaphor and the role of music in his fiction remains virtually unexplored. Beethoven emerged as a controversial, catalyzing force both in Tolstoy's theory of art and in his novelistic practice. Nonetheless, in discussions of the allusions to Beethoven to be found in Tolstoy's works, the artistic manipulation of polemic often is overlooked. What, then, contributed to the dynamics of Tolstoy's reception of Beethoven, how was that reception incorporated into the poetics of Tolstoy's fiction, and how did it shape his moral stance as a writer?

Tolstoy's views on music inevitably grew out of the diversity of musical expression that was a natural part of his surroundings: songs of the mowers, gypsy and folk music, church liturgy, family music-making, chamber music performed by visiting artists. House music remained throughout Tolstoy's life the form of musical activity most readily available to him and that which he valued above all others. Ideologically, the musical life of Yasnaya Polyana thus became an extension of family experience and an expression of communal solidarity. By contrast, institutionalized music, connected to the social season of the capitals and dependent on a patronage of the privileged, acquired in Tolstoy's thinking a negative value.[1]

Tolstoy's aesthetic thinking developed pari passu with his studies as an amateur musician and his youthful theorizing about music. The years preceding the writing of *Childhood* were ones in which Tolstoy began a serious study of piano. In a diary notation of 1847, in keeping with a program of self-discipline, he enumerates as one of his goals "dostignut' srednej stepeni soveršcnstva v muzyke i živopisi" (to attain a middling degree of accomplishment in music and painting). In 1850 he outlines a daily regimen that includes "vse 24 gammy, vse akkordy, arpežio [*sic*] na dve oktavy" (all 24 scales, all chords, arpeggios in two octaves) in addition to learning the fingering for four pages of music.[2]

The same year he put in writing his theoretical ideas on the fundamentals of music. "Tri otryvki o muzyke" (Three Fragments about Music), his earliest attempts to define what music is, can be found in his notebook for June 1850. Only partially completed, the writings consist of three sections: "1) Vremennaja metoda dlja izučenija muzyki [A temporary method for the study of music]; 2) Znanie muzyki sub"ektivnoe i ob"ektivnoe [The subjective and objective meanings of music]; 3) Osnovnye načala muzyki i pravila k izučeniju onoj [The basic principles of music and rules for mastering it]."[3]

In these formulations Tolstoy, the piano student, tries to set forth a concept of music as an autonomous spatial-temporal construct. Thus, in the first he writes:

> Музыка есть выражение отношения звуков между собою по пространству и времени и силе; следовательно, познание музыки состоит в познании способа выражения звуков по пространству и времени, т. е., познание выражения интервалов между звуками по пространству и по времени и по силе.

> Music is the expression of the interrelationship of sounds in space and time and force; therefore, a knowledge of music consists of a knowledge of the expression of sounds in space and time, that is, a knowledge of the expression of intervals between sounds in space and time and force.[4]

He then proceeds in his analysis to a consideration of the arbitrary arrangement of intervals into octaves and the systemization of duration into concepts of musical time:

> Причина понятия о пространстве есть движение; движение же необходимо требует понятия о каких-либо пунктах или моментах. В пространстве музыкальном эти два момента суть верхние и нижние ноты, октавы и пр.—от *до* до *до* и от *ре* до *ре*.

> The cause of the conception of space is movement; movement necessitates the conception of some kind of points or moments. In musical space these two points are the higher and the lower notes, the octaves from *do* to *do*, from *re* to *re*, etc.[5]

This principle then leads to a speculation about musical infinity:

Пространство может представить себе всякий человек неограниченное; поэтому человек может себе представить
неограниченное число октав. . . . Временем между двумя
или несколькими звуками я называю меру протяжения
оных. . . . В музыкальном отношении эти два момента будут
началом и концом какой-либо музыкальной мысли. Так, как
и пространство, человек может себе представить время
неограниченным.

Any person can imagine boundless space; hence, a person can also
imagine a boundless number of octaves. . . . The time between two
or more sounds I call the measure of their duration. . . . In a musical relation these two moments will be the beginning and end of
some musical thought. Just as one can imagine space as boundless, so one can imagine time as boundless.[6]

In a section of the third fragment entitled "A Definition of
Music" (17 June 1850), Tolstoy for the first time anywhere in his
writings then expresses the idea on which his entire aesthetic system rests—namely, that music is an art that transmits emotion:

Есть четвертое значение музыки—значение поэтическое.
Музыка в этом смысле есть средство возбуждать через звук
известные чувства или передавать оныя.

There is a fourth meaning of music—a poetic meaning. Music in
this sense is the means to arouse certain feelings, or to transmit
them, through sounds.[7]

However rudimentary, Tolstoy's explorations in the fundamentals of music are suggestive. The understanding encapsulated
in these statements pointed the way to the means to metaphoriza-
tion. Once music is conceived of as a temporal-spatial phenomenon and a musical score as iconic in its vertical-horizontal representation of that abstraction, music can serve as a metaphor for
perceptions of the empirical world. Once intervals can be projected as a stream of sound—as "boundless octaves"—such an
understanding lends itself itself to comparison of music with
other dynamic processes such as that of unconscious thought.
Moreover, once music is perceived as having a connection to
feeling, musical experience, that is, the way music is heard,
can serve as a correlative for emotions and other extramusical
associations.

The realization that music can be an analogue of feeling reflects Tolstoy's acceptance of an aesthetic premise that extends back from Rousseau to Plato and Confucius. If the Chinese sage is credited with saying, "When touched by the external world, the heart is moved and therefore finds its expression in sounds," and the Greek philosopher with establishing a system of harmonics with a place for every gradation of emotion, it was the French encyclopedist who in the "Essai sur l'origine des langues" (1764) attempted to bestow on a definition of music the authority of the primordial.[8]

The common origin of speech, poetry, and song in the first sounds used by primitive man became the premise for construing music as an art that transmits emotion. Setting forth a systematized affective theory of music in the *Dictionnaire de musique* (1768), Rousseau extolled melody above all, as "an art of imitation by which the mind may be affected with different images, the heart be moved by different sentiments, the passions be excited and calmed; in a word, moral effect be operated, which surpasses the immediate empire of the senses."[9]

The didactic philosophers' assumption that music is an affective art lent itself to equating various emotional states with specific musical elements and assigning to each a moral valuation. The further elaboration of this principle established a connection between music and the running of social institutions: the notion, common to Confucius and Plato, that an orderly harmonics is necessary to an orderly society.

Tolstoy's high regard for vocal as opposed to instrumental music, his preference for uncomplicated, diatonic textures, and his mistrust of chromaticism all reflect an eclectic acceptance of the aesthetics of the French encyclopedists and their didactically minded predecessors. So evident is this attitude in his works that one can cull from them a morphology of musical metaphor. Thus, the human voice in its purity and delicacy is valued as a power, unseen but felt, that transforms moments in the life of listener and performer alike. The song of Steshka the gypsy ("Two Hussars"), Natasha's singing in *War and Peace,* the mowing songs of the harvesters in *Anna Karenina,* even the sound of the carillon in *Resurrection*—all carry a positive moral value. By contrast, the diminished seventh that Natasha hears at her first night at the opera, the unclear harmonic progressions of the "King Lear of the Steppe" fantasy which Levin criticizes, and the glutted texture and frenetic rhythms of "The Kreutzer Sonata" are all X-rated as experiences, because they express the equivocal in music. Except for Wagner, no composer fit more conveniently into this Rousseauean aesthetic morphology than did Beethoven.

Schopenhauer's philosophy, to which Tolstoy was introduced in the 1860s, presented an association of music and emotion that proved especially apposite to the author's own thinking. In chapter 52 of *Die Welt als Wille und Vorstellung* (1818), Schopenhauer advanced the theory that music is an image of individual striving for the fulfillment of all desires that contribute to the pain and travail of human experience—in short, an image of all that is to be understood by the philosopher's concept of the Will. The basis for this connection is the abstract nature of music, wherein it is unique among the arts.[10] Recognizing the essence of music to be that of sound in motion, Schopenhauer evolved a series of analogies that related the strivings of the Will to this principle of dynamism. Melody he regarded as the presentation of individual aspiration that was manifest both in the conscious and in the unconscious life.[11] Harmonic modulation, especially that from and to the tonic, in his view embodied a configuration of desires and temporary satisfactions which are never wholly fulfilled.[12] Schopenhauer thus understood music to be a kind of nondiscursive symbolism that related, but carried further into the more problematic areas of human psychology, the connection between feeling and form. Tolstoy encountered these ideas *after* he had himself undertaken theoretical explorations into the nature of music as a dynamic art, and they thus may have had an impact that was all the more important, given his early writings on the fundamentals of music. The lyricism and narrative terminology of Schopenhauer's excursuses ("[Music] tells . . . the story of the Will illuminated by self-awareness . . . but it expresses still more, it tells its most secret history") must have appealed to Tolstoy's novelistic imagination, for the idea that music tells the story of the Will is incorporated into musical metaphors in *War and Peace* and "The Kreutzer Sonata."[13] Later in life Tolstoy rejected Schopenhauer's theory, but in his fiction the use of musical experience to create psychological metaphor, as well as his appraisal of Beethoven, reflect a reading of Rousseau and Schopenhauer.

Over the years Tolstoy expressed a preference for Bach, Mozart, Weber, Chopin, and Schubert among composers, and his predilections, however seemingly inconsistent, fall within the morphology suggested above. In some cases, Tolstoy's judgment is that of the disinterested listener or performer; in others, that of the novelist intuitively storing up aural impressions which will later be distributed among his fictional characters in the making, in still others, that of the didact, attempting to reconcile the emotional impact of sensory pleasure or distress with the moral function of art. Consequently, Tolstoy's judgments of any one composer from time to time often are contradictory. Chopin, for instance, whose music moved Tolstoy deeply, also is the one composer to whose works Tolstoy responded most objectively. Tolstoy keenly recognized that Chopin avoided both the banality of Mozart's occasional melodic lapses and the preciosity from which Schumann's allusive statement occasionally suffered. Chopin, however, never entered Tolstoy's fictional laboratory, possibly because the abstractness and mercurial improvisational shifts characteristic of that composer's musical idiom never spoke to Tolstoy's literary imagination.

Another interesting example is provided by Carl Maria von Weber, who remained one of Tolstoy's favorite composers and whose music—in piano transcriptions of operas (a commonplace procedure in the nineteenth century), as well as the technically demanding piano sonatas—the novelist prided himself on learning. Weber's *Der Freischütz* (1821) ranks as one of the few operas Tolstoy deeply loved and revered. In Act II, Scene 2, the famous "Wolf Glen" scene, Weber introduced a leitmotif based on a diminished seventh chord to sound the theme of evil—the compact that the hero, Max, makes with the demonic Samiiel in order to gain a free shot that will guarantee his marksmanship in a trial stipulated by his future father-in-law and thus prove his worthiness to marry his sweetheart, Agathe. That leitmotif has

gone down in opera history as a precursor of the device introduced by Wagner in the *Ring* cycle. Weber's diminished seventh,
which Glinka found tiresome, subsequently became a cliché of
the sinister in operatic idiom. Tolstoy indeed parodies the device
in the scene of Natasha at her first opera. Nonetheless, he praised
Der Freischütz without qualification, and it is this attitude that
apparently contradicts the novelist's animus, which he was to express from the late 1870s on, against the "Wagner tendency in
music."

The contradiction, however, is only apparent. *Der Freischütz*
in its depiction of the life of the folk and the idealization of rustic
simplicity has an affinity with Rousseau's aesthetics—as expressed in his *Lettre à d'Alembert* (1758)—of the theater as a
celebration of collective well-being. Moreover, the mythopoeic
subtext of the Weber opera—the portrayal of the bridegroom as
hunter, the affirmation of life lived close to nature as the good
life, the theme of marriage as a communal sacrament conjoining
the individual with the cycles of nature and the group experience—is consonant with Tolstoy's novelistic vision. These motifs
can be discerned in the Levin narrative line of *Anna Karenina,*
particularly in part 2, chapter 15, in the scene in which Levin and
Stiva Oblonsky go hunting and Levin raises the delicate question
of Kitty's plans to marry. (The above remarks, interjected cur-
sorily into this essay, are an integral part of a larger study entitled
"Tolstoy and the Diminished Seventh." In the present discussion
they are meant to do no more than suggest the diversity of
Tolstoy's musical judgments and the surprising philosophical
unity within that diversity.)

Tolstoy's complex and contradictory attitude toward the music of Beethoven can be traced back to his earliest fiction. In a
discarded draft for chapter 11 of *Childhood,* Tolstoy polemicizes
against the excess of allusions to Beethoven in European literature of the 1840s:

Читатель! Заметили ли вы, как все любят сочинения Бетховена, как часто в разговорах вы слышите, что сочинения
этого композитора предпочитают всем другим? Заметили ли
вы, что часто его хвалют [*sic*] и восхищаются им так, что

совестно за тех, которые восхищаются? В романе или повести, ежели кто-нибудь играет, то непременно сонату Бетховена, особенно в французских романах.

Reader! Have you noticed how everyone loves the compositions of Beethoven, how often in conversation you hear that the works of this composer are preferred to those of all others? Have you noticed that often people praise him and are enraptured by him in such a way that one is embarrassed for those who are enraptured? In a novel or tale, especially in French novels, if anyone plays a piece, then, without fail, it is a Beethoven sonata.[14]

That rebuke appears in a draft in which we find the first mention of Tolstoy's fiction of music as an analogue of feeling, the first delineation of the thought processes of a child by means of a musical metaphor, and the first discussion of Beethoven's music. Tolstoy's innovations in the delineation of states of feeling and thought continue in Russian literature the traditions of French psychological prose and, as in Tolstoy's *Childhood-Boyhood-Youth* trilogy, the legacy of eighteenth-century Lockean empiricism with its emphasis on the dissection of sensations. Nonetheless, the drafts for *Childhood*, together with Tolstoy's youthful theoretical writings about music, demonstrate that the novelist's perfection of devices of interior monologue was accomplished in association with an impulse to musical form which he developed into an artistic procedure. A notebook entry for 29 May 1856 shows this impulse spontaneously at work. Coming in from the fields one day, Tolstoy attempted to write down in melodic notation the musical idea that expressed his elation upon seeing a blooming crop of rye: "Est' naslaždenie v mysle, čto vsja, vsja èta zelennaja zemlja—moja. . . . I sto dva-adcat' po-se-em" (There is gratification in the thought that all, all of this green land is mine. . . . And we will sow one hundred and twenty), he confessed. An unbarred triadic melodic sequence in the treble clef followed: g-b-d-e-d-e-d-c. The joyous expression of possession and anticipation of sowing can be found in chapter 32 of *Youth*. The melodic idea was well forgotten—but not the connection of feeling and form.[15]

When it came time to work out a method using music as a psychological metaphor, to delineate below-conscious feeling or thought, Tolstoy sought and found an appropriate correlative. Allusions to Beethoven appear in five of Tolstoy's works: in *Childhood* (1852), where Nikolenka listens to his mother's rendition of the *Sonata Pathétique;* in *Family Happiness* (1859), where Masha plays the *Moonlight* Sonata; in *War and Peace* (1865–1868), where Petya Rostov conducts a symphony; in "The Kreutzer Sonata" (1889), where Pozdnyshev's wife and Trukhachevsky perform a violin-piano duet; in *Resurrection* (1899), where Nekhlyudov listens to the Andante of the Symphony in C Major (the Fifth) in a piano arrangement and the music fills him with tears of tenderness at the prospect of his moral regeneration. All these works reveal a use of Beethoven's music as analogues of feeling. In *Resurrection* the allusion is episodic, while in *Family Happiness* and "The Kreutzer Sonata" it serves a large structural function. In *Childhood, Family Happiness,* and "The Kreutzer Sonata" Tolstoy introduces elements associated with Beethoven's innovations in sonata form or with his compulsive rhythms. In three works, *Childhood, War and Peace,* and "The Kreutzer Sonata," he employs Beethoven's music as correlatives of the unconscious. In each of these the musical metaphor has a connection to a fast movement. Quite obviously, Tolstoy found in Beethoven's scoring of Allegro movements certain features that to his artistic imagination were highly suggestive in delineating the emotional life of his heroes.

ALLEGRO CON BRIO

Chapter 11 of *Childhood,* in the final version, depicts Nikolenka drawing in the parlor at teatime, while his mother plays Field and Beethoven on the pianoforte.[16] The child is very much a nestling attached to his mother; his aesthetic sensibility and perception of reality are still fuzzy. The amorphous self-consciousness of the child is rendered first in a general statement about the music; next, by means of a psychological metaphor:

Maman играла второй концерт Фильда—своего учителя. Я дремал, и в моем воображении возникали какие-то легкие, светлые и прозрачные воспоминания. Она заиграла патетическую сонату Бетховена, и я вспоминал что-то грустное, тяжелое, и мрачное. *Maman* часто играла эти две пьесы; поэтому я очень хорошо помню чувство, которое они во мне возбуждали. Чувство это было похоже на воспоминания, но воспоминания чего? Казалось, что воспоминаешь то, чего никогда не было.

Maman played the second concerto of Field, her own teacher. I drowsed, and in my imagination arose some kind of light, bright, and transparent memories. She began to play the *Sonata Pathétique* of Beethoven and I recalled something sad, heavy, and gloomy. *Maman* often played these two pieces; therefore, I well recall the feeling that they aroused in me. This feeling was like that of remembering, but remembering what? It seemed that one remembered what never was.[17]

The metaphor of music as unspecified recollection is symbolic of the child's amorphous self-consciousness. In the mind of the child the sounds of his mother's playing come to stand for her voice, and, as such, they express the child's connectedness at this very young age to the central figure in his world. The musical metaphor thus is a consummate psychological device in terms of what it leaves unsaid.

By contrast, in the three early drafts for the same chapter, Tolstoy delineates the child's mind through discursive ratiocinative and polemical devices. He has not yet arrived at one suggestive analogue. All three drafts contain the polemic directed against the overuse of Beethoven allusions in literature, which opens with the address to the reader: "Čitatel'! Zametili li vy, kak vse ljubjat sočinenija Betkhovena?" (Reader! Have you noticed how everybody loves Beethoven's works?). This argument leads into a discussion of pictorial representation in music. As illustration, Nikolenka describes a passage in a French novel where the effect of a Beethoven sonata on the fictitious listener elicits images of angels with blue wings, palaces with golden columns, and marble fountains. The child rejects this fantasy as an arbitrary one, appropriate to that particular listener:

В одном французском романе, автор, имя которого очень известно, описывая впечатление, которое производит на него одна соната Бетховена, говорит, что он видит ангелов с лазурными крыльями, дворцы с золотыми колоннами, мраморные фонтаны. . . . Не знаю как другие, но читая это очень длинное описание этого француза, я представлял себе только усилия, которые он употреблял, чтобы вообразить и описать все эти прелести. Мне не только это описание не напомнило той сонаты, про которую он говорил, но даже ангелов и дворцов я никак не мог себе представить. Это очень естественно, потому что никогда я не видал ни ангелов с лазурными крыльями, ни дворцов с золотыми колоннами.

In one French novel, the author, whose name is very well known, describing the impression that a Beethoven sonata produces on him, says that he sees angels with blue wings, palaces with golden columns, marble fountains. . . . I do not know about others, but, reading the very long passages of this Frenchman, I imagined to myself only the strain he exerted to express and describe all of these beautiful things. To me not only did this description not recall that sonata about which he spoke, but I couldn't even imagine angels and palaces. This is very natural, because I never saw angels with blue wings nor palaces with golden columns.[18]

These passages thus become a running discourse on aesthetics which, as Tolstoy himself realized, was inappropriate to the immaturity of his child-narrator.

To prove his point, Nikolenka describes how he *feels* when his mother plays the *Pathétique*. In this version Tolstoy moves from expository discourse to the suggestive psychological analysis that we associate with the metaphor of the final version. Here, the way a child hears a piece of music becomes an analogue for his process of thought. Particularly notable is the development section of the first movement, marked "Allegro," to which Nikolenka responds by noting his almost unbearable apprehension as a listener that the piece or his mother's performance of it may change before the resolution begins that will assure him that all is well. He explicates what he hears, that is, the musical texture of a fugue, by means of an *ostranenie* (defamiliarization) that makes his discourse iconic of the fugal texture itself:

Я успокоился только тогда, когда мотив интродукции высказал все и шумно разрешился в *Allegro*. Начало *Allegro* слишком обыкновенно, поэтому я его не любил. Но что может быть лучше того места, когда начинаются вопросы и ответы! Сначала разговор тих и нежен, но вдруг в басу кто-то говорит такие две строгие, но исполненные страсти фразы, на которые, кажется, ничего нельзя ответить. Однако, нет, ему отвечают и отвечают еще и еще, еще лучше, еще сильнее до тех пор, пока наконец все сливается в какой-то неясный, тревожный ропот. Это место всегда удивляло меня, и чувство удивления было так же сильно как будто я слышал его в первый раз.

My mind was set at ease only when the motif of the introduction said all it had to say and noisily resolved itself into the Allegro. The beginning of the Allegro is too ordinary, therefore I didn't like it. . . . But what can be better than that passage where the questions and answers begin. At first the conversation is quiet, but suddenly in the bass someone speaks two such phrases, stern yet full of passion, to which it seems there can be no reply. However, no, they do answer the bass, and answer and answer, more and more, better still, still stronger, to the point where everything blends into a sort of unclear, agitated rumble. This passage always astonished me, and the feeling of astonishment was as strong as if I had heard it for the first time.[19]

The excitement caused in the child's mind by the successive entries of the subjects continues to be articulated through his discourse:

Потом в шуму *Allegro* вдруг слышен отголосок интродукции, потом разговор повторяется еще раз, еще отголосок, и вдруг в ту минуту, когда душа так взволнована этими беспрестанными тревогами, что просит отдыха, все кончается, и кончается так неожиданно и прекрасно.

Then in the din of the Allegro suddenly is heard an echo of the introduction, then the conversation is repeated once more, again an echo, and suddenly at that moment when your soul is so stirred up by these incessant agitations that you beg for rest, everything ends, and ends so suddenly and beautifully.[20]

Tolstoy wrote two versions of the passage quoted above, with each variant gradually shifting the emphasis from a rational analysis of the Beethoven music to one that is psychological and oblique. It is significant that the echo Nikolenka mentions has a precise musical reference: it is to the reiteration of a motif of three dotted notes heard first in the Grave introduction of the *Pathétique* Sonata. Beethoven's motif becomes Tolstoy's memory metaphor.[21] One variant of *Childhood* shows particularly well the developing psychological direction, although the discourse as yet is too explicit:

> В то время, как я слушаю музыку, я ни об чем не думаю и ничего не воображаю, но какое-то странное сладостное чувство до такой степени наполняет мою душу, что я теряю сознание своего существования, и это чувство—воспоминание. Но воспоминание чего? Хотя ощущение сильно, воспоминание неясно. Кажется как будто вспоминаешь то, чего никогда не было. . . . Чувство музыки не происходит ли из воспоминания о чувствах и переходах от одного чувства к другому?

> While I listen to music I do not think of anything and do not imagine anything, but some kind of strange sweet feeling so fills my soul that I lose consciousness of my own existence—and that feeling is memory. But memory of what? Although the sensation is strong, the memory is unclear. It seems as if one remembers what never was. . . . Does the feeling of music not originate from the recollection of feelings and the transition from one feeling to another?[22]

Preliminaries to this statement occur in Tolstoy's diary for the same period with special urgency, demonstrating how critical it was that the psychological metaphor be valid yet allusive, laconic yet expressive:

> Отчего музыка действует на нас как воспоминание? . . . Почему музыка есть подражание нашим чувствам и какое сродство каждой перемены звука с каким-нибудь чувством? Нельзя сказать.

> Why does music act on us like memory? . . . Why does music imitate our feelings, and what is the relationship between each change in sound and some kind of feeling? One can't say.[23]

The passages above sum up what was to become the Rousseau-ean first principle of Tolstoy's aesthetics, that music is the art of transmitting feelings. Tolstoy began by exploring the mechanism of that connection and the diverse ways in which it could be exploited metaphorically. Gradually, as the drafts reveal, he shed the explicit for the psychologically suggestive. The metaphor of music as an analogue of memory in the allusive, impressionistic formulation of its final version in chapter 11 approaches stream-of-consciousness technique. Tolstoy eliminated from *Childhood* the passages containing Nikolenka's discourse on aesthetics and the depiction of the effect of the Allegro movement of the *Pathétique* Sonata on his child listener. However, they provided important material for the writing of a passage in *War and Peace* that employs another Beethoven score in the construction of a psychological metaphor.

ALLEGRO MAESTOSO

Was sagst du Bruder, zu diesem
künstlich-fügenden Traume?[24]

Jean-Paul Richter

The night before he dies in a partisan raid on a French convoy, Petya Rostov has a dream. Lying half-awake on a wagon in the company of Denisov's men, Petya envisions that he is conducting a symphony. Within the spiritual biography of Petya Rostov, the dream is an *aristeia,* a moment of glory snatched from the history of his ineptitudes: in the army, as a young hussar officer, and at home, where he is constantly underfoot as the youngest of the four Rostov children. The scene appears in the tenth of eleven chapters in book 4, part 3, of *War and Peace* that focus on the partisan contribution to the defeat of the French in 1812.[25]

Petya is depicted as an impetuous child who insists on acting out a charming but foolish ideal of heroism. He attempts to petition the tsar for permission to enlist, only to be jostled and knocked unconscious by the crowd (book 3, part 1, chapter 21); at Vyazma, against the orders of his commanding officer, he rides into the French firing lines and shoots his pistol (book 4, part 3, chapter 8); upon his arrival at the partisan encampment, he begs Denisov to keep him on, again disobeying the terms of his assignment (chapter 10); he pesters Dolokhov to join in the incognito visit to the French officer's camp; finally, during the raid on the convoy, he again gallops ahead of his detachment—to his death (chapter 10).[26]

The drafts of the partisan chapters of *War and Peace* present Petya's desire for heroism in a comparatively simplistic, positive light. It is Petya's commanding officer, for instance, who avoids action, whereas Petya cannot wait to get into battle. The characterization of Petya as a "little hero" is seen especially clearly in the opinions of his fellow partisans: "Govorja s Petej Denisov ne mog ne ulybnut'sja, tak mil emu byl ètot malen'kij geroj" (Speaking with Petya, Denisov could not help smiling, so dear to him was this little hero).[27] By contrast, in the final version, Petya's aspiration is developed as an attitude of mind which he projects onto his associates:

> Но, когда он увидал французов, увидал Тихона, узнал что в ночь непременно атакуют, он с быстротою переходов молодых людей от одного взгляда к другому, решил . . . что Денисов герой, что эсаул герой, что Тихон герой и что ему было бы стыдно уехать от них в трудную минуту.

> But when he saw the French, saw Tikhon, learned that they surely would attack that night, he decided, with the rapidity with which young people change from one view to another, that Denisov was a hero and the *èsaul* was a hero, and that it would be shameful to leave them at this difficult moment.[28]

This more pointedly psychological treatment of Petya's mental state is raised to poetic symbol in the dream passage with which the chapter concludes. The nocturnal visit in which Petya accompanies Dolokhov in spying out the French brings Petya's story to just short of its climax.[29] The action is retarded so that the reader's attention is directed to Petya's state of soul on the night before his death.

The passage shows Petya waiting expectantly for the night to pass and the morning with its promised raid to come. Excited by the adventure from which he has returned, Petya perceives the partisan milieu as an enchanted world. As his dream state deepens, the *realia* of his surroundings are gradually transformed, first into shadowy splotches, then into actual dream images: the hut becomes a black spot, then a cavern; the fire, a red spot, then a monster's eye; and so on. The sky, too, acquires a supernal beauty: Petya's vision creates images of stars and clouds in configurations like cinematographic fade-outs, close-ups, and long

shots, seen in quick succession. The sound of his sword being
sharpened against a stone below the wagon on which he is lying
triggers an aural fantasy. Petya first hears the counterpoint of a
hymn played by an orchestra. His dream state goes on and he
hears what seems to be music of his own composition. Next,
he becomes the conductor of this glorious composition surging
through his mind. He orders the sounds and they obey him. The
work becomes a choral symphony—male and female voices enter. He guides the tempo and the dynamics; the music rises to a
triumphal march as, at this point, the fantasy music, penetrated
by the empirical sounds with which his dream began, mixes with
the hissing of his saber being filed against the stone. Likhachev's
voice intrudes, announcing that the saber is ready. The lightening
sky returns the scene to full reality, and Denisov calls Petya to
ready himself for action. (The extract has been keyed to the
analysis which follows.)

[I: I] Петя должен бы был знать, что он в лесу, в партии
Денисова, в версте от дороги, что он сидит на фуре, отбитой
у французов, около которой привязаны лошади, что под ним
сидит казак Лихачев и натачивает ему саблю, что большое
черное пятно направо—караулка, и красное яркое пятно
внизу налево—догоравший костер, что человек, приходив-
ший за чашкой,—гусар, который хотел пить; *[I: 2]* но он
ничего не знал и не хотел знать этого. *[I: 3]* Он был в волшебном царстве, в котором ничего не было похожего на
действительность. Большое черное пятно, может быть,
точно была караулка, а может быть, была пещера, которая
вела в самую глубь земли. Красное пятно, может быть, был
огонь, а может быть—глаз огромного чудовища. Может
быть, он точно сидит теперь на фуре, а очень может быть,
что он сидит не на фуре, а на страшно высокой башне, с
которой ежели упасть, то лететь бы до земли целый день,
целый месяц—все лететь и никогда не долетишь. Может
быть, что под фурой сидит просто казак Лихачев, а очень
может быть, что это—самый добрый, храбрый, самый чу-
десный, самый превосходный человек на свете, которого
никто не знает. Может быть, это точно проходил гусар за
водой и пошел в лощину, а может быть, он только что исчез
из виду и совсем исчез, и его не было.
[I: 4] Что бы ни увидал теперь Петя, ничто бы не удивило
его. Он был в волшебном царстве, в котором все было
возможно.

[I:5] Он поглядел на небо. И небо было такое же волшебное, как и земля. На небе расчищало, и над вершинами дерев быстро бежали облака, как будто открывая звезды. Иногда казалось, что на небе расчищало и показывалось черное, чистое небо. Иногда казалось, что эти черные пятна были тучки. Иногда казалось, что небо высоко, высоко поднимается над головой, иногда небо спускалось совсем, так что рукой можно было достать его. *[I:6]* Петя стал закрывать глаза и покачиваться.

Капли капали. Шел тихий говор. Лошади заржали и подрались. Храпел кто-то.

—Ожиг, жиг, ожиг, жиг . . . —свистела натачиваемая сабля. *[II:1]* И вдруг Петя услыхал стройный хор музыки, игравшей какой-то неизвестный, торжественно сладкий гимн. *[II:2]* Петя был музыкален, так же как Наташа, и больше Николая, но он никогда не учился музыке, не думал о музыке, и потому мотивы, неожиданно приходившие ему в голову, были для него особенно новы и привлекательны. *[II:3]* Музыка играла все слышнее и слышнее. Напев разрастался, переходил из одного инструмента в другой. Происходил то, что называется фугой, хотя Петя не имел ни малейшего понятия о том, что такое фуга. Каждый инструмент, то похожий на скрипку, то на трубы—но лучше и чище, чем скрипки и трубы—каждый инструмент играл свое и, не доиграв еще мотива, сливался с другим, начинавшим почти то же, и с третьим, и с четвертым, и все они сливались в одно и опять разбегались и опять сливались то в торжественно церковное, то в ярко блестящее и победное. *[II:4]* —Ах, да, ведь это я во сне—качнувшись наперед, сказал себе Петя. —Это у меня в ушах. *[II:5]* А может быть, это моя музыка. Ну, опять. Валяй моя музыка! Ну! . . . — *[II:6]* Он закрыл глаза. И с разных сторон, как будто издалека, затрепетали звуки, стали слаживаться, разбегаться, сливаться, и опять все соединилось в тот же сладкий и торжественный гимн. —Ах, это прелесть что такое! Сколько хочу и как хочу,—сказал себе Петя. Он попробовал руководить этим огромным хором инструментов.

—Ну, тише, тише, замирайте теперь.—И звуки слушались его.—Ну, теперь полнее, веселее. Еще, еще радостнее.—И из неизвестной глубины поднимались усиливающиеся торжественные звуки.—Ну, голоса, приставайте!—приказал Петя. И сначала издалека послышались голоса мужские, потом женские. Голоса росли, росли в равномерном торжественном усилии. Пете страшно и радостно было внимать их необычайной красоте.

[II:7] С торжественным победным маршем сливалась

песня, и капли капали, и вжиг, жиг, жиг . . . свистела сабля, и
опять подрались и заржали лошади, не нарушая хора, а входя
в него.

[I: 1] Petya should have known that he was in the forest with
Denisov's partisan detachment, almost a verst from the road, that
he was sitting on a wagon captured from the French, near which
the horses were tethered, that beneath the wagon was sitting
Likhachev the Cossack, sharpening a sword for him, that the
large black splotch to the right was the watchman's hut and the
bright red splotch below to the left was the dying-out campfire,
that the person who came for a cup was a hussar who wanted to
drink; *[I: 2]* but he knew none of this, nor did he want to know
anything. *[I: 3]* He was in an enchanted world in which nothing
resembled reality. Maybe the large black splotch really was the
watchman's hut, but maybe it was a cave which led into the very
depths of the earth. Maybe the red spot was a fire, but maybe
the eye of an enormous monster. Maybe he really was sitting on
a wagon, but it might very well be that he was not sitting on a
wagon but on a terribly high tower, from which, if he were to fall,
he would fly to the earth for an entire day, an entire month—he
would go on flying and never reach bottom. Maybe it was just the
Cossack Likhachev who was sitting beneath the wagon, but it was
very possible that it was the kindest, the bravest, the most wonderful, finest man in all the world, of whom no one knew. Maybe
it really was that a hussar came for water and went back to the
hollow. But maybe he had simply disappeared, vanished altogether, and was no more.
[I: 4] Nothing that Petya could have seen now would have astonished him. He was in an enchanted world in which everything
was possible.
[I: 5] He looked up at the sky. And the sky was every bit as
enchanted as was the earth. The sky was clearing and over the
tops of the trees clouds were swiftly running, as if baring the stars.
Sometimes it looked as if the sky were clearing and a purer black
sky appeared. Sometimes it seemed that these black splotches
were clouds. Sometimes the sky seemed to be rising high, high
overhead; and then it seemed to sink so low that you could touch
it with your hand.
[I: 6] Petya's eyes began to close and he swayed a little.
Drops dripped from the trees. Quiet talking was heard. The
horses neighed and jostled one another. Someone snored.
"Ozhig, zhig, ozhig, zhig," hissed the saber, which was being
sharpened against the stone. *[II: 1]* And suddenly Petya heard
a harmonious orchestra playing some unknown, triumphantly
sweet hymn. *[II: 2]* Petya was musical, just like Natasha, and

more so than Nikolai, but he had never studied music, had never thought about it, and so the motifs which unexpectedly resounded in his head were to him especially new and captivating. *[II: 3]* The music became more and more audible. The melody grew and passed from one instrument to another. What was being played was what is known as a fugue, although Petya had not the slightest idea of what a fugue is. Each instrument, now sounding like a violin, now like a horn—but better and purer than a violin and a horn—each instrument played its own part, and before having finished the melody, blended with another that began almost the same, and with a third, and with a fourth, and they all blended into one and again separated, and again all blended now into something triumphantly solemn, now into something dazzlingly brilliant and victorious.

[II: 4] "Oh, yes, really, I heard that in a dream," Petya said to himself, lurching forward. "The sounds were in my ears. *[II: 5]* But maybe it is my own music. Now, again! Play on, my own music! Now!"

[II: 6] He closed his eyes. And from different sides, as if from far away, sounds palpitated, began to blend, separated, blended, and again all came together into that same sweet, triumphant hymn.

"Ah, this is something really lovely. Just the way I like it," Petya said to himself. He tried to conduct this enormous orchestra of instruments. "Now softer, softer, die away now." And the sounds obeyed him. "Now then, louder, merrier. Still more, still more joyful!" And from an unknown depth swelled ever more sonorous triumphant sounds. "Now, voices, join in!" commanded Petya. And at first from afar men's voices were heard and then women's. The voices swelled and swelled in balanced, triumphant force and Petya listened to their extraordinary beauty with feelings of awe and joy.

[II: 7] The song blended into a triumphant victorious march and the drops dripped from the trees and vzhig, zhig, zhig . . . the saber hissed, and again the horses jostled one another and neighed, not disturbing the music, but entering into it.[30]

Just as Petya's would-be heroism has not yet been given psychological point in the draft versions of this scene, neither have the poetics of the dream been refined to the symbolism that emerges in the final version. The draft, however, supplies a clue both to the construction of the dream and to the kinds of subtextual meanings implied in the dream itself. Petya's dream music is referred to as a symphony:

и с торжественным, победным маршем сливалась песня, и капли капали, вжиг, жиг, и опять подрались и заржали лошади, не нарушая *симфонии*, а входя в неё.

with a triumphal victorious march the songs blended, the drops dripped from the trees, vzhig, zhig, and again the horses neighed and jostled without disturbing the *symphony* but entering into it.[31]

Thus, from a reading of the drafts we are supplied with a cluster of motifs which in combination give us a boy's aspiration to heroism in the period of the Napoleonic wars, a dream fantasy in which he conducts a symphonic fugue (putting together the two references to the musical idiom), and which he furthermore regards as his own music.

Petya's fantasy is a wish-fulfillment dream—an empowering of impotence. The child who in reality was crushed by the crowd, the young officer who has been scolded for charging into the mêlée, is now fully in command. The musical metaphor of an orchestra conductor is a psychological mimesis of all these former experiences. Petya orders about the sounds (his life) as he has been accustomed to being ordered about. Stated in child language, "èto moja muzyka," this idea is a registering of the mind shaping empirical reality to its own false mold. Petya, the conductor of an orchestra, becomes a composer in this sense. Petya calls the music "his own." But whose is it really? What is the source of the metaphor?

Obviously it is a Beethoven score, but which one, and why? Tolstoy was not above exploiting his anti-Beethoven statements for his own artistic ends. The passage in the draft for *Childhood* that polemicizes against Beethoven allusions in literature is a specific reference to Balzac's novel *Histoire de la grandeur et de la décadence de César Birotteau*. The "rise" of the hero reaches a climax at the end of part 1, where the *petit bourgeois parfumeur*, to mark his elevation to the titulary position of deputy mayor, throws a sumptuous ball. César's emotion at that high point in his life is registered through a musical metaphor: the finale of Beethoven's Fifth Symphony rings in his ears, symbolic of the joy he experiences in the glitter of the ballroom scene. As such, the device is highly ironic, because the ball marks the *apogée* of Birotteau's influence and initiates his *décadence*. In developing his metaphor Balzac introduces the figure of a conductor under whose baton the music issues forth:

> Among the eight [*sic*] symphonies of Beethoven there is a theme glorious as a poem, which dominates the finale of the Symphony in C Minor. When after the sublime magician's slow preparations the inspired conductor, with a gesture of his hand, raises the rich veil from this decoration and calls forth from his baton the transcendent theme toward which the powers of music have all converged, poets whose hearts have throbbed at those sounds will understand how the fête given by César Birotteau produced upon his simple being the same effect that this fecund harmony wrought in theirs.[32]

It is a far cry from Balzac's *parfumeur* to Tolstoy's Petya. Nonetheless, the parallels in the two passages are suggestive. In each, a symphony score supplies the content for a grandiose dream of glory—a state of desire. This is explicitly stated in the Balzac passage: "We are held in the grasp of our secret hopes, which are realized for an instant as we listen."[33] In each, a conductor of an orchestra brings the music into being. In each, the author refers to music as a correlative of the inner life of his fictional characters: "The psychical history of the most brilliant point in the beautiful finale is one of the emotions produced by this festive evening in the soul of César and Constance."[34] In each passage as well, illusory feelings of triumph lead to the construction of a fantasy world. César Birotteau associates Beethoven's music with a grand palatial vista:

> Sculpted golden doors like those of the baptistry at Florence turn on their diamond hinges . . . the eye is lost in splendid vistas: it sees a long perspective of rare palaces. . . . Beings with divine smiles, robed in white tunics bordered in blue, flit lightly before the eyes and show us visions of supernatural beauty.[35]

In Petya's vision, reality is transformed into a fairy-tale world. Developing his metaphor, Tolstoy avoids the association of music and pictorial representation which Nikolenka had so disliked in the Balzac passage with its sculpted golden doors and angels in white tunics. Instead, he makes use of the same kind of *ostranenie* that he employed in chapter 11 of *Childhood*, where discourse mimetic of musical texture is a correlative of a state of mind and feeling. Petya's gestures as he conducts the grand fugue of his symphonic music, marking the entry of each subject, the passing of the theme from instrument to instrument, are reminiscent of Nikolenka's rendition of the "conversation" of the fugal passage in the Allegro of the *Pathétique* Sonata.

César Birotteau heard Beethoven's Fifth Symphony, which Balzac introduced as an analogue for the illusory feelings of glory experienced by his hero. The metaphor in Petya Rostov's dream specified music that is symphonic-fugal-choral in form. Neither Petya Rostov nor any other character in *War and Peace* could have heard Beethoven's Ninth Symphony. It had not yet been written. An allusion to it, therefore, would have been a flagrant anachronism. The most obvious symphony for Tolstoy to have used as his prototype, in terms of its historical associations with the Napoleonic period, is the *Eroica* (op. 55, 1804), were it not that the work lacks both choral and anthem-like elements. The battle piece, *Wellingtons Sieg oder die Schlacht bei Vittoria* (*Wellington's Victory or the Battle of Vittoria*, op. 91, 1813), celebrates a French defeat and introduces a fugal treatment of the British anthem "God Save the King." Tolstoy knew V. F. Odoevsky's story "Poslednij kvartet Betkhovena" ("Beethoven's Last Quartet"), which introduces a reference to *Wellington's Victory* and addresses a question of fugal writing.[36] However, the battle piece uses no voices. In 1868 both the music critic Alexander Serov and Odoevsky had lauded the Ninth Symphony in articles singling out the innovative path of Beethoven's last works.[37] The Ninth, first performed in Russia in 1836, was a work that many readers would have known. Its musical idiom can easily be identified. Despite the anachronism, therefore, the dream music that streams through Petya Rostov's mind seems to have been modeled on the Ninth Symphony—specifically, on the choral-symphonic setting of the anthem-like "Hymn to Joy."[38]

The Ninth Symphony looked back in style to Beethoven's music of the heroic decade and indeed has been called a combi-

nation of a "*sinfonia eroica* and a *hymne de la république*"—
nuances which are felt in Petya's dream music.[39] Petya's aspiration to heroism and the historical moment in which the dream
fugue is placed (the repulsion of the French after Borodino) make
credible an association with the heroic in Beethoven's symphonic
style. Putting the grand nineteenth-century musical concept of
Napoleon and the *eroica* into a metaphor expressing a child's
dream of glory calls attention to a theme implicit in these chapters. War is not what the historians say it is, but the fantasy of
each soldier, or a dream in the mind of a child. The Beethoven
subtext fits ideologically with the polemical direction of the author's opening commentary to the partisan chapters (book 4,
part 3, chapters 1–3), where he states explicitly that it was the
small units—isolated detachments of soldiers, not a massive
army—that strategically outmaneuvered and pushed back the
French.

The heroic dimension of the Ninth Symphony accords as well
with other semantic layers of the metaphor. The music that
streams through Petya's unconscious mind as an analogue of his
Will fits precisely Schopenhauer's statement:

> The unspeakable depth of all music by virtue of which it floats
> through our consciousness as the vision of a paradise firmly be-
> lieved in, yet ever distant from us, . . . rests on the fact that it re-
> stores to us all the emotions of our inmost nature, yet entirely
> without reality and far removed from their pain.[40]

Petya's joy in the dream-fulfillment of his desire and in the enchanted world that his fantasy constructs bears out Schopenhauer's emphasis on the illusoriness of pleasure, which is op-
erative in the manifestations of the Will.[41]

Petya's dream music carries an ethical implication as well. It
links the fantasy-fugue passage to the larger Rostov narrative
line, as it progresses toward restoration and continuity of the
generations. Likhachev sharpens Petya's saber against a stone
and the sounds are immediately transformed in Petya's subconscious into symphonic music. The transformation of a real sound
(that of metal being filed against stone) into the dream music of
Petya's fantasy presumes aural acuity (although acuity is not

obligatory—one can point to Balzac's César Birotteau) and is dependent on Petya's innate musicality. Petya's desire for heroism, endearing in its childishness, irresponsible in its disregard of danger, is a deceptive appraisal of reality. The stone—in reality a soldier's makeshift tool—in the unconsciousness of Petya, an agent releasing other associations, acquires symbolic force as well. By means of this implement Tolstoy fuses the motif of aural acuity with that of deception.

Through his musical ability Petya is bound to the extended Rostov family, which in addition to parents and children includes Denisov, "Uncle," and Anisya Fedorovna. Natasha's untrained, velvety contralto voice is praised in the two major episodes where she sings at home: "V golose ee byla ta devstvennost', netronutost', to neuznanie svoikh sil i ta neobrabotannaja ešče barkhatnost'" (In her voice was that virginal freshness, that unconsciousness of its own power and an as yet untouched velvetiness).[42] Denisov has a "true" voice; "Uncle" sings and plays as do the folk. Petya, we are told in a line of authorial commentary to his dream, "was musical like Natasha, more so than Nikolai, but never studied music." Each of these members of the larger Rostov family fulfills the Rousseauean ideal of *l'homme naturel* as musician—the purity of the music-making of each is equivalent to purity of soul. Each is an agent of a good enchantment.

As we see in scenes focusing on music and the performing arts, the Rostov family group is also bound by experiences linking aural acuity and deceptive perceptions of reality. Tatyana Kuzminskaya in her memoir of the Tolstoy family describes childhood and youth as a period of "poetry and stupidity." In *War and Peace* music is associated with mistakes and crises in the lives of Natasha, Nikolai, and Petya. Tolstoy was a reader of Hans Christian Andersen. In 1857 he translated "The Emperor's New Clothes," a reflection of which can be detected in Natasha's impressions of her first opera. Andersen's story "The Stone of the Wise Man" describes five brothers "in whom the five senses were highly developed both inwardly and outwardly, but in whom one sense had reached a keenness surpassing the other four."[43] That special power leads the brothers to painful experiences and each longs to be less keenly endowed. Something of the Andersen mode of storytelling seems to hover over the fantasy fugue and over chapter 10, into which the dream passage has been set. One is even tempted to claim an Andersen subtext at work: the stone motif, the delineation of Vincent as a little French drummer boy, the tenderness of the men to Petya, Petya's steadfast-tin-soldier model of bravery, and the strain of moral didacticism underneath it all.

The imagery in the visual fantasy of Petya's dream brings to the fore a central meaning of the passage—that of the theme of enchantment, one which is reinforced by the author's reiteration of "on byl v volšebnom mire" (He was in an enchanted world). It is this very theme that links Petya to Denisov, who, before proposing to Natasha at the Rostovs', had sung the romance "Volšebnica mira" (Enchantress of the World).[44] Through the performing arts, moments of enchantment are incorporated into the Rostov home life. The mummers arrive. The young people dress up, assume different guises—ethnic, sexual, age—play at life in a protected world. Within such a protective environment these opportunities for spectacle, musical expression, and play create out of mundane circumstances a fairy-tale realm; when, for instance, they leave for the Melyukovs' in their troikas, Nikolai comments on how the countryside has been transformed by snow into an enchanted kingdom.[45] Play thus is preparation for life, and the implicit charge in *War and Peace* is that the young are to make the transition from childhood to adulthood to carry on the best of what they represent, so that family and communal life will be restored and renewed.

At the same time, the crises in the lives of the Rostov children demonstrate that the young, as a result of their impressionability, can be prey to a dangerous enchantment. In Tolstoy's aesthetics, this peril is linked to the function of music, which as an affective art has the power of ethical agency. In book 3 of *The Republic*, Plato explicitly posits an educative function for music: it is a way of guiding the young through the perils of experience:

> So must we take our youth amid terrors of some kind, and again pass them into pleasures, and prove them more thoroughly than

gold is proved in the furnace, that we may discover whether they are armed against all enchantments, and of a noble bearing always, good guardians of themselves and of the music which they have learned.[46]

Petya, composing and conducting the inner music of his desire, is not armed against enchantment; nor, hearing her first opera, is Natasha against the seductive intent of Anatole Kuragin; nor is even Count Ilya Rostov, who, under the spell of his daughter's singing, forgets midway his orders to his steward. Petya's mistake is the most costly. The fantasy fugue can be read as an apotheosis of a young soul into the world beyond. As such, it is a prefiguration of Petya's death.

One of the most celebrated passages in early nineteenth-century literature associating a death dream with music is to be found in Thomas de Quincey's essay "The English Mail Coach" (1849). Section 3, entitled "Dream Fugue" and marked "Tumultuosissimamente," is a speculation on war and deliverance from destruction, with particular reference to the Napoleonic period.[47] It is presented through the mind of a rider in a mail-coach that is speeding unguided down the wrong side of a road toward an oncoming gig. The imminent collision of two coaches hurtling toward mutual destruction from opposite directions precipitates a series of visions. In the mind of the narrator, the sides of the road along which the coaches are rushing are transformed through the illusion of linear perspective into walls of the nave of a cathedral.[48] The cathedral association is extended into the spectral image of a necropolis, a memento mori of war. A child whose life is endangered by the Napoleonic threat wanders among vaults of fallen warriors. From a bas-relief on a tomb the stone figure of a dying trumpeter comes to life and succeeds in summoning through music the forces of deliverance that will ransom the child from Waterloo. The vision ends with an organ fugue that recapitulates in the mind of the narrator the tumultuous thoughts and emotions of his experience:

> Immediately in trance, I was carried over land and sea to some distant kingdom and placed upon a triumphal car. . . . At a flying gallop our equipage entered the grand aisle of the cathedral. . . . Suddenly we became aware of a city of sepulchres built . . . for the

warrior dead. . . . And now had we reached the last sarcophagus
. . . when we beheld afar off a child. O babe! I exclaimed, shalt
thou be the ransom for Waterloo? In horror I rose at the thought,
but then also in horror rose one that was sculptured on a bas-
relief—a Dying Trumpeter. Solemn from the field of battle he rose
to his feet; and unslinging his stony trumpet, carried it in his
dying anguish to his stony lips. . . . Then was completed the passion of the mighty fugue. . . . The golden tubes of the organ—
threw up as from fountains unfathomable columns of heart-
shaking music.[49]

Many parallels can be drawn between the Tolstoy passage and
the one from de Quincey. They suggest that Tolstoy used the
writing of his predecessor in a highly oblique, eclectic way. What
he distilled from the de Quincey piece is a cluster of motifs that
contribute to the resonance of Petya's dream fugue as an imagined moment of glory before a rendezvous with destruction. The
mail-coach in de Quincey's essay, like the dream music that Petya
hears and conducts, embodies two opposing principles: the
themes of triumphant joy and of destructive power, which are
manifest in the de Quincey text in the form of speed. The triumphal car on which de Quincey's narrator lies in his vision can
be paralleled with the wagon on which Petya sinks into his
dream state. Three elements are notable in each fantasy. The
de Quincey passage features the dynamic movement of the
charging coaches, the fear-filled voices of the riders, and the syn-
thesizing image of the cathedral. Petya's music poetically stands
for a moment when those same elements made up a significant
episode in his life—his attempt to petition the tsar. The surging
crowd behind the tsar's procession, the imploring voices of the
petitioners, and the resting point at Uspensky Cathedral from
which issues a hymn of thanksgiving and salvation make up the
material out of which Petya's music is constructed. Taken together, these elements point to de Quincey's essay as an important literary source for Tolstoy in the writing of Petya's dream.

The decisive link between the two passages, however, is that
of form. De Quincey's dream fugue can be analyzed as prose
written in fairly strict counterpoint, which has been used to give
variety within unity to the dream visions.[50] The dream fugue of
Petya Rostov is also a free contrapuntal composition. It has a po-

etic unity that derives from the central metaphor of the music as the state of desire of the dreamer. In his fantasy Petya is restored beyond the confusion and chaos of real life to a transcendent oneness of self. Tolstoy gave fictional meaning to Schopenhauer's statement that the melody of the Will tells its own story. Since Petya's state of desire is the music, one can say that he is the counterpoint and that the various strands which he forms into "his" music unite the three levels of his thoughts: those related to the present, those of the recent past, and others that reside deep in his subconscious. These are the musical ideas from which the passage is constructed. They are scored by three kinds of semantic material: data of the immediate empirical world, authorial commentary, and dream imagery.

The musical metaphor as an analogue for these levels of thought contains an ellipsis. Unlike Tolstoy's other psychological metaphors—that of landscape, for instance, in which the past is an explicit component, whether it be Prince Andrei's sense of oneness as he gazes at the sky compared to his former sense of the vanity of life or Levin's feeling of self-renewal as he lies on a hayrick and looks up at the clouds compared to his earlier self-dissatisfaction—the musical metaphor does not make explicit Petya's past, his failure to become the hero he had hoped to be. The fantasy-fugue metaphor, counterpointing past and present, itself supplies the missing part. Thus it looks back to Tolstoy's first theorizing about music as a temporal and spatial construct.

The two-part structure of Petya's dream fantasy is iconic of fugal writing. The visual section suggests the spatial contours of music: the aural, the temporal. The sky moves up and down, and the voices do, too, rising and falling. Visually as well as aurally, the fantasy is an interplay of past and present. One can indeed call this passage the double fantasy fugue of Petya Rostov.

Petya's dream fugue consists of two parts of equal length, linked by a short transition passage and concluded by one of similar length. The visual fugue opens with a statement of the first subject—the theme, "Petja dolžen by byl znat'" (Petya should have known) [I: 1], followed by an answer, "No on ničego ne znal" (But he knew none of this) [I: 2]. The first of two countersubjects enters. This is the dream imagery of the campfire scene [I: 3] and is followed by the answer, "Čto by ni uvidal Petja, ničto by ne udivilo ego. On byl v volšebnom carstve" (Nothing that Petya would have seen now would have astonished him. He was in an enchanted world in which everything was possible) [I: 4]. The statement of the second countersubject follows: the dream imagery of the sky, which contains a restatement of the answer, "i nebo bylo takoe že volšebnoe, kak i zemlja" (The sky was every bit as enchanted as was the earth) [I: 5]. A brief bridge passage [I: 6] introduces sounds of the real world—drops from the trees, voices, neighing of horses, snoring—and leads to the onomatopoetic sounds that frame the aural fugue—ožig, žig, ožig, žig—mimetic of Petya's saber being sharpened. Immediately, the first subject enters the dream music, which is heard as an orchestral anthem [II: 1]. It is followed by the answer, the author's comment on Petya's musicality [II: 2], and leads into a development of the first subject, the anthem in fugal form [II: 3]. The countersubject then enters, Petya's acknowledgment of his dream state [II: 4], which in turn provokes the answer "A možet byt', èto moja muzyka" (But maybe it is my own music) [II: 5]. This statement initiates the free development of the subject, the motif of Petya as the conductor of his own symphonic composition, and to the end of the dream the musical idiom changes, from anthem to symphonic-choral fugue, concluding with a march [II: 6]. A bridge passage follows, blending the sounds of the real world and the motif of the first subject [II: 7].

The syntax reinforces the fugal structure of the passage. Nikolenka's discourse in *Childhood* created a mimesis of polyphonic style. Here, Petya's thoughts bring out the fugal entries: "Každyj instrument igral svoe i, ne doigrav ešče motiva, slivalsja s drugim" (Each instrument played its own part, and before having finished the melody, blended with another, [II: 3]. Petya's discourse provides the dynamic markings of the music: "Nu, opjat'. Valjaj moja muzyka! Nu! . . . [II: 5] tiše, tiše, zamirajte teper'. . . . Nu, teper' polnee, veselee. Ešče, ešče radostnee." (Now, again! Play on, my own music! . . . Now! softer, softer, die away now. . . . Now then, louder, merrier. Still more, still more joyful!), [II: 6] which is the explicit expression of his desire.[51]

Musicality is further exploited in the instrumentation of the

The Fantasy Fugue of Petya Rostov

PART I

Subject 1 [I:1]
Answer 1 [I:2]

Countersubject 1 [I:3]
Counteranswer 1 [I:4]
Countersubject 2 and
Counteranswer 2 [I:5]

Bridge Passage [I:6]

PART II

Subject 1 [II:1]
Answer 1 [II:2]
Development of Subject 1 [II:3]

Countersubject 1 [II:4]
Counteranswer 1 [II:5]
Free Development of Subjects
[II:6]

Bridge Passage [II:7]

---

prose itself: the onomatopoeia of the sounds that frame the fantasy fugue; the paronomasia built on the *sl-* of *slivat'sja, sladkij, slaživat'sja,*[52] thus fusing, through a blending of sounds, the idea of the sweetness of the dream and the means of its happening. One can even suggest that in its placement, the double dream fugue, marking a narrative ritardando, leads into a third fugal section, that of the partisan raid itself, the real-life polyphony of battle.

Within *War and Peace* the fantasy fugue of Petya Rostov stands out and then recedes into the larger epic rhythms of the novel. Its self-conscious artifice makes of it almost a musical joke, directed against the cult of Beethoven and against arbiters of realism in literature, and, perhaps, a piece of self-irony, one which came to be written in defiance of an aesthetics that holds that art must be simple. In it Tolstoy revealed a sublime eclecticism compacting into one resonant metaphor semantic meanings of wish-fulfillment, enchantment, and a rendezvous with destruction. The passage represents a peak in the formalistic means through which Tolstoy developed a musical metaphor to symbolize a psychological state. As such, it anticipates the formal experiments of twentieth-century novelists in employing music as a literary device to depict the unconscious.

PRESTO

"The Kreutzer Sonata" (1889) carries to an extreme Tolstoy's creation of a musical metaphor as an analogue for the unconscious. The extremism does not derive from Tolstoy's characterization of Pozdnyshev's obsession with sex as the work of the devil, a conviction which has a long genealogy in literature. Rather, it relates to the premise on which "The Kreutzer Sonata" metaphor has been constructed, namely, that the language of art equivocates: it can be so manipulated as to communicate feelings and attitudes that in fact subvert the ennobling function to which the artistic experience lays claim. Woman may deceive, but the artist ranks as a close second; love may be shameless, but equally so can be a *soirée musicale*. What is at issue is the validity of Pozdnyshev's invective against deceit (in sexual relations as in music), which he biliously pours forth to the passenger on the train in recounting his motive for murder. Consequently, in "The Kreutzer Sonata" the issue of ambiguity in artistic discourse comes to the fore with a prominence that allows the work to be read not only as a tale of the motivation for a crime of passion but as a story of aggression against equivocation in language.[53]

At its simplest, "The Kreutzer Sonata" depicts the breakdown of a marriage, with Beethoven's music serving as the structuring principle of the narrative. In this respect it can be compared to *Family Happiness* (1859), where *Quasi una Fantasia* functions as the lyrical framework for an unfolding of the stages in a story of sexual love and marriage—the very title of the piano sonata is suggestive. By contrast, the performance of the Sonata in A Major in Tolstoy's short novel of 1889 is used structurally to mark not a passing dream but an intensifying phantasmagoria.

The rising action and the climax of the work unfold in moments connected with the playing of the Presto movement (chapters 19–26). Trukhachevsky makes his first visit in chapter 19; the performance of the Sonata by Trukhachevsky and Pozdnyshev's wife exacerbates Pozdnyshev's already highly disturbed psychological state (chapter 23); the murder occurs in chapter 26, after the violinist and Pozdnyshev's wife have been playing string duets. Moreover, the musical texture, the driving dynamic propulsion of the Presto movement, has been incorporated into the syntactical mode of the narration to create a stylistic unity of tone. Whereas in the early draft for *Childhood* and in *War and Peace* the discourse of the listener (Nikolenka, Petya Rostov) was iconic of the Allegro form, Pozdnyshev's narration quivers with questions and interjections, the equivalent of Beethoven's intense rhythmic motifs. One can even suggest that his psychic disintegration allows him to hear, not form in its entirety, but only the smallest rhythmic components of form, to which he reacts acutely.

The theme of equivocation is introduced in Pozdnyshev's prehistory (chapters 1–18). Here, the hypocrisy of sexual relations forms what can be called the ground bass of Pozdnyshev's biography and the motivation for the murder of his wife. Pozdnyshev's first-person narration recapitulates his sexual initiation, his debauchery as a young man, his marriage and family life. His account is shot through with compulsive self-disgust and contempt for the forms of male-female relationships, and its fury is concentrated on marriage. In portraying the growth of Pozdnyshev's obsession Tolstoy fuses the psychological and the polemical.

The poetic equivalent to the sexual polemic is the indictment of the equivocal in musical discourse. Describing how "The Kreutzer Sonata" affects him as a listener, Pozdnyshev questions the intentionality of the composer:

Они играли Крейцерову сонату Бетховена. Знаете ли вы первое presto? Знаете? . . . У! Страшная вещь эта соната. Именно эта часть. И вообще страшная вещь музыка. Что это такое? Я не понимаю. Что такое музыка? Что она делает? И зачем она делает то, что она делает? Говорят, что музыка действует возвышающим душу образом—вздор, неправда! Она действует, страшно действует . . . но . . . не возвышающим душу образом.

They played Beethoven's *Kreutzer Sonata*. Do you know the first Presto? Do you? . . . Oh! It is a terrible thing, that Sonata. And especially that part. And music in general is a dreadful thing. What is it? I don't understand it. What is music? What does it do? And why does it do what it does? They say music has an ennobling effect on the soul—nonsense, that's not true! It has an effect, an awful effect . . . but not of an ennobling kind.[54]

In developing the polemic of his hero Tolstoy plays on the legacy of romanticism, which associated art with demonic powers. In fact, Pozdnyshev pursues an argument introduced by one of the conversationalists in the frame to Odoevsky's story "The Last Quartet of Beethoven," in which Faust describes the uncanny power of music to sneak into the recesses of the soul. Faust exclaims:

Ничья музыка не производит на меня такого впечатления. . . . Веселые темы Бетховена—еще ужаснее: в них кажется, кто-то хохочет—с отчаяния.

No one else's music produced such an impression on me. The happy themes of Beethoven are still more terrible; in them it seems that someone guffaws from despair.[55]

In "The Kreutzer Sonata," the demonic in music is felt as a hypnotic power:

Музыка заставляет меня забывать себя, мое истинное положение; она переносит меня в какое-то другое, не свое положение: мне под влиянием музыки, кажется что я чувствую то, чего я собственно не чувствую, что я понимаю то, чего я не понимаю, что могу то, чего не могу. . . . Музыка действует как зевота, как смех.

Music makes me forget myself, my true situation. It transports me to some situation other than my own. Under the influence of music it seems that I feel what in fact I don't feel, that I understand what I don't understand, that I can do what I can't. . . . Music acts like a yawn, like a laugh.[56]

Under the hypnosis of the Will, music becomes a bestializing force, an agent of the devil. In chapter 26, when he is steeling himself to murder, Pozdnyshev confesses, "Ja čut' bylo ne zarydal, no totčas že d'javol podskazal, 'Ty plač', sentimental'ničaj a oni spokojno razojdutsja'" (I almost sobbed, but at that moment the devil prompted, "You cry, be sentimental, and they will quietly separate"): the demonic is made explicit.[57]

The polemic against the equivocal in music represents a curious amalgam of musical thought. Rousseau discredited instrumental music as an intellectual rather than an emotional form of expression and as a vehicle that served to display technical virtuosity. Fontenelle, after hearing some chamber works which left him unmoved, is alleged to have complained: "Sonata, que me veux-tu?"[58] Tolstoy turned that line into the psychologically significant one of Pozdnyshev's agitated "Čto delaet muzyka?" (What is the music doing?) and under the impact of Schopenhauer's aesthetics insisted that the effect of music on the listener is one of ethical dissolve as a consequence of the hypnosis of the Will. To this idea he added the notion, inherited from didactic aesthetics, that music is an agent that sets in motion a chain reaction: a feeling that originates with the composer is transmitted through his composition to the listener and from him to society at large. Pozdnyshev's statement "V Kitae—muzyka gosudarstvennoe delo" (In China music is an affair of state) takes this idea, the source of which is Confucius, to its extreme.[59] The reality Pozdnyshev seeks to expose under the noble exterior of music is that of the artist as immoralist:

> Разве можно допустить, чтобы всякий, кто хочет, гипнотизировал бы один другого или многих и потом бы делал с ними что хочет? И главное, чтобы этим гипнотизером был первый попавшийся безнравственный человек?

> Can one indeed allow anyone who pleases to hypnotize another or many others and do what he likes with them? And, most important, that this hypnotist should be the first immoral man who shows up?[60]

In this passage Tolstoy adheres to an idea that was impressed on him in conversation with Berthold Auerbach. In a letter of 21 April 1861, Tolstoy recorded the words of the German writer that music is a "Pflichtloser Genuss"—a "povorot k razvraščeniju," "a turning," in Auerbach's opinion, "toward corruption."[61] Ascribing to music the power of ethical agent, Tolstoy attempted to legitimate the sexual polemic with which it was thematically connected. As a result, the poetic force of the metaphor is weakened. The confusion of the ideal and the actual, and the zeal with which the sexual polemic is argued, bring to an impasse the novelist's attempt to treat in poetic terms the question of equivocation in art.

The role of music as a psychological metaphor in "The Kreutzer Sonata" thus focuses attention on the issue of the truth of artistic discourse. Tolstoy's metaphor presumes an idée fixe on the part of Beethoven when he wrote his Sonata, an erotic intentionality which becomes the structural pivot of Tolstoy's story. Pozdnyshev, reacting to the equivocal in music, attempts to project onto the Presto movement one limited idea:

> Разве можно играть в гостиной среди декольтированных дам это [первое] престо? . . . Эти вещи можно играть только при известных, важных, значительных обстоятельствах, и тогда, когда требуется совершить известные, соответствующие этой музыке важные поступки. Сыграть и сделать то, на что настроила эта музыка. А то несоответственное ни месту, ни времени вызывание энергии, чувства ничем не проявляющегося, не может не действовать губительно.

> Can that first Presto be played in a drawing room among ladies in low-necked dresses? . . . Such things should be played only on certain important, significant occasions and then only when certain important actions answering to such music are wanted. Play it then and do what the music has moved you to do. Otherwise, an awakening of energy and feeling unsuited both to the time and place, to which no outlet is given, cannot but act harmfully.[62]

Suzanne Langer has said that "music that is invented while the composer's mind is fixed on what is to be expressed is apt not to be music."[63] Beethoven's Sonata contains a more expansive musical idea than the one that Pozdnyshev imputes to it. Several years after the publication of his novel, Tolstoy tried to concede that he had misjudged the piece. On one occasion he returned to the position, enunciated in *Childhood*, that music can transmit only a general emotive power. On another he tried to conceal his blunder by imputing the eroticism he felt the music expressed to an interpretation of the work given by student performers.[64]

Nonetheless, the generating artistic idea of the story as Tolstoy wrote it is one that associates language and desire. Is the question of consummation as projected through innuendo one of misplaced semantics? Langer asserts that music, though clearly a symbolic form, is an "unconsummated symbol."[65] Put another way, the symbol defies completion. Langer's statement illuminates what can be perceived as the failure of "The Kreutzer Sonata" as musical metaphor. In exposing the erotic component in social relations, in driving a polemic against equivocation in music, Tolstoy paradoxically restricts the power of language as an instrument of truth. In this respect Pozdnyshev's story can be read as a metaphor for an aggression against linguistic ambiguity—it can even be understood as a crime of passion against the duplicity of language. Not surprisingly, the aggressive didacticism of the discourse and the association of Beethoven's music with a critique of the symbol-making power of the unconscious provide a link from "The Kreutzer Sonata" to the position Tolstoy argued in "What Is Art?" (1897).

Calling for an art of ethical vision and universal accessibility, one which, if not religious in a theological sense, would elevate the individual to a community of life and feeling with his fellow man, Tolstoy in his polemical tract reiterated Rousseau's principle that art transmits emotions and stressed the idea that this process can best be accomplished by simplicity and sincerity of expression:

> Искусство есть деятельность человеческая, состоящая в том, что один человек сознательно известными внешними знаками, передает другим испытываемые им чувства, а другие люди заражаются этими чувствами и переживают их.

> Art is a human activity wherein one person consciously by certain external signs transmits to others the feelings that he experiences and other people are infected by these feelings and experience them.[66]

The emphasis on an ideal of communication and solidarity required reconciliation of the affective power of music with its function. In so doing Tolstoy rejected Schopenhauer's aesthetics of music, attacked impressionist painters, symbolist poets, "decadent" composers, and swept into that indictment his own practice as a novelist.

Before bringing "What Is Art?" to an uneasy close, Tolstoy confessed how hard it had been to write and eventually complete. Why had this been so? The difficulty relates not only to the magnitude of the task itself—formulating a definition of art within the context of a history of aesthetics—but goes back to a central theme of the tract: the issue of equivocation in art. If "The Kreutzer Sonata" had expressed obliquely the author's own anger directed against what is problematic in artistic discourse, Tolstoy's philosophical prose also allowed him to conceal the real enemy: himself. Here, Tolstoy found his antagonists among the creators of works of art that he considered difficult, inaccessible to a broad public, and immoral.

A major adversary was Beethoven. Ascribing the musical idiom of the late sonatas, quartets, and symphonies to the composer's physical and psychological difficulties, Tolstoy attributed to Beethoven a loss of melodic inspiration for which he claimed the composer compensated by writing thick harmonic textures. The singing of old women—"real art"—Tolstoy preferred to the confusing modulations of the Sonata for Piano in A Major, Op. 101.[67] The Ninth Symphony and the late quartets were given especially harsh treatment. In his tract Tolstoy envisioned a moral regeneration of the arts that could be realized only through universalization of every phase of the artistic experience. Judged according to this standard, the Ninth Symphony fell short. Tolstoy pointed out the flaws in the choral section, asserting that Beethoven had chosen a text on the theme of brotherhood, Schiller's "Hymn to Joy," and then had written music that could be felt only by the musical elite:

Девятая симфония . . . считается великим произведением искусства . . . Имеет ли это произведение . . . свойство соединять в одном чувстве всех людей? . . . Не только не вижу того, чтобы чувства передаваемые этим произведением, могли соединить людей, не воспитанных специально для того, чтобы подчиняться этой сложной гипнозитации, но не могу даже представить себе толпу нормальных людей, которая могла бы понять из этого длинного и запутанного искусственного произведения что-нибудь, кроме коротеньких отрывков, тонущих в море непонятного.

The Ninth Symphony is considered a great work of art. . . . Does this work possess the means to unite all people in one feeling? . . . I not only don't see that the feelings transmitted by this work could unite all people who have not been specially educated to subjugate themselves to this complex hypnosis, but I cannot imagine a crowd of normal persons who could understand out of this long and confused artificial work something other than short fragments, drowning in a sea of incomprehensibility.[68]

Nonetheless, preaching his own criterion of brotherly feeling, Tolstoy did not hesitate to argue ad hominem, linking Beethoven's alleged melodic deficiencies to the composer's deafness:

Среди часто по заказу, второпях писанных бесчисленных произведений его есть, несмотря на искусственность формы, и художественные произведения; но он становится глух, не может слышать и начинает писать уже совсем выдуманные, недоделанные и потому часто бессмысленные, непонятные в музыкальном смысле произведения.

Among his innumerable compositions, which often were hastily written to order, there are a few that, despite an artificiality of form, are artistic works, but then he becomes deaf, cannot hear, and begins to write works that are quite contrived and unpolished and therefore often musically meaningless and incomprehensible.[69]

What the novelist found most unforgivable, however, was that Beethoven had spawned Wagner:

И вот является Вагнер, который . . . в критических статьях, восхваляет Бетховена, именно последнего периода, и приводит эту музыку в связь с мистической теорией Шопенгауера . . . о том, что музыка есть выражение воли.

And now Wagner comes along, who . . . in his critical articles praises Beethoven, specifically the works of the last period, and connects this music to the mystical theories of Schopenhauer . . . that music is an expression of the Will.[70]

Thus, the final thrust of his argument is directed against the tonality of Beethoven's music, which opened the way to the extreme chromaticism of the neoromantic composers. In Tolstoy's view, harmonic instability expressed the precarious morality of both the composer who wrote such music and the patron who gave it public acclaim. Repudiating Wagner, Tolstoy of necessity turned on Schopenhauer as well.

It has been suggested that Tolstoy's arguments reveal the influence of the Russian musicologist A. D. Ulybyshev (1794–1857), to whom the novelist had been introduced in 1857. Ulybyshev's biography of Beethoven, published simultaneously in French (Paris) and German (Leipzig), had created something of a stir in circles that were enthusiastically pro-Beethoven.[71] The indirection of the title, *Beethoven, ses critiques et ses glossateurs,* concealed the unrestrained polemic of the text, which had been written explicitly to quell the mythic resonance of the Beethoven cult and to sever any lingering connection between Beethoven and liberal social and political currents. In so doing, the author attempted to demonstrate that Beethoven, far from continuing the legacy of Haydn and Mozart, had deflected musical thought into false harmonic directions and thus initiated its decline. Questioning Beethoven's genius, Ulybyshev criticized the works of the last period, associating Beethoven's taste "pour les dissonances anti-euphoniques" with the composer's loss of hearing and his psychic disturbances:

> Thus again it is the zealots of the impossible who have sympathized with an impossible music and who have seen themselves in the disorder of an inspiration which age and suffering have enfeebled, which the ear has not guided for ten years, and which strange hallucinations have managed to corrupt at its source.[72]

Tolstoy certainly would have been aware of the mixed critical response to Beethoven's last works. He would not necessarily have had to rely on a work published in the 1850s. Nonetheless, stripped of their political and social allusions and projected into a low rather than a high rhetorical style, Tolstoy's arguments in "What Is Art?" are similar to Ulybyshev's detractions.

Particularly striking is the emphasis of each on the fallibility of Beethoven's inner ear. Ulybyshev claimed that Beethoven, having lost even the "mémoire des sons," had retreated into a world of imaginary audition that was highly suspect: "he gave himself up to the illusions of an ideal music unrelated to real music." [73] Tolstoy also questions the reliability of the inner ear, stating that imagined sounds cannot be substituted for those that can be verified:

Я знаю что музыканты могут воображать звуки и почти слышать то что они читают; но воображаемые звуки никогда не могут заменить реальных, и всякий композитор должен слышать свое произведение.

I know that musicians can imagine sounds and almost hear what they read; but imagined sounds can never substitute for real sounds and each composer should hear his work. [74]

The inner ear is the symbol-making power of the composer. Once again, through another's voice—that of Ulybyshev—Tolstoy seeks a way to throttle equivocation, even at the expense of the ideal of compassion underlying his tracts.

Mean-spirited and inattentive, Tolstoy's anti-Beethoven arguments contrast sharply with his informal writing on the nature of music. His use of musical metaphor would be inconceivable without this gift of aural acuity, which he so artfully and polemically manipulated. [75]

Paradox remained a constant feature of Tolstoy's statements about Beethoven. Marking familiar junctures in his spiritual evolution, they range from the praise of the young traveler in Europe: "Francuzy igrajut Betkhovena k moemu udivleniju kak bogi" (To my surprise the French play Beethoven like gods, 1857); to reproof of the pedagogue organizing a school at Yasnaya Polyana: "Ja ubedilsja čto Puškin i Betkhoven nravjatsja nam ne potomu čto v nikh est' absoljutnaja krasota, no potomu čto my takže isporčeny kak Puškin i Betkhoven" (I became convinced that Pushkin and Beethoven please us not because they represent absolute beauty but because we are as corrupted as Pushkin and Beethoven were, 1862); to the final mockery of the detractor: "Kakoe by oblegčenie počuvstvoval vse, zapertye v koncerte dlja slušanija Betkhovena poslednikh sočinenij, esli by vmesto ikh zaigrali trepaka, čardaš, ili tomu podobno" (What a relief everyone would feel who had been locked up in a concert hall to listen to the late works of Beethoven, if instead they played a *trepak* or a *csárdás*, or something like that, 1896).[76] Curiously enough, early and late Tolstoy come together in *Resurrection*. Nekhlyudov, listening to a piano transcription of the Fifth Symphony, feels welling up inside him a spontaneous kinship with all men and, on the strength of that feeling, a momentary self-satisfaction. The emotion of reconciliation is one associated with the Andante movement of Beethoven's Symphony No. 5 in C Minor. In describing the effect of the music on Nekhlyudov— "on počuvstvoval ščipanie v nosu ot umilenija" (He felt a tickling in his nose from tender emotion)—Tolstoy makes use of an early avowal of his own feelings. Nekhlyudov's reaction in fact is a restatement of a phrase from a letter to A. A. Tolstaya in 1857: "A ja skverno tupymi pal'cami razygrivayu Betkhovena, i prolivaju slëzy umilenija" (Badly, with my clumsy fingers, I play Beethoven, and I shed tears of tender emotion).[77] Nekhlyudov's response is thus Tolstoy's fictional adieu to Beethoven. As such it suggests less the writer's reconciliation to Beethoven's symphonic style than an admission prompted by artistic necessity. To it must be juxtaposed such repudiations of Beethoven as the one below, found in his last tract on art, "O tom čto nazyvajut iskusstvom" (On What Is Called Art), published posthumously:

Большинство музыкальных произведений в подражание бессмысленным произведениям Бетховена суть набор звуков, имеющих интерес для изучивших фугу и контрапункт, но не вызывающий никакого чувства в обыкновенном слушателе.

A majority of musical works that imitate Beethoven's senseless compositions are a collection of notes, of interest to those who have studied fugue and counterpoint, but they do not arouse any feelings in the ordinary listener.[78]

What could be more inconsistent than that the disciple of Rousseau and the exponent of all that is natural in art should expend so much effort in constructing a passage of symbolic prose around the metaphor of a fugue, only to castigate fugal form in "On What Is Called Art"? Abusive and often illogical, Tolstoy's attacks against the so-called forerunner of the decadent in music read like an exorcism that failed—not of the artist, nor of the didact within, but of the competing claims of each, which he could not resolve.

Giving form to the reveries of the mind and soul, Tolstoy's technique of musical metaphor joined art and life, consequently intensifying the writer's skepticism regarding the morality of art, and of language as an instrument of truth. Artistically, musical metaphor became incorporated into the larger body of his symbolism of ethical choice. "Čto takoe muzyka?" (What is music?) Tolstoy continued to ask, even to the very end of his life. "Stenografija čuvstv" (the stenography of feelings), he replied. In Beethoven's music Tolstoy found the means to transcribe in fiction the mind's voice—memory, aspiration, desire. Musical metaphor contributed to the making of Tolstoy's personal mythology of the enchantment of art. "The very nature of the musical medium," claimed the noted twentieth-century composer Carlos Chavez, "so utterly suitable to take on the shape of our emotions, makes music an ideal instrument of magic."[79] Can it be that, from the very outset, Tolstoy in his reception of Beethoven was expressing the mistrust of one magician for another?

NOTES

1. Tolstoy's diaries and those of his wife provide a full record of the importance of music in the life and thought of the Tolstoy family. See also A. B. Gol'denvejzer, *Vblizi Tolstogo* (Moscow, 1923); *Lev Tolstoj i muzyka*, comp. Z. G. Palijukh and A. V. Prokhorov (Moscow, 1977); and S. L. Tolstoj, *Muzyka v žizni otca: Očerk bylogo* (Tula, 1938), pp. 382–408.

2. *PSS* 46:31, 36.

3. *PSS* 1:241–45.

4. *PSS* 1:241. All translations of Tolstoy passages are mine, unless otherwise indicated.

5. *PSS* 1:244.

6. *PSS* 1:244.

7. *PSS* 1:245.

8. *The Wisdom of Confucius*, ed. Lin Yutang (London, 1957), p. 208; J.-J. Rousseau, "Essai sur l'origine des langues," *Oeuvres complètes*, vol. 12 (Paris, 1825), chaps. 12–15 and 19.

9. J.-J. Rousseau, *Dictionnaire de musique* (Paris, 1786), p. 277.

10. "Thus music is distinguished from all the other arts in that it is

not the image of the appearance of the Will, but the direct image of the Will itself." Arthur Schopenhauer, *Sämtliche Werke*, vol. 1 (Stuttgart, 1960), p. 366.

11. "Finally, in the melody . . . I recognize the highest stage of the objectification of the Will, the conscious life and the endeavor of man." Schopenhauer, *Sämtliche Werke*, 1 : 362.

12. "So consequently the melody is a continual fluctuation, a thousandfold deviation from the tonic, not only to the consonant intervals, but to every tone . . . yet a final return to the tonic always follows." Schopenhauer, *Sämtliche Werke*, 1 : 363. This illusion was explicated later by Edmund Gurney (1847–1888): "Music may project on the mind faint intangible images of extra-musical impulse and endeavor. . . . The ease and spontaneity of the motion, the certainty with which a thing known or dimly divined as about to happen does happen, creating a half-illusion that the notes are obeying a controlling force of one's own desire, may similarly open up vague channels of association with other moments of satisfaction and attainment." Cited by G. Epperson, *A Study of the Philosophic Theory of Music* (Ames, Iowa, 1967), p. 348.

13. Schopenhauer, *Sämtliche Werke*, 1 : 362.

14. *PSS* 1 : 180.

15. *Lev Tolstoj i muzyka*, p. 54.

16. See chap. 11, "Zanjatija v kabinete i gostinoj," *PSS* 1 : 30–33. The dynamic marking of the first movement of the *Pathétique* Sonata, Op. 13, reads "Allegro di molto è con brio."

17. *PSS* 1 : 31.

18. *PSS* 1 : 177.

19. *PSS* 1 : 182.

20. *PSS* 1 : 182.

21. Rudolph Réti in his analysis of the Beethoven piano sonatas points out that this echo is an important element in the architectonics of the *Pathétique* Sonata. "At first glance, it may appear that the . . . structural continuity in the *Grave* . . . has drawn to a close. . . . However, going deeper into the musical substance one discovers that . . . the *Allegro* represents an intentional repetition of the shapes and phrases of the *Grave*." See Rudolph Réti, *Thematic Patterns in the Sonatas of Beethoven*, ed. Deryck Cooke (New York, 1967), p. 17. While repetition may be characteristic of many musical compositions, here Tolstoy isolated a precise musical element in a particular Beethoven sonata and transformed it into a psychological metaphor.

22. *PSS* 1 : 182. This passage appears with slight variation in an earlier draft, where Tolstoy included the line:

Когда я слышу музыку, я не думаю—мысль совершенно умирает, воображение тоже не рисует мне никаких образов и находится в совершенном бездействии—сознание физического существования уничтожается, но я чувствую что я живу и живу полно и тревожно.

When I hear music, I don't think—thought completely dies, imagination also doesn't draw me any pictures and is completely inactive—an awareness of physical existence is blotted out, but I feel that I live and that I live fully and agitatedly. *PSS* 1 : 180.

23. *SS* 19:76.
24. "What sayest thou, brother, to this ingeniously put-together dream?" J.-P. Richter, *Traumdichtungen* (Leipzig, n.d.), p. 27. Translation mine.
25. *SS* 7:168–70.
26. *PSS* 15–16:89–134. In addition to the details in the characterization noted above, variant no. 276 gives two names for Tolstoy's hero, Petrusha and Petya.
27. *PSS* 15–16:166.
28. The psychological delineation is conveyed through wordplay on *geroj* and its derivatives. *SS* 7:156–57.
29. For Petya's expedition to the French with Dolokhov, see book 7, part 3, chapter 9. *SS* 7:162–66.
30. See *SS* 7:168–70; cf. the translation by Louise Maude and Aylmer Maude (New York, 1942), pp. 1170–71.
31. *PSS* 15–16:132–33 (emphasis added).
32. H. de Balzac, *La grandeur et décadence* [*sic*] *de César Birotteau* (Montreal, n.d.; first published 1837), p. 215.
33. Balzac, *César Birotteau*, p. 216.
34. Ibid., p. 208.
35. Ibid., pp. 216–17.
36. V. F. Odoevskij, "Poslednij kvartet Betkhovena," in *Russkie noči* (Leningrad, 1975), p. 81. Beethoven to Luisa: "Pomniš' li ty, kogda v Vene . . . ja upravljal orkestrom moej Vaterlooskoj Batalii? . . . Krugom batal'nyj ogon', pušečnye vystrely. . . . èto do sikh por lučšee moe proizvedenie, nesmotrja na ètogo pedanta, Vebera." (Do you recall when in Vienna I conducted my own *Waterloo Battle* [*Wellingtons Sieg*]? . . . Battle fire all around, cannon shots [Beethoven's speech refers to the scoring of the work, which includes ratchets to simulate gunfire, and actual cannon]. . . . It is up to now my best composition, despite that pedant, Weber.) Section 2 ("Siegessymphonie") was written as a fugue. Jakob Gottfried Weber (1779–1839), editor of the journal *Cäcilia*, faulted Beethoven on his counterpoint. Odoevskij confused the Wellington victory that actually inspired Beethoven's *Battle of Vittoria* with the later, more decisive victory at Waterloo.
37. See G. Bernandt, *V. F. Odoevskij i Betkhoven* (Moscow, 1971), p. 43, for brief comments on these articles, both of which laud the innovations in the Ninth Symphony.
38. A twentieth-century example lends support for the point of view expressed in this essay that the last movement of Beethoven's Ninth

Symphony is the prototype on which Tolstoy based Petya's dream music: Anthony Burgess's use of the Ninth Symphony as a metaphor for depicting the stream of thought of the main character, Alex, in *A Clockwork Orange* (London, 1962), p. 49.

39. See Maynard Solomon, *Beethoven* (London, 1977), p. 311.

40. Schopenhauer, *Sämtliche Werke*, 1:368. Translation mine.

41. The dynamic markings for the last movement of the Ninth Symphony range from Andante maestoso to Allegro energico to Prestissimo. Petya's music comes closest to an Allegro maestoso in its ironic symbolization of his aspiration to the heroic. See in this regard Schopenhauer's statement that "an Allegro maestoso with its large-scale periods . . . symbolizes loftier, nobler strivings and eventual attainment of some distant goal." Schopenhauer, *Sämtliche Werke*, 1:365.

42. *SS* 5:69.

43. Hans Christian Andersen, "The Stone of the Wise Man," in *The Complete Andersen*. Vol. 2: *The Longer Stories* (New York, 1949), pp. 248–62. Tolstoy had translated "The Emperor's New Clothes" in 1857; he included the tale in *Azbuka* (1872) and in *Detskij krug čtenija* (1901). Cf. as well his notebook entry for 16/28 February 1857: "Delo literatury i slova—vtolkovat' vsem tak, čtob rebenku poverili" (The concern of literature and writing—is to explain everything in such a way that they would believe a child), i.e., as they believed the child in "The Emperor's New Clothes." *PSS* 47:202.

44. *SS* 5:67. In the second scene in which she sings (book 2, part 55, chapter 10), Natasha is referred to in language associated with enchantment: "Kak budto obojdja svoe carstvo i ispytav svoju vlast' i ubedivšis' čto vse pokorny no čto vse-taki skučno, Nataša pošla v zalu, vzjala gitaru i stala v basu perebirat' struny" (Having as it were reviewed her kingdom, tested her power, and made sure that everyone was submissive but that all the same it was dull, Natasha went to the ballroom, picked up her guitar, and began to pluck the bass strings). *SS* 5:305.

45. "'Gde èto my edem?' podumal Nikolaj. 'Po Kosomu lugu, dolžno byt': No net. Èto čto-to novoe, čego ja nikogda ne vidal. . . . Èto čto-to novoe i volšebnoe . . . vot kakoj-to volšebnyj les s perelivajuščimisja černymi tenjami i blestkami almazov.'" ("Where are we headed?" thought Nikolai. "It should be the Kosoi meadow before us. But no—this is something new and which I never have seen. . . . This is something new and enchanted . . . here is some kind of enchanted forest with intermingling black shadows and glittering diamonds.") *SS* 5:313–15.

46. Plato, *The Republic*, trans. B. Jowett (New York, 1941), p. 123.

47. Thomas de Quincey, "The English Mail-Coach," in *Tales and Prose Phantasies* (Edinburgh, 1890), pp. 270–329.

48. Ibid., pp. 312–13.

49. Ibid., Section 3, "Dream-Fugue," pp. 322–26.

50. See Calvin S. Brown, Jr., "The Musical Structure of de Quincey's Dream-Fugue," in *Musical Quarterly* 24, no. 3 (1948): 341–50. Brown calls attention to the *Traumdichtungen* of Jean-Paul Richter, which de Quincey translated. One of the characters in "Emmanuel's Dream Vision" asks the question "Was sagst du Bruder . . .?" cited in the epigraph to the Petya Dream Fugue section, which may have suggested, via the pun on *fügen*, de Quincey's device of contrapuntal form.

51. *SS* 7:168–70.

52. *SS* 7:168–70.

53. *SS* 12:132–212. The focus of the discussion in the text is on the use of musical metaphor and the theme of equivocation in art as it is projected in "The Kreutzer Sonata" and as it unwittingly, in the opinion of this writer, intensified Tolstoy's personal dilemma concerning the function of art. Therefore, the larger issue of Tolstoy's sexual ethos and the autobiographical referents that contributed to the inception of the story are not a part of the discussion. Rather, the issue of an autobiographical referent has been treated as a question of semantics. For an informative survey of the literature elicited by the sexual thematics of "The Kreutzer Sonata," see Peter Ulf Møller, *Postlude to The Kreutzer Sonata: Tolstoi and the Debate on Sexual Morality in Russian Literature in the 1890's* (Leiden, 1988).

54. *SS* 12:192.

55. Odoevskij, "Poslednij kvartet Betkhovena," p. 85. Faust goes on: "Ja uveren, čto muzyka Betkhovena dolžna byla ego samogo izmučit'" (I am sure that Beethoven's music must have tormented the composer himself).

56. *SS* 12:193.

57. *SS* 12:202.

58. Quoted by J.-J. Rousseau in his article "Sonata," in the *Encyclopédie* of 1748. See Peter Le Huray and James Day, *Music and Aesthetics* (Cambridge, England, 1981), p. 4.

59. *SS* 12:193. "The music of a peaceful and prosperous country is quiet and joyous and the government is orderly; the music of a country in turmoil shows dissatisfaction and the government is chaotic." See *The Wisdom of Confucius*, p. 28.

60. *SS* 12:193.

61. *SS* 19:246.

62. *SS* 12:193–94.

63. S. K. Langer, *Philosophy in a New Key* (Cambridge, 1957), p. 240.

64. According to P. I. Biryukov, Tolstoy allegedly commented to the Czech violist Oscar Nedbal (1874–1930), who visited Yasnaya Polyana in 1895, that he never would have written "The Kreutzer Sonata" had he heard the work in performance by "blagorodnye muzykanty"—in this context, "first-rank musicians"—but, he continued, "V slyšannom

mnoju ispolnenii dvukh plokho igravšikh muzykantov ona proizvela na menja vpečatlenie èrotičeskogo proizvedenija" (In the performance that I heard given, by two musicians who played badly, it produced on me the impression of an erotic composition). Cited in *Lev Tolstoj i muzyka*, pp. 133–34. S. L. Tolstoy also reports that his father subsequently repudiated his belief in the erotic nature of Beethoven's Sonata for Piano and Violin: "Lev Nikolaevič otkazalsja ot mysli, čto èta melodija izobražaet čuvstvennost', tak kak . . . muzyka ne možet izobrazat' to ili drugoe čuvstvo, a liš' čuvstva voobšče" (Lev Nikolaevich repudiated the idea that this melody depicts sensuality, since . . . music cannot depict this or that feeling, but only feelings in general). In *Lev Tolstoj i muzyka*, p. 134.

65. Langer, *Philosophy*, p. 240.

66. *SS* 15:87.

67. *SS* 15:176. "A meždu tem, pesnja bab byla nastojaščee iskusstvo, peredavavšee opredelennoe i sil'noe čuvsto. . . . 101-aja že sonata Betkhovena byla tol'ka neudačnaja popytka iskusstva ne soderžaščaja nikakogo opredelennogo čuvstva" (Nonetheless, the peasant women's songs were real art, transmitting a definite and strong emotion. . . . Beethoven's Sonata Opus 101 was only an unsuccessful artistic attempt, possessing no definite emotion at all).

68. *SS* 15:198.

69. *SS* 15:154.

70. *SS* 15:155.

71. In his diary for 5 January 1857 Tolstoy had recorded that at the home of F. M. Tolstoy (a music critic and no relation) he had met Ulybyshev. See Nikolaj Gusev, *Letopis' žizni i tvorčestva L. N. Tolstogo* (Moscow, 1958), p. 138. N. D. Kashkin suggested that Tolstoy had read Ulybyshev's work in the 1850s: *O Tolstom: vospominanija i kharakteristika predstavitelej različnykh nacij*, vol. 1 (Moscow, 1911), pp. 108–9.

72. A. D. Oulibicheff [Ulybyšev], *Beethoven, ses critiques et ses glossateurs* (Paris, 1857), p. 347. Translation mine.

73. Ibid., p. 277.

74. *SS* 15:154.

75. See Tolstoy's comment on vocal pitch and emotion in his letter of 16 January 1905 to S. A. Tolstaya (cited in *Lev Tolstoj i muzyka*, p. 201), and a similar statement formulated by Roger Sessions in *The Musical Experiences of Composer, Performer and Listener* (New York, 1962), p. 282. Tolstoy's awareness of a prediscriminatory response to music that is made manifest in vocal pitch anticipates the statements of Sessions.

76. *Lev Tolstoj i muzyka*, pp. 65, 85, 165.

77. Tolstoy to A. A. Tolstaya, 18 August 1857. *SS* 17:168. Tears and a tickling in the nose were for Tolstoy signs of the affective power of art. The transcription of that physiological reaction to music can be as-

cribed to two sources. The first is the letter to A. A. Tolstaya cited here.
The second is a letter to A. A. Fet of 11 May 1870 in which Tolstoy expressed how much he had been moved by reading "Majskaja noč'," a
copy of which the Russian poet had enclosed in a letter (*SS* 17:338):

> Я получил ваше письмо, любезный друг Афанасий Афанасьич,
> возвращаясь потный с работы с топором и заступом. . . . Развернув
> письмо, я—первое—прочел стихотворение и у меня защипало в
> носу: я пришел к жене и хотел прочесть, но не мог от слез умиления.

I received your letter, kind friend Afanasy Afanas'ich, when I returned
sweaty from work with an axe and spade. . . . After opening the letter, I—
first of all—read the poem and felt a tickling in my nose; I went over to
my wife and wanted to read it to her but couldn't from tears of tender
emotion.

Nekhlyudov's reaction appears in *SS* 13:479:

> Когда же хозяйка . . . вместе с бывшим директором департамента
> сели за фортепиано и заиграли хорошо разученную ими Пятую
> симфонию Бетховена, Нехлюдов почувствовал давно не испытан-
> ное душевное состояние полного довольства собой, точно как будто
> он теперь только узнал, какой он был хороший человек. Рояль был
> прекрасный, и исполнение симфонии было хорошее. По крайней
> мере, так показалось Нехлюдову, любившему и знавшему эту сим-
> фонию. Слушая прекрасное *Andante*, он почувствовал щипание в
> носу от умиления над самим собою и всеми своими добродетелями.

When the mistress of the house, . . . together with the former director of
the department, sat down at the piano and played Beethoven's Fifth
Symphony, which they had thoroughly mastered, Nekhlyudov felt a spiritual state that he had for a long time not experienced, of complete self-
satisfaction, precisely as if he had only now discovered what a good
person he was. The piano was excellent, and the performance of the Symphony was good. At least it seemed so to Nekhlyudov, who loved and
knew this symphony. Listening to the beautiful Andante, he felt a tickling
in the nose from tender emotion over himself and all his virtues.

78. *SS* 15:384.
79. Carlos Chavez, *Musical Thought* (Cambridge, Mass., 1961),
p. 44.
     I would like to thank the staff of the Morrison Music Library, Uni-
versity of California, Berkeley, for their assistance with the Beethoven
scores and the Ulybyshev materials, Ruth Aubrey for typing the manu-
script, and my family for listening to a *haus* reading of the first draft of
this paper, August 1986.

Love, Death, and Cricketsong

Prince Andrei at Mytishchi

John Weeks

Despite the vastness of *War and Peace,* or perhaps even because of it, certain passages of the novel stand out in particular relief. One of the most memorable of these concerns Andrei Bolkonsky's deathbed epiphany in the village of Mytishchi and his subsequent reconciliation there with Natasha Rostova.[1] Most readers will no doubt agree with Konstantin Leont'ev's praise: "This depiction of a half-dreaming, half-waking state, of the alternation of feverish delirium with lucidity is so beautiful, so profound and so true that I am at a loss for words to express my amazement!"[2] Leont'ev, however, reproaches Tolstoy for his use of onomatopoeia (*zvukopodražanie*), a device the critic finds irksome and maladroit.[3] In doing so, he overlooks the central role of sound texture in this passage. Onomatopoeia is but one of many acoustical effects the novelist deploys in order to convey the extraordinary psychological state—by turns delirious and pellucid—in which Andrei passes his final days. It is not the object of this essay to take issue with Leont'ev's objection to what he considered a hypernaturalistic "tic." Rather, an attempt will be made to analyze Tolstoy's use of aural texture to convey an impression of Andrei's unusual mental state. The ultimate aim of this analysis is to gain some insight into the way in which Tolstoy understood perception, memory, and understanding to be interrelated.

In obedience to the principle of recapitulation which shapes so much of *War and Peace,* the events that inform Andrei's epiphany are related from three points of view, creating a trio of distinct openings.[4] The first might be designated "Natasha's opening." Shortly after the Rostov family arrives in Great Mytishchi, Natasha learns that Andrei is lying, seriously wounded, only a few yards away. She has not seen him since the collapse of their engagement, and she feels burdened with guilt. Though she is told that Andrei's life is not in danger, Natasha becomes alarmed when she is refused permission to see him. She resolves to visit the dying man secretly at night, after the other Rostovs have gone to sleep.

> For a long time Natasha listened attentively to the sounds that reached her from inside and outside the room and did not move. First she heard her mother praying and sighing and the creaking of her bed under her, then Madame Schoss's familiar whistling snore and Sonya's gentle breathing. Then the countess called to Natasha. Natasha did not answer.
> "I think she's asleep, Mamma," said Sonya softly.
> After a short silence the countess spoke again but this time no one replied.
> Soon after that Natasha heard her mother's even breathing. Natasha did not move, though her little bare foot, thrust out from under the quilt, was growing cold on the bare floor.
> As if to celebrate a victory over everybody, a cricket chirped in a crack in the wall. A cock crowed far off and another replied near by. The shouting in the tavern had died down; only the moaning of the adjutant was heard. Natasha sat up.
> "Sonya, are you asleep? Mamma?" she whispered.
> No one replied.

Since it is, of course, difficult to distinguish objects in the dark, Natasha relies on aural cues to determine what is happening around her. However, Tolstoy's obvious emphasis on sounds in this passage is motivated by considerations beyond the requirements of realism or plot development. As we shall see, many of the details mentioned here—the chirping of the cricket, the noises in the courtyard, the adjutant's moaning—will become leitmotifs in the unfolding of Prince Andrei's spiritual drama.

Convinced that the others are sound asleep, Natasha quietly gets up and tiptoes to the door. Pausing there for a moment, she becomes aware of a sound unlike those catalogued so far. "It seemed to her that something heavy was beating rhythmically against all the walls of the room: it was her own heart, sinking with alarm and terror and overflowing with love." Since Natasha fears for Andrei's life, the fact that her heart is pounding comes as no surprise. Yet Natasha does not immediately recognize the source of the sound. For a moment she has the distinct sensation that the beating emanates from "something" (*čto-to*) in the room with her. Tolstoy is here using his favorite procedure, defamiliarization (*ostranenie*), on an almost microscopic scale. And although the "naive" reading is speedily replaced by a more prosaic explanation, a residue of the former remains in the emphasis given to the alarm, terror, and love that pervade Natasha's heart. As so often happens in Tolstoy, a physical sensation seems to require interpretation in emotional or spiritual terms. What is striking in the fiction of this inveterate moralist is the way Tolstoy heightens the physicality of a sensation before elucidating it; he thereby implicitly rejects both psychological and physiological reductionism in constructing his model of human nature. Instead, Tolstoy offers his own synthesis, in which sensory perceptions play an epistemological, educative, and even—with the proper stimulus—a metaphysical role.

In the next paragraph, "something" of a quite different order dominates Natasha's (and the reader's) attention; different both because it is a visual phenomenon and because it will carry us into the realm of metaphysics. Natasha confronts the physical reality of death.

> She opened the door and stepped across the threshold and onto the cold, damp earthen floor of the passage. The cold she felt refreshed her. With her bare feet she touched a sleeping man, stepped over him, and opened the door into the part of the hut where Prince Andrei lay. It was dark in there. In the farthest corner, on a bench beside a bed on which something was lying, stood a tallow candle which had burned itself down into the shape of a large mushroom.[5]

The dread that fills Natasha as she gazes on this new "something" (*čto-to*) causes her to hesitate before approaching the bed. This time the ritardando, from the moment Natasha catches sight of Andrei's form until she finally comes close enough to

make out his face, stretches over three full paragraphs. Like a
veteran film director, Tolstoy slows the tempo and invests the
process of unriddling this *čto-to* with a suspense that is oddly po-
tent; after all, the reader does know full well who is lying on the
cot. But Tolstoy is not concerned with surprising us at this stage
in the plot; rather, he has used Natasha's experience of percep-
tion-plus-delayed-recognition to rehearse the pattern of Andrei's
more complex experience, which is about to be related. Having
therefore performed her duty as far as the plot is concerned,
Natasha can now be excused for the moment; Tolstoy benefi-
cently allows the former lovers to see one another, and even to
touch, but their first verbal exchange is now cinematically post-
poned, as the next of our three openings commences.

With the second opening, the "epiphany" chapter formally
begins.[6] But Tolstoy offers a further delay, for the point of view is
still not handed to Andrei. It might be called the doctor's point of
view, because it shows how Andrei's companions perceive his
physical and mental condition after the battle of Borodino and
during the subsequent, arduous evacuation to Mytishchi:

> Seven days had passed since Prince Andrei found himself in the
> ambulance station on the field of Borodino. His feverish state and
> the inflammation of his bowels, which were injured, were in the
> doctor's opinion sure to carry him off. But on the seventh day he
> ate with pleasure a piece of bread with some tea, and the doctor
> noticed that his temperature was lower. He had regained con-
> sciousness that morning. The first night after they left Moscow
> had been fairly warm and he had remained in the *calèche,* but at
> Mytishchi the wounded man himself asked to be taken out and
> given some tea. The pain caused by his removal into the hut had
> made him groan aloud and again lose consciousness. When he
> had been placed on his camp bed he lay for a long time motionless
> with closed eyes. Then he opened them and whispered softly:
> "And the tea?" His remembering such a small detail of everyday
> life astonished the doctor. He felt Prince Andrei's pulse, and to his
> surprise and dissatisfaction found it had improved. He was dissat-
> isfied because he knew by experience that if his patient did not die
> now, he would do so a little later with greater suffering. Tim-
> okhin, the red-nosed major of Prince Andrei's regiment, had
> joined him in Moscow and was being taken along with him,
> having been wounded in the leg at the battle of Borodino. They
> were accompanied by a doctor, Prince Andrei's valet, his coach-
> man, and two orderlies.

The salient feature of this passage and of the point of view it embodies is its precise definition of time and place. "Seven days" have elapsed since Andrei lay "in the ambulance station on the field of Borodino"; "on the seventh day," Andrei eats a piece of bread and drinks some tea, having regained consciousness "that morning"; during "the first night after they had left Moscow," it is warm, but "at Mytishchi," Andrei asks to be carried indoors and given tea. The living, rather than the dead or dying, so concern themselves with the exact delineation of time and space; it is in this second opening passage, devoted to such a careful identification of these circumstances, that Andrei's companions from the world of the living take their places around him. The doctor checks his pulse, the valet brings him tea, Timokhin lies wounded in the corner.

The doctor, who may be regarded as emblematic of the passage as a whole, occupies a middle position between Natasha and Andrei. Although he knows a great deal more than they do about Andrei's moribund condition from a technical standpoint, he is completely incapable of understanding, as they eventually will, the transformation going on within his patient. Tolstoy is perhaps treating the poor doctor unfairly (the novelist's disdain for the medical profession was notorious), but the rest of Andrei's entourage fare no better. Their incomprehension of Andrei is expressed with great economy in the exchange between the feverish prince and Timokhin:

> They gave Prince Andrei some tea. He drank it eagerly, looking with feverish eyes at the door in front of him as if trying to understand and remember something.
> "I don't want any more. Is Timokhin here?" he asked.
> Timokhin crept along the bench to him.
> "I am here, your excellency."
> "How's your wound?"
> "Mine, sir? All right. But how about you?"
> Prince Andrei again pondered as if trying to remember something.
> "Couldn't one get a book?" he asked.
> "What book?"
> "The Gospels. I haven't one."
> The doctor promised to procure it for him and began to ask how he was feeling.

The confusion over Andrei's request for a copy of the *Evangelie* is telling. He knows what he wants, but the others have no direct access to his mind.[7] Inwardly preoccupied as he is, Andrei clarifies his request to Timokhin only with the greatest effort. A little later, Andrei, who is once again in severe pain, unaccountably asks that the Gospels be placed underneath him as a bolster. His companions naturally conclude that the sick man has started to rave again, but Andrei's bizarre request contains an obvious *podtekst*. The introduction of the Gospels at this point anticipates the impending shift in focus from Andrei's physical to his metaphysical condition. Understandably, the latter dimension is inaccessible from the external vantage point of the doctor's opening. Thus, his fellow officers see Andrei staring at the door to the hut "as if trying to understand and remember something." Just as Natasha did earlier, Andrei struggles to decipher the identity of a mysterious *čto-to*. Unlike Natasha, however, Andrei (who is wrestling with an unknown quite different from those his ex-fiancée encountered) brings to bear not only his cognitive and perceptual faculties but also his memory. The linking of these three actions of the mind will shortly assume crucial importance. And the reference to the door is a dual prefiguration: it looks ahead to Natasha's entry, which occurs at the end of the chapter following Andrei's meditation on love, and to Andrei's later dream of the closed door through which death would come for him.[8]

Now begins the third and final opening, in which the events already related concerning him are recapitulated from Andrei's point of view:

> The first time Prince Andrei understood where he was and what was the matter with him and remembered being wounded and how was when he asked to be carried into the hut after his *calèche* had stopped at Mytishchi. After growing confused from pain while being carried into the hut he again regained consciousness, and while drinking tea once more recalled all that had happened to him, and above all vividly remembered the moment at the ambulance station when, at the sight of the sufferings of a man he disliked, those new thoughts had come to him which promised him happiness. And those thoughts, though now vague and indefinite, again possessed his soul. He remembered that he had now a new source of happiness and that this happiness had something to do with the Gospels. That was why he asked for a copy of them.

The uncomfortable position in which they had put him and turned him over again confused his thoughts, and when he came to himself a third time it was in the complete stillness of the night. Everybody near him was sleeping. A cricket chirped from across the passage; someone was shouting and singing in the street; cockroaches rustled on the table, on the icons, and on the walls, and a big fly flopped at the head of the bed and around the candle beside him, the wick of which was charred and had shaped itself like a mushroom.

The notation of time and place here bears a superficial resemblance to that exactitude Tolstoy had displayed everywhere in the novel, up to and including the other two openings. It could be argued that Andrei's reckoning of time differs from ours only in the units of measurement: in place of day and night he substitutes swoons and returns to consciousness. However, a closer look at the Russian text reveals a different pattern in the organization of time, one which is, unfortunately, obscured in the Maude translation.

В первый раз князь Андрей понял, где он был и что с ним было, и вспомнил то, что он был ранен и как *в ту минуту,* когда коляска остановилась в Мытищах, он попросился в избу. Спутавшись *опять* от боли, он опомнился *другой раз* в избе, когда пил чай, и *тут опять,* повторив в своем воспоминании все, что с ним было, он живее всего представил себе *ту минуту* на перевязочном пункте, когда, при виде страданий нелюбимого им человека, ему пришли эти новые, сулившие ему счастье мысли. И мысли эти, хотя и неясно и неопределенно, *теперь опять* овладели его душой. Он вспомнил, что у него было *теперь* новое счастье и что это счастье имело что-то такое общее с Евангелием. Потому-то он попросил Евангелие. Но дурное положение, которое дали его ране, новое переворачиванье *опять* смешали его мысли, и он *в третий раз* очнулся к жизни уже в совершенной тишине ночи. Все спали вокруг него. (Emphasis added)

Tolstoy's Russian here exhibits a density of paradigmatic connections that makes the text almost a poem in prose. Note, for example, how the passage has suddenly become saturated with synonyms for "moment": "v pervyi raz," "v tu minutu," "drugoi raz," "tu minutu," "teper'," "v tretii raz." An equally important set of temporal markers stresses the idea of recurrence: "opiat'" (twice), "tut opiat'," "teper' opiat'." These last two phrases represent the intersection of the two temporal hierarchies; both might be translated "once again." Andrei's chronometer is indeed sharply different now from the one people ordinarily use. Instead of a Heraclitean flux, time has become for him an array of contemporaneous shining moments. Andrei lives, as T. S. Eliot put it, "at the still point of the turning world."

Yet there remains a perceptible forward movement in the passage. Andrei's path has ceased to be a progression in time in order to become an ascension in spirit. He regains consciousness three times after arriving in Mytishchi. The first time, he realizes where he is and recalls the circumstances of his wounding at Borodino. He asks to be carried into the hut, but the pain of the transfer overwhelms him and he passes out again. The second time he comes to his senses, he asks for some tea. This time he recalls the entire scene in the field hospital at Borodino: how he lay next to his personal enemy, Anatole Kuragin, and how the spectacle of the other man's physical suffering moved him to pity and forgiveness. Associated with this memory is Andrei's dawning awareness of a "new happiness" (*novoe sčast'e*) which "had something to do with the Gospels." He therefore requests a copy of the Gospels, but loses consciousness again before it can be brought to him. The third and last time he recovers, it is already late at night. At this point the text does not explicitly indicate that Andrei remembers anything; instead, he seems to be absorbed in registering a variety of sensory impressions of his surroundings. However, he will shortly resume his meditations on the nature of happiness and love, precisely where he left off before swooning.

Andrei recalls, in succession, where he is, what has happened to him, how he felt when he saw Kuragin in agony at the ambulance station, and what—spurred by that pathetic sight—he has come to understand by the notion of happiness. The shift from material to moral concerns is paralleled by the sequence of his requests. He asks, in turn, for conveyance into the hut, a cup of tea, and a copy of the Gospels. As it was with Andrei's train of recollections, the text is silent about any requests he might have wanted to make on awakening the third time, in the middle of the night. In this case there is an obvious, matter-of-fact explanation: the others are all asleep. But even while awake they have failed Andrei more than once; their rough handling has twice caused him to lose consciousness, while his request for the Gospels has so far gone unmet. There simply is no more to be asked of them. The further Andrei advances spiritually, the further he leaves them behind, caught in the web of their mundane concerns.[9] This night will be Andrei's equivalent of Christ's vigil in Gethsemane (not for nothing will his meditations falter momentarily over the question, "And why was the Son . . . ?"), and the others have shown themselves unable to keep watch with him. Until Natasha rejoins him, Andrei's solitude is not only physical and moral, but total.

His most significant act, the only one of which he is capable at present, has been to remember. Words sharing the same root as the Russian word for memory (*pamjat'*) occur four times here: "vspomnil," "he recalled" (twice), "vospominanie," "recollection," and "opomnilsja," "[he] regained consciousness." The word *opomnilsja* is interesting for the way it demonstrates the convergence of memory and understanding. To regain consciousness, the root of the Russian word implies, is to understand, to recollect, where one is. This verb, although it is used here in its literal sense, serves to reinforce the passage's motif of memory. And when Tolstoy substitutes a synonym for *opomnilsja,* the whole complex having to do with memory suddenly resonates with new significance.

Curiously, the substituted verb does not contain any form of the root for "memory." The third time Andrei becomes conscious again, we read, "on v tretii raz *očnulsja k žizni.*" The Maude version ("he came to himself a third time") has lost an important connotation of the phrase, which is better captured by the colloquial English "he came back to life." The latter idiom seems commonplace enough both in English and in Russian, but the reference to life, at a time when Andrei's grasp on it looks increasingly precarious, is far from accidental. Tolstoy would have us realize that Andrei is "coming back to life" in an extraordinary sense. To understand just what sort of revival Tolstoy is alluding to, as well as what part is played in it by memory, we have to go back to a scene that occurred hundreds of pages earlier in the novel.

We recall how, at the end of 1811, less than a year before Napoleon led his armies into Russia, the Rostovs have gathered at the family estate of Otradnoe to celebrate Christmas.[10] One evening Natasha and Nikolai try to cheer themselves up by exchanging reminiscences about their childhood. It quickly becomes a game, the object of which is to remember events further and further back in time. When the music tutor, Dimmler, approaches and asks what the preoccupied young people are talking about, Natasha gives the unexpected reply, "my filosofstvuem" (We're philosophizing). She then carries the game she and Nikolai have been playing a crucial step forward. In hushed tones she says to Nikolai and Sonya, "You know, I think . . . that when you remember like that, you remember, remember everything, you remember all the way back to what was earlier, before you were on the earth." Sonya calls this process of remembering metempsychosis, but it is really Plato's doctrine of anamnesis paraphrased. The connection with Plato becomes firmer when Natasha goes on to say, in reply to Sonya's incorrect gloss, "No, you know, I don't believe that we have been in animals. . . . But I know for sure that we were angels there some place, and were here, and from that remember everything."

This conception of memory, so artlessly expressed by Natasha, presupposes that the human soul is immortal (or at least that it endures for many lifetimes), and Natasha goes on to state this as a simple fact. In the space of half a page, the heroine of *War and Peace* restates several of Plato's most important ideas about epistemology and ontology! However, by not going beyond the affirmation of the soul's immortality, Natasha leaves unstated a major corollary that Plato develops. He argues that all men remember, however dimly, their prenatal existence among the divine Ideas and, moreover, know that they will return to the celestial sphere after death. Yet, illogically, they fear to die. The philosopher should welcome death as a way of returning to that divine realm of which we on earth retain a hazy recollection. This is what Socrates meant (in the *Phaedo*) when he said, as he calmly awaited his own execution, "Death is an awakening."[11]

It is this metaphysical connection between memory and the immortality of the soul that comes into play when Andrei awakens, for the third time, to "life." Whereas on the two previous occasions we were told specifically what Andrei remembers, the text is now silent on this score precisely because the contents of his present recollections are ineffable. As Natasha would put it, Andrei has "remembered all the way back"—to God.

Memory has brought Andrei to the threshold of epiphany. He has long since left all his present companions far behind. Now Andrei parts company with Plato as well: he will travel the rest of the way to his goal as a Christian. This shift away from pagan thought has as an immediate consequence the reduction of the role of memory in Andrei's spiritual development. Henceforward its duties will be taken over by other faculties of the mind, notably perception. I do not mean to suggest that we can make the crude equations paganism = memory; Christianity = perception. Nevertheless, we cannot ignore the role that pain and other physical sensations play in the decidedly Christian turn Andrei's thought now takes. Andrei's *new* happiness makes its reappearance at the same time that he requests a copy of the Gospels (the *New* Testament). Not coincidentally, Andrei is said to pass out for the second time after being turned over in bed; the Russian is "novoe perevoračivan'e" (being turned *anew*).[12] The re-turning in question is strictly physical, yet it evokes ancient metaphysical associations with the idea of the circle, while the adjective *novoe*, "new," in the present context inevitably links these associations to the Gospels.[13] Andrei's physical agony in being turned is thus a figure for the metaphysical agony of being reborn in spirit.

It is very much with the condition of Andrei's soul that Tolstoy wishes us to be concerned, and he now provides an almost clinical analysis of the dying man's psychic state:

> His mind[14] was not in a normal state. A healthy man usually thinks of, feels, and remembers innumerable things simultaneously, but has the power and will to select one sequence of thoughts or events on which to fix his whole attention. A healthy man can tear himself away from the deepest reflections to say a civil word to someone who comes in and can then return again to his own thoughts. But Prince Andrei's mind was not in a normal

state in that respect. All the powers of his mind were more active and clearer than ever, but they acted apart from his will. Most diverse thoughts and images occupied him simultaneously. At times his brain suddenly began to work with a vigor, clearness, and depth it had never reached when he was in health, but suddenly in the midst of its work it would turn to some unexpected idea, and he had not the strength to turn it back again.

This passage offers an important corrective to the commonsense judgment (on the part of the doctor and the others in Andrei's entourage) that Andrei has "gone out of his mind" with fever and pain. Tolstoy makes clear that Andrei is not at all in an irrational state. Except for the brief spells during which he is overpowered by delirium, "all the powers of his mind were more active and clearer than ever." His powers of perception, in particular, have reached a state of preternatural acuity. The main difference between Andrei in his present condition and Andrei as he was prior to Borodino consists in the fact that he can no longer control the activity of his mind. This may not be a normal state, but neither is it a typical form of illness. Indeed, the comparison between the "healthy" man and the "sick" prince is laced with irony; our received ideas about health suffer from the same limitations as the doctor's understanding of disease. Andrei may not be able, just now, to "tear himself away from the deepest reflections to say a civil word to someone who comes in," but this is because he has more momentous work to accomplish. Once this is done, he will indeed be capable of greeting the one who will come in (Natasha), and in a way profoundly more important than "civil."

For Andrei, thought has become not an activity but a state of being, induced and modified by stimuli external to his will. The ordering of three passages in the text is significant in this regard. First, at the conclusion of Andrei's opening, Tolstoy describes how Andrei awakens in the middle of the night and how he hears, feels, and sees various things: a chirping cricket, rustling cockroaches, someone shouting and singing, a "fat, autumnal fly" plopping on his pillow, and a tallow candle burned down in the shape of a large mushroom. Next, the novelist defines Andrei's spiritual state in the passage beginning "His mind was not in a normal state," which has just been discussed. Finally, he quotes Andrei's interior monologue, which conveys his epiphanic experience. Without the intermediate passage describing the condition of Andrei's psyche, we would pass directly from the catalogue of the external circumstances he perceives to the interior monologue in which he resumes his meditation on the nature of love. We would be fully justified in concluding that Andrei has *willfully* redirected his attention away from his surroundings to a spiritual object of contemplation. As the text stands, however, we know that Andrei's will plays no part in what is happening. Something induces Andrei's train of thought, but what? The ultimate answer, inasmuch as we have reached the verge of a revelatory experience, can never be stated with certainty. However, it makes sense to look for the proximate cause of Andrei's meditations in the catalogue of sensory stimuli headed by the chirping cricket. To a man whose soul "is not in a normal state," such physical stimuli might combine to produce quite unphysical impressions. The paradox is that the physical stimuli are here shown to produce moral impressions; we have arrived at the unexpected idea of a kind of *synaesthesia of moral perception*. In the same way that we may experience the tactile sensation of heat as loud or blinding, we may also— Tolstoy would have us believe—experience terrible pain as moral knowledge. (This was the meaning, as we saw earlier, of Andrei's "being turned anew.")

Tolstoy goes even further than this. Implicit in the structure of Andrei's epiphany as Tolstoy depicts it is the daring assertion that the chirping of a cricket, the plopping of a fly, the drunken singing of an unseen stranger, and the guttering of a fungiform candle can somehow coalesce to produce in Andrei's febrile soul the sensation, that is to say, the direct knowledge, of divine love. Stated in this way, the connection between these sensory perceptions and moral insight appears tenuous, if not preposterous. Note, however, the interplay between them during Andrei's meditation:

> "Yes, a new happiness was revealed to me of which man cannot be deprived," he thought as he lay in the semidarkness of the quiet hut, gazing fixedly before him with feverish, wide-open eyes. "A happiness lying beyond material forces, outside the ma-

terial influences that act on man—a happiness of the soul alone, the happiness of loving. Every man can understand it, but to conceive it and enjoin it was possible only for God. But how did God enjoin that law? And why was the Son . . . ?"

And suddenly the sequence of these thoughts broke off, and Prince Andrei heard (without knowing whether it was a delusion or reality) a soft whispering voice incessantly and rhythmically repeating "piti-piti-piti," and then "ti-ti," and then again "piti-piti-piti," and "ti-ti" once more. At the same time he felt that above his face, above the very middle of it, some strange airy structure was being erected out of slender needles or splinters, to the sound of this whispered music. He felt that he had to balance carefully (though it was difficult) so that this airy structure should not collapse; but nevertheless it kept collapsing and again slowly rising to the sound of whispered rhythmic music—"it stretches, stretches, spreading out and stretching," said Prince Andrei to himself. While listening to this whispering and feeling the sensation of this drawing out and the construction of this edifice of needles, he also saw by glimpses a red halo round the candle, and heard the rustle of the cockroaches and the buzzing of the fly that flopped against his pillow and his face. Each time the fly touched his face it gave him a burning sensation and yet to his surprise it did not destroy the structure, though it knocked against the very region of his face where it was rising. But besides this there was something else of importance. It was something white by the door—the statue of a sphinx, which also oppressed him.

Just when Andrei reaches the point of trying to understand Christ's sacrifice on the Cross ("And why was the Son . . . ?"), the chirping of the cricket obtrudes upon his consciousness. In his present condition it is not a cricket that he hears but a "whispering music." This music provides accompaniment to the strange sensation Andrei has that a delicate edifice of pins or splinters is rising from his face. Andrei also perceives, "in snatches" (*uryvkami*), the candle, the rustling cockroaches, and the buzzing fly, which causes a burning sensation about his face.

A significant item is now added to this catalogue of external details: the white statue of a sphinx. This detail provides the clue we need in order to understand what is happening to Andrei; clearly, he has begun to be delirious again. Yet the demands of art are also served here: the sphinx is an apt image for the puzzle Andrei is trying to solve within himself. Externalized in this fashion, Andrei's unanswered questions ("But how did God enjoin that law? And why was the Son . . . ?") draw attention to themselves once again, via his delirium-racked sense of sight. Andrei now tries to reassert his previous, lucid perception of his surroundings in order to suppress the delirium and concentrate once again on the answer to these questions:

> "But perhaps that's my shirt on the table," he thought, "and that's my legs, and that is the door, but why is it always stretching and drawing itself out, and 'piti-piti-piti' and 'ti-ti' and 'piti-piti-piti' . . . ? That's enough, please leave off!" Prince Andrei painfully entreated someone. And suddenly thoughts and feelings again swam to the surface of his mind with peculiar clearness and force.

Andrei here oscillates rapidly between lucidity and delirium. When delirium overtakes him the "piti-piti-piti" of the cricket becomes part of his disorientation; when lucidity returns, however, Andrei's sensory perceptions recede from the text and his "thoughts and feelings" about love "swim to the surface" again.

Have Andrei's senses parted company with his active mind? He has always displayed a propensity for abstraction, for being divorced from this world of sensations. However, he never manages to dwell, even temporarily, in the sphere of the Absolute to which he feels drawn—until he is wounded at Austerlitz. The proximity of physical dissolution enables Andrei to obtain his first glimpse of the Absolute. Now, after Borodino, slowly dying and in great pain, Andrei is once again able to contemplate the realm of the eternal and the infinite. And pain plays a crucial role in this breakthrough; his "being turned anew," as we should remind ourselves yet again, began with it. Andrei, a Bolkonsky, is such an inveterate rationalist that only the two serious wounds he receives can halt the great engine of his ratiocinative faculties. The significance of the physical perceptions that are secondary to his excruciating pain is twofold. On the one hand, they combine with his delirium to disrupt the blessed vision which he struggles to maintain; on the other hand, during his moments of relative lucidity they stimulate that same vision. In the passage last quoted, Andrei responds with exasperation to the "piti-piti-piti" of the cricket. Immediately thereafter, his meditation on love recommences (still outside his will) and reaches its climax. Is this merely a juxtaposition? In discussing the mechanics, so to speak, of an epiphany, we cannot expect to find logical connections. However, a significant piece of evidence in the text links the love of God to that inexorable cricket.

Andrei's epiphany climaxes in this moving passage:

> "Yes—love," he thought again quite clearly. "But not love which loves for something, for some quality, for some purpose, or for some reason, but the love which I—while dying—first experienced when I saw my enemy and yet loved him. I experienced that feeling of love which is the very essence of the soul and does not require an object. Now again I feel that bliss. To love one's neighbors, to love one's enemies, to love everything, to love God in all His manifestations. It is possible to love someone dear to you with human love, but an enemy can only be loved by divine love. That is why I experienced such joy when I felt that I loved that man. What has become of him? Is he alive? . . .
>
> "When loving with human love one may pass from love to hatred, but divine love cannot change. No, neither death nor anything else can destroy it. It is the very essence of the soul. Yet how many people have I hated in my life? And of them all, I loved and hated none as I did her." And he vividly pictured to himself Natasha, not as he had done in the past with nothing but her charms which gave him delight, but for the first time picturing to himself her soul. And he understood her feelings, her sufferings, shame, and remorse. He now understood for the first time all the cruelty of his rejection of her, the cruelty of his rupture with her. "If only it were possible for me to see her once more! Just once, looking into those eyes to say . . ."
>
> "Piti-piti-piti and ti-ti and piti-piti-piti boom!" flopped the fly. . . . And his attention was suddenly carried into another world, a world of reality and delirium in which something particular was happening.

His meditation breaks off again when the cricket returns to the foreground of his consciousness and the fly plops loudly next to his ear. Thus, the culminating moment of Andrei's vision is framed by the cricket's "whispering music," and we may reasonably assume that the insect sang all the time Andrei was thinking as well. Bearing this in mind, consider the sound texture of the following excerpt from the passage just quoted (emphasis has been added to the pivotal word *ljubit'*, "to love"):

"*Любить* ближних, *любить* врагов своих. Все *любить*—*любить* Бога во всех проявлениях. *Любить* человека дорогого можно человеческой любовью; но только врага можно *любить* любовью божеской.*"

"To *love* one's neighbors, to *love* one's enemies, to *love* everything, to *love* God in all His manifestations. It is possible to *love* someone dear to you with human love, but an enemy can only be *loved* by divine love." [15]

Is it not possible to hear an echo of "piti-piti-piti" in the regular tattoo of *ljubit'-ljubit'-ljubit'* in this passage? Circumstantial support for this contention can be found in the similar way Tolstoy uses the related words *tjanetsja, rastjagivaetsja, tjažel,* and *vtjagival* to convey an aural impression of the viscous, undulating rhythm of Andrei's delirium (*bred*). In this instance Tolstoy makes the connection explicit (not once but twice) in the text: "O, kak tjažel ètot neperestajuščij bred" and "bred vtjagival ego v svoju oblast'." Just as Andrei himself unconsciously repeats forms of the word group *tjanetsja* at each onset of his delirium, the reader unconsciously senses the association that is being made. In the light of this example of an almost musical motif, the hypothesized link between the cricket's "piti-piti-piti"—itself explicitly identified in the text as "whispering music"—and Andrei's vision of divine love becomes less farfetched.

Further evidence for this argument is found in two scenes from the novel which, though they are written in a very different key, exhibit a structure similar to that of Andrei's epiphany scene. In the first, Pierre—who has just been reproaching himself for being afraid at Borodino—has an unusual dream about the meaning of courage under fire:

Afterwards when he recalled those thoughts Pierre was convinced that someone outside himself had spoken them, though the impressions of that day had evoked them. He had never, it seemed to him, been able to think and express his thoughts like that when awake.

"To endure war is the most difficult subordination of man's freedom to the law of God," the voice had said. "Simplicity is submission to the will of God; you cannot escape from Him. And *they* are simple. *They* do not talk, but act. The spoken word is silver but the unspoken is golden. Man can be master of nothing while he fears death, but he who does not fear it possesses all. If there were no suffering, man would not know his limitations, would not know himself. The hardest thing [Pierre went on thinking, or hearing, in his dream] is to be able in your soul to unite the meaning of all. To unite all?" he asked himself. "No, not to unite. Thoughts cannot be united, but to *harness* all these thoughts together is what we need! Yes, one *must harness* them, *must harness* them!" he repeated to himself with inward rapture, feeling that these words and they alone expressed what he wanted to say and solved the question that tormented him.

"Yes, one must harness, it is time to harness."

"Time to harness, time to harness, your excellency! Your excellency!" some voice was repeating. "We must harness, it is time to harness. . . ."

It was the voice of the groom, trying to wake him.

For the reader, who has also experienced the way external sounds can impinge on dreams, Pierre's vision of a new way to unite mankind immediately dissolves into comedy.

In the second scene, Petya Rostov has given his saber to a Cossack to sharpen and is now napping prior to the partisans' sortie against the French encamped nearby:

Petya's eyes began to close and he swayed a little.

The trees were dripping. Quiet talking was heard. The horses neighed and jostled one another. Someone snored.

"*Ozheg-zheg, Ozheg-zheg . . .*" hissed the saber against the whetstone, and suddenly Petya heard an harmonious orchestra playing some unknown, sweetly solemn hymn. Petya was as musical as Natasha and more so than Nikolai, but had never learned music or thought about it, and so the melody that unexpectedly came to his mind seemed to him particularly fresh and attractive. The music became more and more audible. The melody grew and passed from one instrument to another. And what was played was a fugue—though Petya had not the least conception of what a fugue is. Each instrument—now resembling a violin and now a horn—but better and clearer than violin or horn—played its own part, and before it had finished the melody merged with another instrument that began almost the same air, and then with a third and fourth; and they all blended into one and again became separate and again blended, now into solemn church music, now into something dazzlingly brilliant and triumphant.

"Oh—why, that was in a dream!" Petya said to himself, as he

lurched forward. "It's in my ears. But perhaps it's music of my own. Well, go on, my music! Now!"

He closed his eyes, and, from all sides as if from a distance, sounds fluttered, grew into harmonies, separated, blended, and again all mingled into the same sweet and solemn hymn. "Oh, this is delightful! As much as I like and as I like!" said Petya to himself. He tried to conduct that enormous orchestra.

"Now softly, softly die away!" and the sounds obeyed him. "Now fuller, more joyful. Still more and more joyful!" And from an unknown depth rose increasingly triumphant sounds. "Now voices join in!" ordered Petya. And at first from afar he heard men's voices and then women's. The voices grew in harmonious triumphant strength, and Petya listened to their surpassing beauty in awe and joy.

With a solemn triumphal march there mingled a song, the drip from the trees, and the hissing of the saber, "*Ozheg-zheg-zheg . . .*" and again the horses jostled one another and neighed, not disturbing the choir but joining in it.

Petya did not know how long this lasted: he enjoyed himself all the time, wondered at his enjoyment and regretted that there was no one to share it. He was awakened by Likhachev's kindly voice.

"It's ready, your honor; you can split a Frenchman in half with it!"

The humor of this scene is good-natured and indulgent, quite unlike the satirical mirth of the preceding one. Tolstoy was, after all, at all times more charitable toward the innocent illusions of childhood than he was toward the vain delusions of adults. Yet in both of these comic scenes is the same undertone of seriousness, for Pierre has just witnessed the carnage of the battle of Borodino and Petya is about to ride off to meet his own death. In theme, then, as well as in structure, these two episodes may rightly be regarded as seriocomic parodies of the scene at Mytishchi.

Unlike Pierre, Andrei and Petya are about to die. They are, therefore, given dispensation to hear the music of the spheres. For Petya, it comes in the form of a dream about a heavenly orchestra. For Andrei, the music is more subdued; in fact, it is reduced to a "whisper." Yet whether the hymn swells to symphonic volume or subsides to a nocturne it is the same universal song. Who is the singer for Andrei? A cricket. The music, which Petya heard as something "dazzlingly brilliant and triumphant [*pobed-*

noe]" and, later, as a song mingling with a "solemn triumphal [*pobednym*] march," is performed at Mytishchi by this lowliest of God's creatures, "[a]s if to celebrate a victory [*pobedu*] over everybody."

We first heard the cricket's plangent melody as Natasha tip-toed out of her family's lodgings, and it is fitting that she now reappear on the scene. Fitting, moreover, because Andrei's epiph-any has come to an end and he is now prepared to solve the iden-tity of this new "sphinx" looming before him. Thus, in the larger scheme of things, when Andrei's meditation breaks off for the last time it is not so much disrupted by the cricket's chirping and the fly's flopping on his pillow as it is redirected by forces outside his will. Tolstoy is careful to show, with the greatest psychologi-cal realism, how Andrei resists this forcible transfer of his atten-tion: "Prince Andrei wished to return to that former world of pure thought, but he could not, and delirium drew him back into its domain." Note that reality and delirium have now become in-distinguishable for Andrei ("And his attention was suddenly car-ried into the other world, the world of reality and delirium"). Previously, they were as separate in his mind as they normally appear to the rest of us ("without knowing whether it was in the delirium or in reality that he heard this").[16] By trying willfully to push delirium away he succeeds only in exacerbating his pain and losing consciousness. Hence, Andrei's single act of will in the whole revelatory chapter is not only impotent but is a posi-tive hindrance to the attainment of his goal, that of returning to the world of pure thought. No other lesson is driven home so relentlessly in *War and Peace* as this one: that *will* hinders understanding, and willful behavior fails to achieve its pur-poses. Andrei is now in the hands of God (as he always was), and he can no more will a return to his epiphanic vision than the fly landing helplessly on the pillow beside him can cease doing so. "My Father, if it be possible, let this cup pass from me; nevertheless, not as I will, but as Thou wilt." This is the true answer, which Andrei is now almost ready to receive, to the question, "And why was the Son . . . ?" And it is God's will that Andrei be drawn back into the physical world for a short while longer, in order to impart some fragment of the divine love he has glimpsed to Natasha, the woman he has wronged with his hatred.

For some time now, she has been watching for her cue just outside the door. At last, having kept Natasha—and us—in suspense long enough, Lev Nikolaevich Tolstoy, with all the magisterial authority of a cinema *auteur,* issues the long-awaited gesture.

NOTES

1. In the Russian text, book 3, part 3, chaps. 31–32; book 11, chap. 15 of the Maude translation. All citations from the original are as given in *SS.* In excerpts from the Maude translation I have changed "Andrew" to "Andrei" and "Nicholas" to "Nikolai."

2. "Èto izobraženie polusna i poluprobuždenija, poperemennogo perekhoda iz gorjačečnogo breda v sostojanie pravil'nogo soznanija—do togo prekrasno, do togo gluboko i pravdivo, čto ja ne nakhožu podkhodjaščikh slov dlja vyraženija moego izumlenija!" K. Leont'ev, *Analiz, stil' i vejanie: O romanakh gr. L. N. Tolstogo* (Providence, 1965), p. 41.

3. Ibid., pp. 41–42.

4. For a discussion of Tolstoy's handling of time in *War and Peace,* see Nicholas O. Warner, "The Texture of Time in *War and Peace,*" *Slavic and East European Journal* 28 (1984): 192–204. Patricia Carden has explored Tolstoy's debt to Plato's ideas on the epistemological function of memory, in "The Recuperative Powers of Memory: Tolstoy's *War and Peace,*" in John Garrard, ed., *The Russian Novel from Pushkin to Pasternak* (New Haven, ca. 1983), pp. 81–102. The present essay was inspired by and is dedicated to Professor Carden, to whom goes most of the credit for its strengths. The responsibility for its faults rests solely with me.

5. I have made a slight revision (regarding the mushroom) in the Maude translation in order to bring out the identity of the details in this scene and the later one in which Andrei surveys the same objects.

6. In the Russian text, chap. 31 ends with Andrei silently extending his hand to Natasha and chap. 32 begins by retracing Andrei's path from the battlefield dressing station to the hut in Mytishchi. In the Maude translation the Russian chaps. 30, 31, and 32 are subsumed as unnumbered sections, set apart by blank lines, within chap. 15.

7. The misunderstanding may be even greater than the Maude translation indicates. "Nel'zja li dostat' knigu?" would have been better rendered as "Couldn't [some]one get *the* book?" (emphasis added). In the latter version the gulf separating Andrei from Timokhin and the others widens significantly.

8. Natasha's appearance has already been recounted from *her* point of view, in the previous chapter. The reader, who will experience her second entry with a bit of déjà vu, is thus also involved by Tolstoy in the process of understanding and *remembering*.

Andrei's dream is described in book 4, part 1, chap. 16 in the Russian text (book 12, chap. 4 in the Maude translation).

9. We learned, in the doctor's opening, that Andrei actually requested tea twice, once when he asked to be carried into the hut and again when he recovered from the ensuing swoon. The doctor marveled at Andrei's ability, in his present condition, to remember such a trivial matter. In the sequence of Andrei's spiritual development, however, this form of memory represents only the first stage. Since he must transcend all worldly attachments, even memory may be harmful, when it serves to strengthen such attachments. The doctor, who necessarily possesses keen powers of recall regarding the symptoms of disease and the minutiae of his patients' conditions, is therefore trapped in false consciousness. Memory, then, is a polyvalent notion; to the *pamjatlivost'* that so impressed the doctor may be opposed that as-yet-unnamed, metaphysical variety of recollection in which Andrei is about to engage.

10. The scene appears in book 2, part 4, chap. 10 of the Russian text (book 7, chap. 10 of the Maude translation).

11. Patricia Carden gives a thorough analysis of the Otradnoe scene and its sources in Plato's thought in "The Recuperative Powers of Memory," pp. 83–85. I have quoted her revised versions of the two speeches by Natasha. Socrates' famous aphorism is of course quoted verbatim by Andrei just before he dies (book 4, part 2, chap. 16 in the Russian text; book 12, chap. 4 in the Maude translation).

12. Again, the Maude translation, though accurate as to the basic sense, loses some of the overtones of the Russian: "The uncomfortable position in which they had put him and *turned him over again* confused his thoughts" (emphasis added).

13. Platon (!) Karataev's renowned *kruglost'* is related to this mystical tradition of associating the figure of the circle with God. Likewise, Pierre's stripped and ineffectually turning cognitive screw symbolizes the fact that he is striving after knowledge of the Absolute, but in the wrong way.

14. The Russian word *duša*, as Hugh McLean noted to me after reading the original version of this paper, presents a vexed problem for the English translator. "Mind" is too narrow a rendering, while "soul" is a shade too theological in most instances; in the present passage, "psyche" is perhaps the best equivalent. Nevertheless, since Tolstoy invokes Christian dogma elsewhere in this chapter, "soul" will be appropriate in some places.

15. The Maude translation of this passage has been slightly revised

in order to reproduce Tolstoy's insistent repetition of the infinitive form *ljubit'*, "to love." The Soviet-mandated spelling of "God" (*Bog*) with a lowercase letter has also been emended.

16. I have varied the Maude version of these two lines slightly: "And his attention was suddenly carried into *another* world, *a* world of reality and delirium"; and "without knowing whether it was *a delusion or reality*" (emphasis added). As with the earlier reference to the Gospels (*the* book), the use of the definitive article sharpens the dichotomy stated here, as Tolstoy probably intended. The Russian phrases are, respectively: "I vnimanie ego vdrug pereneslos' v drugoj mir dejstvitel'nosti i breda," and "ne znaja, v bredu ili v dejstvitel'nosti on slyšit èto."

The Dichotomy Between Flesh and Spirit

Plato's Symposium in Anna Karenina

Irina Gutkin

As far back as 1918, in his critical biography of Lev Tolstoy, George Rapall Noyes pointed out Tolstoy's indebtedness to Plato's philosophy.[1] Although a few articles have been written recently that deal with the Platonic contribution to Tolstoy's thought, the issue still awaits systematic analysis.[2] In her article on the Platonic element in Tolstoy's art and psychology, Donna Orwin focuses on Tolstoy's perception of the conflict between individual freedom and responsibility and notes some similarities and differences between Plato's and Tolstoy's interpretation of this conflict. In sketching the history of Tolstoy's interest in Plato, Orwin itemizes references to Plato's name and works in Tolstoy's writings, including his diaries, letters, and novels. As for *Anna Karenina*, Orwin mentions that in that novel Tolstoy "takes up the Platonic theme again," but she finds that it receives a "shorthand" treatment in the form of a "minor but crucial character named Platon" who appears at the end of the novel.[3]

A closer analysis, however, reveals the intrinsic presence of Plato's ideas on the nature of love in the subtext of *Anna Karenina*. These ideas not only contribute to the philosophical basis of the novel, but also provide an ideological liaison between the two seemingly unconnected plot lines of *Anna Karenina* and, to a great extent, determine the novel's hierarchy of characters. Among the philosophical questions that tormented Lev Tolstoy throughout his life the dichotomy between flesh and spirit in human nature probably ranks second only to the meaning of death. This dichotomy is especially manifest in love. Tolstoy's focus on this contradictory aspect of human nature is apparent in several of his works: present in *Childhood,* central in *Family Happiness,* important in *The Cossacks,* and recurrent throughout *War and Peace.* An analysis of Tolstoy's writings, published and unpublished, from the early 1870s suggests that the problem of the duality of human nature—the proportion of flesh and spirit in an individual's psyche—was not only central in his private ruminations but had become a theme calling for treatment in art.

In her diaries of that time, Sofya Andreevna commented on Tolstoy's persistent study of Greek philosophers and writers, including Plato. Tolstoy, she said, yearned to write "a work so pure, gracious, in which there would be nothing excessive—like all Greek literature, the entire Greek school. He is dreaming of writing a novel about life in old Russia."[4] In fact, Tolstoy conceived of a novel set in the time of Peter the Great. The famous sentence "vse smešalos' v dome Oblonskikh" (everything was in a state of confusion at the Oblonsky household) was recast from drafts of the novel set during the time of Peter the Great.[5] About this novel Tolstoy wrote: "I am not going to judge people. I am only going to depict a struggle between lust and conscience [*pokazyvat' bor'bu meždu pokhot'ju i sovest'ju*]."[6] Although Tolstoy abandoned the novel, he by no means abandoned that obsessive theme; it lies at the core of *Anna Karenina.*

In his preoccupation with the dichotomy between spirit and flesh Tolstoy looked to philosophy, and particularly to Plato, for concepts and answers. The dichotomy in human nature is, of course, a theme that has been addressed by many philosophers, with some of whom Tolstoy was familiar—for instance, Schopenhauer and the Old and New Testaments. As a self-made philosopher, however, Tolstoy preferred to bore through the history of philosophical thought to reach the roots of an idea. Philosophers of antiquity such as Plato, the founding father of Idealism, were therefore important to Tolstoy. He was familiar with the *Dialogues;* he listed the *Phaedo* and the *Symposium* as having had a "great influence" on him between the ages of twenty and thirty-five.[7] Later, when reading Plato in his newly acquired Greek, Tolstoy probably chose dialogues, such as the *Symposium,* that he had previously read in French.

The *Symposium* is mentioned at the beginning of *Anna Karenina:* in the dialogue between Oblonsky and Levin at the restaurant (1.10), Levin refers to Plato's definition of two kinds of love.[8] This notion of two forms of love is also present in other dialogues (for example, the *Gorgias*); Plato's dialogues are topical, however, and the *Symposium* is devoted explicitly to the problem of love. Here the distinction is made between a common and an ideal love. It is first introduced on a mythological level:

> as there are two goddesses there must be two loves. . . . The elder one, having no mother, who is called the heavenly Aphrodite— she is the daughter of Uranus; the younger, who is the daughter of Zeus and Dione—her we call common; and the Love who is her fellow-worker is rightly named common, as the other Love is called heavenly.[9]

According to Plato, myth serves a symbolic function, and he incorporates Greek mythology into the *Dialogues.* The *Symposium* is full of mythological allusions that augment the artistic merits of the dialogue. Similarly, Tolstoy incorporates the *Symposium,* particularly the idea of two loves, into the subtext of *Anna Karenina,* which juxtaposes the love of the flesh (common love) with ideal, spiritual love. The two are conventionally called Platonic and non-Platonic (sexual) love, or by the Greek terms *agape* and *eros:*

> Not every love, but only that which has a noble purpose, is noble and worthy of praise. The Love who is the offspring of the common Aphrodite is essentially common . . . and is of the body rather than of the soul—the most foolish beings are the objects of this Love which desires only to gain an end, but never thinks of accomplishing the end nobly, and therefore does good and evil quite indiscriminately.[10]

In the restaurant, Oblonsky and Levin are enjoying an elegant meal. The setting is similar to that of the *Symposium,* which is presented as taking place at a banquet—actually the title of the dialogue, συμπόσιον, can be translated as "banquet" or "feast" (Russian *pir*) and was so known to Tolstoy—in which the participants are enjoying both physical and intellectual pleasures, that is, eating while they engage in philosophical discourse on love. In trying "to distinguish the character of the two Loves" Plato draws a moral distinction, for he considers morality to be a necessary condition for achieving beauty in life:

> Now actions vary according to the manner of their performance. Take, for example, that which we are now doing, drinking, singing and talking—these actions are not in themselves either good or evil, but they turn out in this or that way according to the mode of performing them; and when well done they are good, and when wrongly done they are evil.[11]

The Oblonsky-Levin dialogue at the restaurant follows this associational chain of food, pleasure, love, and morality. Stiva orders a lavish dinner, demonstrating his epicurean tastes, while he talks about the pleasures of life. The conversation turns to matters of love and related moral issues. Levin invokes the notion of two loves in trying to refute Stiva's excuses for adultery. Stiva justifies the affair that caused the disarray in his family: "My wife is aging, but I am full of life." At first Levin, "a man of one piece," refutes this vigorously and, by adhering to the Platonic distinction, takes a nonconformist stance. Suddenly, however, he recalls "his own sins and the internal struggle he had lived through" and thus remembers that he, too, is made of flesh.

The Oblonsky-Levin dialogue follows the logical development in the *Symposium*. In the latter, the next speaker, a physician, moves the discourse one more step by saying that "in all . . . things human as well as divine, both loves ought to be noted as far as may be, for they are both present." In his speech, the notion of the dichotomous nature of human love is introduced: the speaker compares love to a symphony in which harmony is achieved by proper "arrangement of the notes of higher and lower pitch" (that is, harmonious love requires the right proportion of the composite elements).

The restaurant dialogue, during which Levin quotes from the *Symposium*, sets the pattern for the Levin-Oblonsky relationship throughout the novel, and Tolstoy uses the elements of this pattern with remarkable consistency. Easygoing Stiva is concerned with pleasures of the body, mainly those involving women and food. Levin, on the other hand, has little interest in gourmet repasts or in the operettas at which Stiva meets his female friends. He denounces extramarital love affairs, comparing an adulterous man to a person who, coming from a party, steals a loaf of bread. (Levin uses the word *kalač,* which denotes a rich bread traditionally served in Russia on special occasions such as religious holidays and weddings.) Bread as a symbol of the flesh is an ancient one; in Christian tradition it is used thus in the Eucharist. In addition to Oblonsky and Levin's inability to reach a consensus on moral issues, the *kalač* theme is a recurrent element in the pattern of the friendship. At the first banquet the rift between the two friends is already marked: "Although they were dining together, drinking wine which should have drawn them even closer to each other, each was thinking only about his own problems, and each had nothing to do with the other" (1.10). In all their meetings following this pattern, the two friends reach a point at which they can no longer understand one another; the problem of love generally serves as the point of contention.

The next meeting between Oblonsky and Levin (2.14) has a different setting: Stiva visits Levin in the country at Levin's ancestral estate. However, the same pattern of the relationship is observable. The housekeeper and the cook go out of their way to treat Stiva appropriately. To their great dismay, however, Levin orders dinner to be served without their special *pirožki,* because these are not ready on time. Stiva enjoys the meal all the same. The conversation turns to the same subjects: the pleasures of life and the problems of love. Stiva tells of a new, tempting "kalač" he has found, a "woman of the Ossian type." Again Levin listens silently, but "despite all the effort which he made, he could not by any means get himself to enter the soul of his friend and to understand his feelings and the charms of studying such women" (2.14).

In the next encounter (4.11–4.13), the elements of the banquet pattern are dispersed through several chapters. Stiva plays host at a dinner party at his house to which Levin is invited. This situation excludes the possibility of repeating the pattern, which has been structured on a tête-à-tête. Yet Tolstoy incorporates the familiar elements. Stiva is late to the party because he has gone to see his new passion, this time not an "Ossian type" but a timid young ballerina (4.7). The dinner at the Oblonskys constitutes one of the key points in the development of the novel's plot: Levin proposes to Kitty again and this time is accepted. In connection with Levin's proposal the *kalač* curiously reappears. Early the next morning Levin waits impatiently for a proper visiting hour to arrive so that he can make a formal proposal to Kitty's parents. He finds himself in a state of euphoria. To pass the time, he orders some coffee, which comes with a *kalač:* "Levin tried to have a sip of coffee and to put the *kalač* into his mouth, but his mouth decidedly did not know what to do with the *kalač*. Levin spit the *kalač* out, put on his coat, and went out to walk again" (4.15). Thus, Levin seems to reject the *kalač*, the pleasures of the flesh; at any rate, he cannot yet associate them with the virginal Kitty. In his marriage to Kitty he must try to bring *eros* and *agape* together.

With Levin striving toward higher love, the rift between the two friends widens. In their last meeting modeled on the banquet pattern (7.11), they cannot reconcile their differences. This time their meeting is at a hunting party. Stiva visits Levin's estate, where the entire Oblonsky family enjoys Levin's hospitality. In this episode Tolstoy portrays Stiva "from below" by introducing a complementary character, Vasya Veslovsky. Vasya is a grotesque Stiva, a parody of Stiva. Stiva is sincere; Vasya is naive. Oblonsky has a "stately and well-groomed" figure; Veslovsky is fat (the peasants mistake him for a woman in pants). Stiva has some notion of morality, expressed in his motto, "The main thing is to observe the sanctity of your home" (7.11); Veslovsky overtly flirts with Kitty, his host's wife.

However, Stiva also behaves like Veslovsky. While Levin is hunting, the two of them eat all the food, a supply meant to last for three days, leaving Levin hungry. Then at night they lightheartedly go to frolic with peasant girls. When Levin reproaches him, Stiva answers along familiar lines: "It will do my wife no harm, and I'll enjoy myself" (7.11).

During the night the two friends attempt to resume their usual dialogue. The author-narrator, whose tone grows more didactic toward the end of the novel, comments on the inability of the two friends to communicate: "Recently there had been established something like a secret hostility between the two brothers-in-law, as though, since they had married sisters, a rivalry had arisen between them as to which was managing his life better" (7.11). Thus, Tolstoy maintains that Oblonsky's and Levin's respective outlooks are two distinctive and opposing ways of love and of life.

The Platonic juxtaposition of the two loves is significant not only in the Oblonsky-Levin friendship but also in the two main plot lines, Anna-Vronsky and Kitty-Levin. Many critics find these two plot lines insufficiently connected. The *Symposium*'s ideas seem particularly relevant to understanding the relationship of both couples and the tension that binds the two otherwise independent plot lines. Tolstoy builds this tension by juxtaposing the more Platonic love of Kitty and Levin with the explicitly erotic passion of Vronsky and Anna; he emphasizes the desires of flesh in one couple and the spiritual features in the other.

Anna and Kitty, the two rival heroines, are opposed to each other in physical terms. Anna has a full, stately figure; Kitty is consistently portrayed as slim, almost gaunt. This can of course be explained by the difference in age: Anna is a St. Petersburg grande dame of about thirty; Kitty, a budding eighteen-year-old girl. But Anna's fullness also signifies the experience of flesh in contrast to the virginal Kitty. In the ball scene (1.22–1.23), where the two rivals encounter one another face to face, Tolstoy accentuates this physical difference:

[Анна] была прелестна в своем простом черном платье, прелестны были ее полные руки с браслетами, прелестна твердая шея с ниткой жемчуга, прелестны вьющиеся волосы расстроившейся прически, прелестны грациозные легкие движения маленьких ног и рук, прелестно это красивое лицо в своем оживлении; но было что-то ужасное и жестокое в ее прелести.

[Anna] was charming in her simple black dress, charming were her round full arms in bracelets, charming was her firm neck with a thread of pearls, charming was the curly hair of disarranged coiffure, charming were the light gracious movements of her small feet and hands, charming was this lovely face in its excitement; but there was something terrible and cruel in her charm. (1.23)

The insistently repeated adjective *prelestna,* "beguiling or charming," is closely related to the verb *prel'ščat',* which means not so much "to charm" as "to beguile, tempt, seduce, enchant, or ensnare," with the connotation of temptation to evil. Tolstoy indicates this directly: "Da, čto-to čuždoe, besovskoe i prelestnoe v nej" (Indeed, there was something alien, devilish and charming in her, 1.23).

In this ballroom scene Kitty appears as a fragile butterfly: "The skirt of her gossamer dress gathered as a cloud around her slim waist; one bare, thin, soft, girlish arm, helplessly sunk into the folds of her pink tunic" (1.23). Besides her full figure, Anna's dark, curly hair is probably the most important feature in her portrait; Kitty has blond hair. Tolstoy plays inconspicuously on the conventional romantic opposition between the two rival heroines. The function of the dark-haired one is to tempt the hero, to lead him from the right path; the blond heroine is usually a sublime, unattainable creature, and her function is that of a guiding star.

As for the rival males, the few examples already given demonstrate the nature of the Oblonsky-Levin relationship and illustrate Levin's ascetic leanings. In his first appearance, Vronsky gives the impression of a polished salon-knight (1.14). His inner world is obscure at the beginning, but soon his "animal personality" reveals itself. Tolstoy stresses Vronsky's animal nature by means of a parallel character, just as Veslovsky mirrored the grosser qualities of Stiva.

Vronsky is obliged to act as a guide to a European prince (4.1). The prince is a man of pleasure who travels to tickle his dulled senses, obsessively seeking pleasure. In Russia he indulges himself in all the most exotic, "Russian" pleasures, but of these the best, ironically, are "French actresses, a ballerina, and champagne with the white seal" (4.1). As his guide Vronsky participates in all the prince's dissipations. Yet he detests the prince: "Vronsky unwillingly recognized himself" in that "stupid piece of beef," and "what he saw in this mirror was not flattering to his self-esteem" (4.1).

Anna also recognizes this animal streak in Vronsky. When he

states that people like the prince "despise everything except animal pleasures," Anna retorts, "But you all like these animal pleasures, don't you?" (4.2). Anna resents and mistrusts this animal tendency in her lover; she is jealous of Vronsky because she rightly sees a threat to their love in his animal nature.

The *Symposium* sheds some light on why Anna's love for Vronsky is doomed from the beginning:

> Evil is the vulgar lover who loves the body rather than the soul, inasmuch as he is not even stable, because he loves a thing which is in itself unstable, and therefore when the bloom of youth which he was desiring is over, he takes wing and flies away, in spite of all his words and promises; whereas the love of the noble disposition is lifelong, for it becomes one with the everlasting.[12]

Anna and Vronsky's love unfolds as stormy passion. The theme of eroding and unstable beauty runs through the novel. Stiva justifies his extramarital affairs by claiming that his "wife is aging." During her visit to Vronsky's estate, Dolly thinks that, no matter how beautiful Anna is, Vronsky can find a more enticing woman, as her own husband has done (7.3). Dolly indirectly predicts Anna's tragic end; in Anna's last-minute desire to commit suicide jealousy plays a large role. In one episode, Vronsky sees Anna as "a drooping flower, the beauty of which he can hardly recognize, for which he had cut and killed it" (4.3).

Anna does, however, share this character trait with Vronsky. After her talk with Dolly (6.24), Anna meets Vronsky in her bedroom and interprets as a sexual invitation a look that was not intended that way: "Vronsky gave her an attentive look. He was looking for the traces of that talk, which he knew she . . . must have had with [Dolly]. . . . He took her hand and looked inquiringly into her eyes. She, having understood his look differently, smiled at him." In the presuicide monologue Anna admits to herself that she is jealous and that she suffers from unsatisfied appetite.

In the words of Plato, this love passion, the "love of the body rather than the soul, strives only to achieve an end."[13] These words explain the tragic sense of doom present in Anna's relationship with Vronsky. Sensual desire constitutes the focus of their love, and, once satisfied, this sole driving force is withdrawn, leaving the love dead. This explains the scene in part 2, chapter 11, which presumably refers to the consummation of their love for the first time. The overtones of death are explicitly present in this scene:

> [Vronsky] had a feeling that a murderer must have when he sees the body from which he took away life. This body, from which he took away life, was their love, the first period of love. . . . Shame for her spiritual nakedness was crushing her and was transmitted to him. But despite all this horror of a murderer facing the body of the victim, it was necessary to cut into pieces, to hide this body, it was necessary to use what the murderer had acquired by his murder. (2.11)

Tolstoy departs from Plato's ideas. Plato discounted heterosexual love as low and common: homosexual love as love of the higher sort, between pupil and teacher, is implied in the *Dialogues*. Although Tolstoy narrates the Kitty-Levin love more in a Platonic vein, he nevertheless portrays their relationship as having a strong erotic side. Their marriage is biologically fruitful: Kitty gives birth to a son. Kitty is not devoid of a physical (sexual) side, as the following dialogue (6.5) testifies. After she sees that nothing has come of Varenka and Koznyshev's walk in the woods, Kitty has the following exchange with Levin:

—Ну, что?—спросил ее муж, когда они опять возвращались домой.
—Не берет,—сказала Кити [. . .].
—Как не берет?
—Вот так,—сказала она, взяв руку мужа, поднося ее ко рту и дотрагиваясь до нее нераскрытыми губами,—Как у архиерея руку целуют.
—У кого же не берет?—сказал он, смеясь.
—У обоих. А надо, чтобы вот так . . .
—Мужики едут . . .
—Нет, они не видали.

"Well, what about it?" asked her husband on their way back home.
"It isn't biting," said Kitty. . . .
"What do you mean 'isn't biting'?"
"This is what I mean," said Kitty, taking her husband's hand

and just touching with closed lips. "The way one kisses a bishop's hand."

"Who isn't biting?" he said, laughing.

"Neither. This is how it should have been." . . .

"Some peasants are coming." . . .

"They didn't see."

For Tolstoy, however, the union of souls is crucially important, and he emphasizes the presence of such union in Kitty and Levin's love by focusing on the spiritual aspect of their relationship. On the morning of the formal proposal, when Levin spits out the *kalač,* his state is described as follows: "He did not eat anything for the whole day, had not slept for two nights, spent several hours outdoors in the frost without a coat, and he felt himself not only to be fresh and healthy as never before but he felt himself completely independent of his body: he moved without any muscular effort and felt as if he could do anything" (4.15).

In another instance, the narrator describes Levin's feelings toward his wife after their marriage: "along with her, now, when the thought of her pregnancy did not leave him for a minute, he felt that, still new for him and blissful, completely free of sensuality, joy of being close to the woman he loved. . . . In her voice, and also in her look, there was softness and seriousness, similar to that which one meets in people constantly concentrated on one dearly loved work" (6.3). Even though Levin does not find the ideal meaning of life and sense of peace that he hoped marriage would bring him, both Kitty and Levin improve through their marriage.

The Platonic concept of two loves shapes the hierarchy of characters in *Anna Karenina.* Tolstoy maintained that an ideological connection lay at the foundation of the novel: "I am proud of the architecture—the vaults are joined in such a way that it is impossible to notice where the seam is. The connection . . . is based not on the plot or on the relationships (acquaintances) between the characters but on an inner connection."[14]

Tolstoy demonstrates the fascinating variations created by the dichotomy between spirit and flesh. In one of the drafts Anna says that "if there are as many minds as there are heads, then there are as many kinds of love as there are hearts." [15] With the exception of Anna, all the characters basically fit into one of the two categories, flesh or spirit. Anna's tragedy partly stems from the fact that both forces are strongly present in her nature. The relationship of Varenka and Sergei Ivanovich Koznyshev is an example of another extreme, where passionate desire is lacking. Their marriage seems plausible and desirable but does not materialize (6.4). Both Varenka and Sergei Ivanovich are characterized as highly spiritual: Varenka lives almost like a nun, and Sergei Ivanovich is a philosopher. They share one feature: in the days of their youth, they had each experienced a sublime and unsatisfied love. A man with whom Varenka was in love was married to a woman of his mother's choice; Koznyshev's fiancée died.

Although Varenka and Sergei Ivanovich admire one another and seem well matched, their union cannot be realized. In his own words, Sergei Ivanovich "reasons coldly"; his feeling for Varenka is not "a flash of desire or of passion." If he "could choose by pure reason, he could not find anything better" than Varenka (6.4). But cold reason proves insufficient to sustain the tension, and the situation, so heavily charged with expectations, disintegrates.

All the characters associated with Vronsky's world lead lives similar to his, unstable and insignificant. Vronsky's mother, once a famous beauty, had a series of lovers; his brother, a family man, keeps a mistress. While the mistress of Petritsky, Vronsky's friend, is trying to obtain a divorce, Petritsky is already involved with another woman:

> In [Vronsky's] Petersburg world, all the people were divided into two utterly opposed sorts. One was the lower sort: vulgar, stupid, and above all, ridiculous people who believe that one man should live with one wife to whom he was lawfully married; that a girl should be innocent, a woman modest, a man manly, self-controlled, and strong; that one should bring up one's children, earn one's bread, pay one's debts—and various similar absurdities. This was the class of old-fashioned and ridiculous people. But there was another sort of people, real people. . . . Above all, one ought to be elegant, beautiful, generous, bold, happy, to abandon oneself to every passion without blushing, and to laugh at everything else. (1.34)

The juxtaposition of the two loves and two life-styles is reinforced by other mythological elements of Russian cultural tradition such as the opposition of the two capitals: St. Petersburg is heavily populated by people with "animal personalities," while Moscow, though a Babylon to Levin, still serves as a dwelling place for the remaining patriarchal families such as the Shcherbatskys. The Slavophile myth of the corrupt West as the incarnation of the material, versus spiritual Russia, is undoubtedly present in the mythological basis of *Anna Karenina*. But most important is the opposition, subtly running through the novel, between the country and the city: Levin flees the city and escapes to his family estate, where he was born and reared and where his parents lived in an ideal union (1.27).

Levin's idealization of the country is present in a puzzling episode in part 3, chapter 11. Levin is enviously observing the teamwork of the young peasant Ivan Parmenov and his wife. He asks Ivan's father whether the couple have any children, to which the father replies that they have been married over two years but do not have any children because "the whole first year of their marriage [his son] did not understand anything and was bashful" ("Kakie deti! God celyj ne ponimal ničego, da i stydilsja"). Peasants were sometimes married off in their early teens, but obviously this was not the case with these two, since Ivan's wife is described as a blossoming beauty with full breasts.[16]

The peasant characters belong integrally to Levin's world of the patriarchal countryside; consequently, they are idealized and spiritualized. Levin experiences a revelation (8.10) when he hears about a peasant who "lives not for his belly, but for his soul." The name of this spiritual peasant is Platon (Plato) (notably, also the name of another idealized peasant from *War and Peace*, Platon Karataev).

Plato interpreted knowledge not as acquired but as the soul's recollection of the realm of pure Ideas. The love for these Ideas is the driving force of a virtuous existence, allowing one to ascend from physical to spiritual love in this realm. In the *Symposium*, Socrates outlines this spiritual process. Plato depicted the highest stage of spiritual cognition as an ecstatic revelation:

He who has been instructed thus far in the things of love, and who has learned to see the beautiful in due order and succession, when he comes toward the end will suddenly perceive a nature of wondrous beauty. . . . He who from these ascending under the influence of true love, begins to perceive that beauty is not far from the end. And the true order of going, or being led by another to the things of love, is to begin from the beauties of earth and mount upwards for the sake of that other beauty, using these as steps only, and from one going on to two, and from two to all fair forms, and from fair forms to fair practices, and from fair practices to fair notions, until from fair notions he arrives at the notion of absolute beauty, and at last knows what the essence of beauty is.[17]

To a great extent Levin's development fits this outline. Though his youth remains outside the novel's chronological frame, enough evidence exists in the text to assume that he lived as a "common man." The diaries of those days, which he gives to Kitty, reveal that he was not much different from Oblonsky. In his desire to marry Kitty he seems driven by the intrinsic need of human nature to extend its existence. He understands a decent, purposeful life as a family life, modeled on the life of his parents.

In the *Symposium* the idea of sexual drive is defined as a need to procreate, that is, as longing for eternal existence. Yet Levin undergoes his worst crisis when he is happily married, and the things he expected to experience—such as a feeling of love toward his child and a sense of peace and of a meaningful life—do not come easily to him.

But he has all the qualities of a virtuous man: these, according to Plato, are courage, right opinion, and the pursuit of wisdom through knowledge. He has a built-in moral guide; his soul is open to remember and reflect absolute beauty, which, according to Plato, is ever-present in the world. At the moment of revelation Levin meditates on his search for knowledge:

I was looking for the answers to my question. But thinking could not give me the answer to that question—it is disproportionate to the question. The answer was given to me by life itself, by way of my knowledge of what is good and what is evil. But this knowledge I did not acquire in any way, for it was given to me as to all, *given,* because I could not get it anywhere. Where did I get this? Was it really by reason that I came to understand that one should love one's neighbor and should not choke him? They told it to me in my childhood, and I joyfully believed it, because they said that which already was in my soul. Reason discovered the struggle for survival and the law requiring us to choke everyone who prevents me from satisfying my desires. (3.12, emphasis Tolstoy's)

Obviously, Tolstoy extends Plato's concept of love to include the Christian tradition. Levin's attainment of the Absolute is the attainment of faith in God, and this understanding of ideal love as total self-sacrifice to humanity is exemplified by Christ's life.

During the 1870s Tolstoy experienced a deep creative and moral crisis, and from this emerged Tolstoyanism as a crystallized philosophy. Tolstoy's crisis finds a certain measure of expression in the character of Levin: The notion that God is love, which Tolstoy stressed in his later years, is embryonic in Levin's inner monologue.[18] *Anna Karenina* is particularly important to an understanding of Tolstoy's work because more than any other novel it reflects the direction of his development through the 1870s.[19]

The dichotomy of flesh and spirit continued to fascinate Tolstoy. The moral imperative to subdue the flesh to the spirit, forcefully expressed in *Anna Karenina,* grew more crucial and absolute in Tolstoy's later life and work. To his *Commentary on the Gospels* he gave the bold subtitle "Victory of the Spirit over the Flesh," "Pobeda dukha nad plot'ju."

NOTES

1. George R. Noyes, *Tolstoy* (New York, 1918), p. 234.
2. See, for example, Donna Orwin, "Freedom, Responsibility, and the Soul: The Platonic Contribution to Tolstoi's Psychology," *Canadian Slavonic Papers* 25 (December 1983): 501–17; and Patricia Carden, "The Recuperative Powers of Memory: Tolstoy's *War and Peace,*" in John Garrard, ed., *The Russian Novel from Pushkin to Pasternak* (New Haven, ca. 1983), pp. 81–102.
3. Orwin, "Freedom," p. 515.
4. Nikolaj Gusev, *Letopis' žizni i tvorčestva L. N. Tolstogo* (Moscow, 1958), p. 381.

5. Originally it read "vse smešalos' v carskoj sem'e."
6. See N. N. Ardens [Apostolov], *Tvorčeskij put' L. N. Tolstogo* (Moscow, 1962), p. 352.
7. Tolstoy to M. M. Lederle (no. 374), 25 October 1891, in *Tolstoy's Letters, 1880–1910*, 2 vols., trans. R. F. Christian (London, 1978), 2:486.
8. Hereafter, references to and quotations from *Anna Karenina* are given by part and chapter; hence 1.10 refers to part 1, chap. 10.
9. *Symposium*, in *The Dialogues of Plato*, trans. Benjamin Jowett vol. 7 (Chicago, 1952), p. 153.
10. Ibid.
11. Ibid.
12. Ibid., p. 167.
13. Ibid.
14. Tolstoy to S. A. Rachinsky, 27 January 1878, in *PSS* 62:377.
15. *PSS* 18:146.
16. In fact, Sofya Andreevna adjudged this description offensive and in her edition of the novel found it necessary to change "breasts" to the more neutral "bosom" (*polnye grudi* to *polnaja grud'*). See V. A. Ždanov and E. E. Zajdenšnur, "Tekstologicheskie pojasnenija," in L. N. Tolstoj, *Anna Karenina* (Moscow, 1969), p. 839.
17. *Symposium*, p. 175.
18. See I John 4:8.
19. Plato's was not the only philosophy that was influential in the formation of Tolstoy's philosophical outlook; Schopenhauer is most often cited as a primary influence. But Plato can in turn be considered a primary influence on Schopenhauer. In a letter to Nikolai Strakhov, Tolstoy managed to put Plato and Schopenhauer side by side in an anti-Western camp: "Purely intellectual philosophy is an ugly Western product; neither the Greeks—Plato—nor Schopenhauer, nor the Russian thinkers understood it this way" (Tolstoy to N. N. Strakhov, 13 September 1871, in *Tolstoy's Letters*, 1:239).
   In another letter to Strakhov, Tolstoy again set "Plato, Schopenhauer, and all religious teachings" apart from "philosophy": "Plato is sharply distinguished from all the others, in my opinion, by the correctness of his philosophical method. Schopenhauer is the closest of all to him. . . . [They] do not correct their listeners' simplest primitive concepts, but seek the meaning of life without dividing into their constituent parts the essential things which make up the life of every man" (Tolstoy to N. N. Strakhov, 30 November 1875, *Tolstoy's Letters*, 1:285). This aspect of Plato's philosophy, the interpenetration of the basic elements of human nature (body, soul, and reason), appealed to Tolstoy.

Death and Resurrection in *Anna Karenina*

Andrew Wachtel

If it can be said that Lev Tolstoy had a single favorite theme throughout his career as a writer, that theme is death and resurrection. He treated this subject with obsessive frequency in a long series of fictional and autobiographical works. It is, for example, the premonition of death that leads the writer of *A Confession* to reexamine his life; he vows to begin it anew, rejecting all that he had previously believed and accomplished. In *War and Peace*, Prince Andrei decides to change the course of his life after the epiphany he experiences while lying, half dead, on the field at Austerlitz. In *Resurrection*, the theme is treated on a purely ethical/metaphysical plane. Nekhliudov's soul, spiritually dead at the beginning of the novel, gradually comes to life in the course of Katia Maslova's trial. Finally, the plot of *The Living Corpse* hinges on the supposed death of Fedor Vasilievich Protasov. He has, of course, only pretended to commit suicide; he is actually still alive, but can only live a secret and miserable existence on the margins of his former world.

Given Tolstoy's propensity for using the theme of death and resurrection, it is perhaps not surprising that it plays a role in *Anna Karenina* as well; in fact, in the course of the novel each of the main characters dies and is resurrected. However, the mere presence of deaths and resurrections in the novel is not particularly important. What is crucial for the structure of *Anna Karenina* is that this typically Tolstoyan theme is played out simultaneously in two diametrically opposite dimensions. The deaths and resurrections of Kitty and Levin take place in a context of Christianity, while those of Anna and Vronsky occur against a background of classical Greek and Roman idolatry. These mutually exclusive contexts ensure that the consequences of the deaths and resurrections in the novel will be entirely different: for Kitty and Levin resurrection leads to happiness, a rich family life, and fecundity; for Anna and Vronsky it leads to despair and new death. Thus, the subtext of death and resurrection points to certain similarities linking all four main characters while, at the same time, it emphasizes the gulf separating Kitty and Levin from Anna and Vronsky.

The first character to experience death and resurrection is Kitty. After having turned down Levin and been jilted by Vronsky, she begins to decline: "She was sick, and with the approach of spring her health became worse." [1] Tuberculosis is suspected and, as the nineteenth-century reader knew (and would see again in this very novel), the disease was a clear sign of early death. Talking with Dolly a bit later, Kitty says frankly, "I am dying of love for him [Vronsky]" (2.3). Despite these omens, however, Kitty does not die. Her return to health is presented as a resurrection and transfiguration: "She found that comfort in the fact that, thanks to this new acquaintance, a completely new world, which had nothing in common with her past one, opened up for her; an exalted sublime world, from the height of which she could look calmly at her past" (2.33). Her spiritual rebirth is accompanied by a resurrection of her physical strength and "Kitty returned home to Russia cured" (2.35).

Later in the novel, while she is in labor, Kitty undergoes a second death and resurrection. She cries out, "No, this is horrible! I will die, die!" (7.15). Although cries of this sort may not be unusual during labor, within the context of the novel's deaths and rebirths Kitty's words are significant. She does not die, of course, and her second resurrection is accompanied by the birth of a son, an event that further emphasizes the underlying mythological pattern.

Vronsky's death and resurrection occur in part 4. After leaving the dying Anna, Vronsky returns home to mull over his position. He takes up a revolver and "he made an effort to think and understood that he was on the floor and, having seen the blood on the tiger skin and on his hand, he understood that he had shot himself" (4.18). Although the shot misses his heart, he brushes death. "He lay between life and death for several days" (4.23). He fully recovers only during the trip to Italy. After Anna's death Vronsky undergoes a second death and resurrection. Vronsky's mother tells Sergei Ivanovich about the scene that followed Anna's suicide: "I just don't know what happened there, but they brought him home like a corpse" (8.4). His second resurrection is effected by his decision to go fight in Serbia.

Anna's death and resurrection are similar to those of Vronsky and Kitty. She has premonitions a few days before giving birth to Vronsky's daughter. "I won't live through this. . . . I know it, and I know it for certain. I will die" (3.4). About to give birth, she sends a telegram to Karenin: "I am dying, I request, beg you to come" (4.17). When Karenin returns, Vronsky tells him, "She is dying. The doctors say there is no hope" (4.17). Then Anna herself half-deliriously, says, "I don't fear him, I fear death. . . . I am in a rush because I've no time. I've been left only a little time to live, the fever will begin now and I won't remember anything. I am dying now. I know that I will die" (4.17). Against all odds, however, Anna does not die, and she too returns to health gradually. Like Vronsky, she does not fully recover until the trip to Italy.

Levin does not come as close to physical death as do the other main characters, although there is one essentially comic scene in which he is almost shot while hunting with Stiva and Vasya Veslovsky (6.9). In addition, he contemplates death and suicide a number of times in the course of the work. More important, he experiences the process symbolically, through the death of his brother Nikolai. During the ten days that Levin and Kitty spend in the hotel where Nikolai lies dying, Levin has ample time to contemplate the meaning of death. The narrator relates Levin's thoughts after Nikolai's death: "The appearance of his brother and the closeness of death renewed in Levin's soul the feeling of horror before the inscrutability and, at the same time, the closeness and inescapability of death that had overcome him on that autumn evening when his brother had come to visit him" (5.20). He does not feel sadness, however. "But now, thanks to the closeness of his wife, this feeling did not lead him to despair; despite death, he felt a necessity to live and to love" (5.20). This psychological rebirth is emphasized by the fact that during the vigil over Nikolai the first signs of Kitty's pregnancy become apparent. Although neither she nor Levin realizes it at the time, Nikolai's death and the conception of new life are inextricably linked. Levin's thoughts immediately after the birth of his son strengthen this mystical link: "He knew and felt only that what had happened was like what had happened a year ago at the deathbed of brother Nikolai in the hotel in the county seat. But that was grief—this was joy" (7.14).

Levin is fated to have lingering doubts and new problems that will lead him to the brink of suicide (8.9), but his resurrection (which is completed on the last page of the novel) clearly began with the death of his brother. He realizes this himself: "And he quickly repeated to himself the whole train of his thought over the last two years, the beginning of which had been the clear obvious thought of death at the sight of his beloved, hopelessly ill brother" (8.12).

Although all four of the main characters "die" and are resurrected, this basic mythological subtext has two alternative projections in *Anna Karenina*. The motivation for the disparate results becomes apparent if we realize that Levin and Kitty are linked to biblical traditions, while Anna and Vronsky are tied primarily to the traditions of Greek and Roman classicism and idol worship. The deaths and resurrections of Levin and Kitty occur in a Christian context in which God ultimately rewards them with happiness and bucolic tranquility. Anna and Vronsky are condemned, by a mixture of the Christian God and classical fate, to die despairing.

From the beginning of the novel there are hints that Levin thinks of Kitty in religious terms. After seeing her at the skating rink he begins to create a picture in his mind's eye:

> When he thought about her he could imagine her vividly, in her
> entirety, in particular the splendor of that little blond head, with
> its expression of childlike goodness and clarity, so freely placed on
> her stately, maidenly shoulders. The childlike expression of her
> face in conjunction with the fine beauty of her figure created her

special splendor, which he remembered well. But what always amazed him unexpectedly about her was the expression in her eyes, meek, peaceful, and just, and, in particular, her smile, which always carried Levin into a magical world where he felt himself moved and softened the way he could remember himself on rare days of his early childhood. (1.9)

Thanks to the blond hair, slender figure, childlike expression, expression of the eyes, and smile, the portrait resembles a Madonna of Fra Filippo Lippi or of Botticelli. The fact that Konstantin feels himself transported back to early childhood upon seeing her is important as well. For Tolstoy, early childhood was the most perfect time of life, because the infant has not yet been corrupted by the influences of civilization and sexuality. Childhood, as depicted in Tolstoy's first published work, *Childhood,* is time in paradise, and the image of Levin looking up at a virgin from the position of an infant strengthens associations with iconographic portraits of the Madonna and Child.[2] Consciously or unconsciously, Tolstoy realized the content of this picture. When publishing the novel in book form he made several small but significant changes from the serial publication. He changed the adverb modifying "placed" from "proudly" (which would have been incompatible with the character of the Virgin) to "freely." Even more important, he added the word "maidenly," "devich'ikh," to the description.[3]

Kitty's resurrection is brought about through the "muscular Christianity" of Madame Shtahl and Varenka. In fact, Kitty is reproached by her mother for being too religious. Kitty does not agree at the time, but the arrival of her father with his light-hearted attitude turns her away from Madame Shtahl. She realizes that her religion cannot be like that of Madame Shtahl or Varenka, because it is a natural extension of herself. She is angry at herself for trying to emulate Varenka: "That was all pretending, because it was invented and not from the heart" (2.35). Although Kitty remains a believer, her faith does not desiccate, like that of Madame Shtahl or even that of Varenka. This innate understanding allows Kitty to look with indifference on Levin's professions of unbelief. "She was religious, never doubted in the truths of religion, but his external unbelief did not touch her in the least. She knew his whole soul through love, she saw what she wanted in his soul, and it made no difference to her that that state of the soul was called nonbelieving" (4.16). As she develops, Kitty loses her earlier virginal attributes but retains all of her Christian virtues, becoming a fecund exemplar of womanhood in the Tolstoyan version of Christianity. The basic Christian underpinnings of meekness and simplicity that characterize her are emphasized by Levin, who, after seeing all that she has done to make Nikolai more comfortable, says immodestly, "Thou hast hid these things from the wise and prudent, and hast revealed them unto babes" (5.19).

While Kitty's connection to biblical times and to Christianity lies somewhere below the novel's surface, Levin's concern with theological problems is apparent throughout *Anna Karenina.* His thoughts at the confession, during the wedding service, and in the philosophical passages at the end of the novel show him in active search of God. His final acceptance of the one God, the God of the Jews, Moslems, or Christians, places his resurrection firmly in the monotheistic religious tradition. He cannot agree with the Russian Orthodox Church ritual (indeed, in order to be resurrected he must escape that ritual), but his resurrection falls well within the bounds of Christianity as seen by Tolstoy.[4]

The turn toward belief is slow, but it continues throughout the novel, from almost complete skepticism at the time of his confession to his thoughts as he watches his dying brother: "If you do exist, make this man recover . . . and you will save both him and me" (5.20). While Kitty is giving birth, Levin's prayer is more fervent and far less doubting: "God have mercy!! Forgive, help!—he somehow suddenly, unexpectedly pronounced the words which had come to his lips. . . . Now, at this moment, he knew that everything . . . did not in the least prevent him from turning to God" (7.13). As Kitty's agony continues, Levin's prayers become ever more those of a believer. More important, just as his mental portrait of Kitty did at the beginning of the novel, his prayer recreates his early childhood. " 'Lord forgive and help,'—he continuously repeated to himself; despite his long and seemingly complete estrangement, he felt that he was turning to God as trustingly and as simply as he had at the time of his childhood and early youth" (7.14). The final stages of Levin's resurrection occur on the last page of the novel. "I will still not understand through my intellect why I pray, yet I will pray—but now my life—is not only not senseless, as it was before, but it has an unquestionable sense of good" (8.19). For both Kitty and Levin, resurrection is within the context of Christianity as Tolstoy interpreted it, and it leads to happiness and life.

The resurrections of Vronsky and Anna, by contrast, take place on the novel's Greco-Roman side. Vronsky is linked to classical times through the steeplechase. Horse racing in a hippodrome is a classical practice, and Tolstoy provides a number of details to emphasize the situation's Roman character. Vronsky competes against two horses who are mentioned by name, Gladiator and Diana (2.25). In the social conversation before the race, Betsy says that she will not come again and is answered by an unidentified woman, "If I had been a Roman, I wouldn't have missed a single circus" (2.28). Finally, in the middle of the race, after a number of serious falls have occurred, an unidentified voice says, "The only thing missing is the circus with lions" (2.29). Later, after Anna and Vronsky have returned to Russia from Italy, the connection is made again. Speaking with Yashvin, Anna says, "Were the races nice this year? Instead of those I saw the races on the Corso in Rome" (5.31). Greece—at least its sensual side—is not neglected either.[5] When Vronsky, who has become exhausted by squiring a foreign prince around Petersburg, speaks with Anna, she says to him, "This morning Liza stopped in to see me . . . and told about your Athenian party" (4.3).

Vronsky's participation in the elections for the position of marshal of the nobility is an important element of the classical context. The election was of special importance, and the process has a distant flavor of Athenian democracy or republican Rome, with its groups of well-dressed, wealthy citizens with the power to debate and vote.[6] In addition, both Stiva and Vronsky equate the elections with the steeplechase and thus, indirectly, with classical times. First Stiva says, "It's sort of like horse races. You could bet on them" (6.30). A bit later the narrator relates Vronsky's thoughts: "The elections themselves so attracted him that he thought he would run himself if he were married before the next three-year term—in sort of the same way that, having won a prize with a jockey, he had wanted to jump himself"

(6.31). Vronsky's active participation is, of course, contrasted with Levin's incomprehension and indifference. In fact, Levin views the entire scene as the enactment of some kind of ancient mystery, and his confusion when he has to vote by placing a sphere in a hidden box is not surprising.

Anna's connection to classical times, especially to classical and neoclassical tragedy, is very strong. The ground for such a link is prepared in a conversation with Betsy. Betsy tells her, "You see, it is possible to look at one and the same thing tragically and make it a torture, or to look simply and even gaily. Perhaps you tend to look at things too tragically" (3.17). In the early part of the novel she faces the love/duty conflict typical of neoclassical tragedy. She loves Vronsky but is married to Karenin and must choose between them. Once the choice is made her tragic fate is sealed, but Tolstoy raises the tragedy one more level by complicating the rather unconvincing love/duty theme (unconvincing because in the 1870s the choice of love no longer guaranteed destruction, as it had in the seventeenth and eighteenth centuries). The conflict becomes one of love for Vronsky and love for her son, Serezha. The two are mutually exclusive, and in the scene where Anna finally understands this she truly becomes a tragic heroine.

Speaking to Dolly, Anna says, "It seems that I love two beings equally—Serezha and Aleksei—but I love them both more than myself" (6.24). The narrator then provides what can only be called stage directions: "She came out to the center of the room and stopped in front of Dolly, pressing her hands to her chest. In her white peignoir her figure seemed particularly tall and wide. She bent her head and looked from under her brows" (6.24). Dolly, of course, fulfills the role of the counselor who is present merely to motivate what is essentially a soliloquy by the central figure. Anna's death is clearly that of a classical tragic heroine; faced with a situation caused by her tragic flaw and from which there is no escape, she commits suicide.

The single mythic conception of the novel also contains a dichotomy between the moral and the physical. Christian—or at least Tolstoy's version of Christian—resurrection leads to happiness and to self-knowledge; through their experiences, which are as much moral as physical, Kitty and Levin become better human beings. The classical resurrection of Anna and Vronsky leads only to despair and death. Although they are given the same chance as Kitty and Levin, their resurrection is purely physical; they turn away from the moral regeneration that should accompany the recovery of their physical strength.[7] Anna and Vronsky do experience a temporary moral resurrection; this can be seen in the changes in their view of Karenin. When Anna is in labor, Vronsky leaves her house convinced that she is dying. The narrator relates his thoughts: "The husband, the deceived husband, who had seemed a pitiful being until now, an accidental and slightly comic impediment to his happiness, had suddenly been called by her, raised to a height that inspired servility, and on that height the husband appeared not evil, false, or comic, but good, simple, and majestic. Vronsky could not help but feel this" (4.18). Anna experiences a similar transformation at the sight of her husband. "I need only one thing: Forgive me, forgive me completely! I am horrible, but nanny told me: the holy martyr—what was her name?—she was worse. I will go to Rome, there's a desert there. . . . Go away, you are too good" (4.17). Their moral regeneration is short-lived, however. As soon as they see each other again their plans to separate are thrown over and they decide to go to Italy. The contrast between Anna's half-delirious vow to go to Rome as a penitent and the way in which she actually goes there is, of course, striking and ironic.

As opposed to the life in a rural paradise that Kitty and Levin enjoy, Anna finds death by the railroad, that most powerful nineteenth-century symbol of urbanization, Westernization, and secular society. Vronsky's death (or, at least, planned death, for he says to Sergei Ivanovich, "In order to die one doesn't need a recommendation" [7.5]) is that of a classical warrior. Both deaths are, however, tinged with biblical associations as well as with classical ones. This hints at the fact that Vronsky and Anna have turned away from the Christian world of which they should have been a part. In addition to being connected with classical times, they are tied to apostasy. Anna and Vronsky are not punished merely because they have sinned (after all, Stiva and Betsy Tverskaya have also sinned, and they are not punished), but because they continued to do so despite having understood that they were sinning. They were shown the light of repentance and they turned their backs on it.

Their apostasy is most apparent if we compare Levin's reaction to Mikhailov's portrait of Anna with his earlier reaction to his own mental portrait of Kitty. Entering Anna and Vronsky's apartment, he looks around: "A second reflector lamp was burning on the wall and it illuminated a large full-length portrait of a woman. . . . Levin looked at the portrait, which under the bright illumination stood out from the frame, and could not tear himself away from it" (7.9). The woman in the picture looks out at him "triumphantly and tenderly." From this description it is clear that Mikhailov has treated Anna as an icon and that the portrait has been hung as such.[8] It is constantly illuminated from below and stands out from its surrounding frame. The expression of tenderness mixed with triumph is characteristic of some iconic portraits of Christ and the Virgin. Unlike his mental picture of Kitty, however, Anna's picture does not return Levin to childhood. Anna's role is not that of the Virgin but that of the seducer. The blasphemous use of her portrait is merely one more proof of that. Moreover, Anna's unbelief does not issue from the same source as Levin's. Kitty was not afraid of Levin's unbelief, because she saw love in his soul. But Anna's unbelief comes from hatred. "What are these churches, that ringing, and this lie for? Only to hide the fact that we hate each other" (7.24).

Another sign of Anna and Vronsky's apostasy is their attachment to things Western European, as opposed to Russian. They feel at home in Italy. Kitty and Levin hurry home to the Russian countryside after having seen or done what they had to in Europe, but in that same Russian countryside Anna and Vronsky live a European life. Even Dolly, who speaks to her children in French, is struck by this on her visit to Anna. "Everything that she saw . . . produced the impression of abundance and foppishness and of that new European luxury about which she had read only in English novels but had never seen in Russia (6.19). The war in which Vronsky plans to die is a crusade in some sense, although his own motives for going are not religious. The war against the Turks was a war to free Constantinople, which had been both the capital of the Eastern Roman empire and the capital of Eastern Christianity. That war fascinated and deeply disturbed Tolstoy, and it is quite possible that the combination of Christian and Roman associations implicit in the "cause" was the reason.[9] The war, which seems to receive an inordinate amount of attention in the novel's final pages, is important because, like Anna's prayer while committing suicide, it symbolizes a partial and incomplete synthesis of classical traditions with Christianity. One cannot worship both the Christian God and the idols of classical times (or those of the modern Western secular society), and it is this unresolved dichotomy of belief that dooms both Vronsky and Anna.

Perhaps the most interesting aspect of the novel's mythological subtext is its absence in the early drafts. All scenes of death and resurrection (as well as the biblical and classical contexts of these scenes) were substantially reworked in the course of the novel's composition. For example, Vronsky's suicide attempt was completely modified: in the early drafts his wounds are not at all life-threatening.[10] Except for the telegram, the scenes of Anna's labor do not contain any mention of death.[11] The horses' names and most of the social conversation are absent from the scenes at the racetrack.[12] In short, it seems that Tolstoy realized the existence of the mythological subtext only after he had done extensive work on the novel. There are two possible explanations for this. He may have realized that he had written two separate novels with little to connect them and have added the subtext as a kind of glue. More probably, the mythic level appeared organically (after all, as I have already noted, death and resurrection was a constant theme in Tolstoy's work). Having noticed the appearance of this subtext, Tolstoy merely shaped it by adding details and strengthening its component parts where necessary. The outbreak of the Serbian war was as much a godsend to Tolstoy as to Vronsky, for it allowed the novel to close with a symbolic event that tied up the loose ends of the mythic subtext.

Having seen how the mythological conception of the novel works, we are now in a position to throw some light on a question that has cropped up frequently in discussions of *Anna Karenina:* the function and meaning of the epigraph. First of all, it is necessary to point out that in Russian realism the epigraph is practically unknown.[13] The first major Russian novel since the time of Pushkin to have an epigraph was Dostoevsky's *The Devils.* It has two: from Luke 8:32–36 and from Pushkin's lyric "Besy" (The Devils). *Anna Karenina* follows a few years later. Thus, a serious, even cruel, epigraph such as "Vengeance is mine; I will repay" must have been rather shocking for Tolstoy's contemporary reader. The epigraph establishes the presence of a strong monophonic voice, which is set in opposition to the polyphony that seems to reign within the novel. It suggests that there is a being outside, looking down, who has the power to pronounce and execute judgment. This being may be God with power over man or an author with power over his characters. Tolstoy is not Flaubert attempting to erase his obvious presence from the text. By choosing such an epigraph he is asserting his moral presence as an element of the novel's structure.

The fact that the epigraph is from the Bible allows an interpretation of the novel not as a work of realistic fiction but as a biblical text with a moral message. Just as certain events and situations in the Old Testament were interpreted by Christian theologians as prefigurations of events in the New Testament, so death and resurrection, repeated in various combinations and with varying results in *Anna Karenina*, can be seen as a mythic paradigm; each use of the paradigm acts as a prefiguration of the next one. The fact that the quote used for the epigraph appears twice in the Bible itself (Deuteronomy 32:35–36 and Romans 12:19) makes it an exemplar of such an interpretive possibility. The chief argument against such an interpretation is that the epigraph appeared in Tolstoy's drafts before characters corresponding to Kitty and Levin had been created. This fact has caused Eikhenbaum, among others, to conclude that the epigraph is relevant only to Vronsky and Anna.[14] It seems to me unlikely that a writer as painstaking as Tolstoy would have retained an epigraph that pertained to only two of his four major characters, especially considering the unusualness of an epigraph and, therefore, the extreme weight it could have been expected to have. The fact that the epigraph appeared before Levin and Kitty does not necessarily mean that it has no relevance to them. It is noteworthy that the original epigraph was not the same as the final version: it said simply "My vengeance." Unquestionably, the

God who metes out vengeance to Vronsky and Anna is a God of vengeance. They have turned their backs on him. They have not learned from their experience, so they must die. The first part of the epigraph refers to them.

When Tolstoy looked up the second half of the epigraph in the Bible (which, as Eikhenbaum shows conclusively, he must have done),[15] he probably read not only the quotation for which he was searching but the surrounding texts as well. In Deuteronomy the line is embedded in a section contrasting God's vengeance on those who turn away from him with his mercy to his own people. As opposed to Anna and Vronsky, Kitty and Levin have turned to God; in so doing they have become worthy of his mercy and are saved.[16] Just as the theme of death and resurrection developed in the course of the novel's composition, so too did the meaning of the epigraph. In acquiring its second half and its biblical context it came to represent the same kind of single conception with two projections as did the mythological subtext. Like the subtext, the epigraph came into being organically and was modified or reinterpreted to embrace the novel's disparate halves.

Any great novel is a complicated system of ideas operating simultaneously on many strata. There is always, however, some kind of underpinning that unifies the novel's various levels. Tolstoy himself said, "We need people who would show the senselessness of the search for independent thoughts in a work of art and who would constantly lead the reader to the endless labyrinth of linkages that make up the stuff of art, to the laws that serve as the basis of those linkages." [17] In *Anna Karenina* Tolstoy helps the reader to discover the unity of his work by including a host of details that lead to the discovery of biblical and classical themes in the novel. Because of the wealth of detail on all levels of *Anna Karenina*, however, it is easy to overlook the unifying themes. They are nevertheless present, and the most basic one is that of death and resurrection; the experience of death and resurrection is simultaneously a common thread linking all of the main characters and a litmus test, the results of which separate Levin and Kitty on the one hand from Anna and Vronsky on the other.

NOTES

1. *PSS* 18:124. Volumes 18 and 19 of the Jubilee Edition contain the text of *Anna Karenina*. Hereafter all citations from the novel will be by book and chapter number e.g., 4.13, and will be included in the text. All translations are my own.

2. The view of childhood as paradise of course echoes Rousseau. For the relation of Tolstoy's views to those of Rousseau, see A. Divil'kovskij, "Tolstoj i Russo," *Vestnik Evropy* (June 1912): 59–79, and (July 1912): 125–53. See also Milan M. Markovitch, *Jean-Jacques Rousseau et Tolstoï* (rpt. Geneva, 1975). A quote from Tolstoy's early novel *Detstvo* seems to echo the author's views even if it is placed in the mouth of Nikolai Irten'ev: "Happy, happy irretrievable time of childhood! How can one not love, not cherish its memories. Those memories freshen, exalt my soul" (chap.15).

On the Madonna cf. Richard Gustafson: "For Tolstoy the archetypal presence—of Mother or God the Father—brings consolation, peace, and security" (Richard F. Gustafson, "The Three Stages of Man," *Canadian-American Slavic Studies* 12 [Winter 1978]: 484).

3. *PSS* 18:468. The departures from the text of the novel as it appeared serially are to be found on *PSS* 18:459–548.

4. It is rather difficult to define just what Christianity meant to Tolstoy, especially since his attitude toward the problem evolved throughout his life. However, an early diary entry (4 March 1855) contains some central axioms of Tolstoy's belief that remained true for much if not all of his life. "Yesterday a conversation about divinity and faith led me to a great, gigantic thought, to the realization of which I feel capable of dedicating my life. This thought—the creation of a new religion, in accordance with the development of mankind, a religion of Christ, but cleansed of faith and mystery, a practical religion which does not promise future bliss, but which provides bliss on earth." What Kitty sees in Levin is precisely the presence of Christian ethics without church dogma.

5. Tolstoy does not dismiss all aspects of the Greek tradition, only those that go contrary to Christian ethics. For a more fully developed description of the place of Greek thought in the novel see the chapter by Irina Gutkin in this volume.

6. The narrator says, "These elections, due to many circumstances and to the individuals participating in them, attracted the attention of society. Much was said about them and many prepared for them. Moscow, Petersburg, and even foreign residents who never came to elections arrived for these elections" (6.25).

7. Iu. Lotman talks about the opposition between resurrection with moral regeneration (which he sees as characteristic for Tolstoy's charac-

ters) and resurrection without moral regeneration. In *Anna Karenina* such an opposition occurs within the text of a single novel. See Ju. M. Lotman, *Roman v stikhakh Puškina "Evgenij Onegin"* (Tartu, 1975), pp. 100–101.

8. Joan Grossman finds the portrait even more central to the construction of the novel. She sees the painting in general and Levin's appreciation and understanding of it in particular as expressions of a symbolic link between the two central characters. See Joan Delaney Grossman, "Tolstoy's Portrait of Anna: Keystone in the Arch," *Criticism* 1 (Winter 1976): 1–14.

9. See Boris Eikhenbaum, *Tolstoy in the Seventies,* trans. Albert Kaspin (Ann Arbor, 1982), p. 123. He quotes a letter from S. A. Tolstaya, for example: "Here, the only thoughts we have now, the only interests, are war and more war. . . . Levochka felt strange about the Serbian War; for some reason he did not look at it the way everyone else did, but from his own personal, partly religious point of view; and now he is saying that the war is real and it troubles him."

10. *PSS* 20:355.

11. *PSS* 20:352–53.

12. *PSS* 20:221–26.

13. A quick glance through the works of Gogol, Goncharov, Pisemsky, early Dostoevsky, early Tolstoy, and Turgenev shows that the epigraph was a device rarely used by these writers. Although Dostoevsky used them in *Poor Folk* and *White Nights,* and Turgenev used them for a few stories (as did Tolstoy in "Two Hussars"), they were practically unknown in the novel for a period of approximately twenty years.

14. Eikhenbaum, *Tolstoy,* p. 146.

15. Ibid., pp. 144–45. Eikhenbaum shows that Tolstoy took the epigraph from Schopenhauer's German version of the biblical passage in *The World as Will and Idea,* which Tolstoy had been reading at the time. Only later did Tolstoy go back to the Slavonic Bible to get the correct quotation.

16. This interpretation is strengthened by the fact that the verb *vozdati* in Church Slavic has usually a positive connotation. See *Slovar' cerkovno-slavjanskogo i russkogo jazyka,* vol. 7 (St. Petersburg, 1847), p. 145. The definition given there is neutral or positive: "1. cerk., otdavat', vozvraščat' . . . ; 2. delat' vozmezdie, okazyvat'." The example quoted is from II Chronicles 6:23: "Opravditi pravednago, *vozdaja* emu po pravde ego," which in the King James version reads, "and by justifying the righteous, by *giving* him according to his righteousness." Similarly, the word *vozdanie* is defined as "vozmezdie, nagrada."

17. *PSS* 62:268–69.

"Words, Idle Words"

Discourse and Communication in Anna Karenina

Joan Delaney Grossman

Tolstoy prided himself on following Russian literary tradition
faithfully in at least one regard: the refusal of its best fiction writers to fit their productions neatly into existing generic forms. His
master in this regard was of course Pushkin. Long ago Boris
Eikhenbaum pointed to the importance of Pushkin's artistic
prose, in particular his fragmentary experiments in the society
tale, for the genesis of *Anna Karenina*.[1] While demonstrating
Tolstoy's thematic debt to "The Guests Gathered at the Dacha"
and "At the Corner of a Small Square," Eikhenbaum noted a
contribution of Pushkin's even more significant for Tolstoy's
future work. "The basic point of contact between Tolstoy and
Pushkin defined in that initial moment of work on *Anna
Karenina* was the need for a clear-cut artistic system founded on
the principle of higher realism."[2] Whatever Tolstoy's newest
novel owed to the society tale of the 1830s, he did not, as his first
draft might have suggested, simply continue where Pushkin left
off his exploration of the genre. Rather, Pushkin's experimental
model inspired Tolstoy's attack on problems confronting his own
artistic system. The example of Pushkin's rapid, unadorned narrative apparently pointed him toward a new, more direct method
of narration and in particular a new manner of rendering psychological experience. Among his instruments in the latter
project were certain models provided by the society tale.

Hindsight shows the society tale of the 1820s and 1830s as
a seedbed for themes and plots that had more illustrious careers

in European literatures later in the century. In Russia, while it provided ingredients for such major contemporary works as Lermontov's *A Hero of Our Time* and Pushkin's "Queen of Spades," the society tale stopped well short of developing into a serious independent genre. That some of its elements appeared in the works of all the major novelists from Turgenev to Dostoevsky needs no proof and merely illustrates the process of literary evolution. More interesting than their simple presence in the works of later authors are the uses these authors sometimes found for the earlier generic forms. Thus the manner in which Tolstoy adapted such elements for *Anna Karenina* throws interesting light on certain aspects of his later narrative art.

Relations between the sexes in the exclusive cosmopolitan milieu known as high society provided the society tale's usual subject matter, while clashes between individual human emotions and social mores provided its basic plot motivation. As one authority has defined it, the society tale is "a work in which 'society' appears as a structuring element, defining the basic conflict, the dynamic of plot development, relations among characters, the principle of character construction, and the general emotional tonality of the whole work."[3] A common plot, already threadbare by the 1840s, centered on the pursuit of a beautiful society matron by an attractive and fashionable man under the interested eyes of society.[4] While *Anna Karenina* was originally conceived in that form, Tolstoy, predictably, burst its mold. This he did by adding thematic and plot elements diverse enough to alter the original genre almost beyond recognition. Of particular interest, then, is his purposeful retention and utilization of certain features of the smaller genre within the larger form he was creating.

Tolstoy used a variety of techniques in *Anna Karenina* to explore his heroine's mental and emotional states just before and following her surrender to Vronsky. Clearly he believed that such an act involved a profound disturbance in a personality like hers, which, unlike her brother Stiva's or her friend Princess Betsy's, was in essence deeply moral. Evidence of this disturbance mounts throughout the novel, reaching its first climax in her delirium after childbirth. Tolstoy's obvious fascination with Anna's moral and psychological turmoil is closely intertwined with his concern to find new means for portraying it. One striking feature of the relationship between Anna and Vronsky is the degree to which both are forced out of accustomed modes of thinking and feeling. As each begins to function at new and deeper emotional levels, habitual patterns of communication become less possible and communication itself becomes more problematic. Both to dramatize this experience, especially in the case of his heroine, and to demonstrate the artistic problem it posed, Tolstoy made innovative use of the society tale's conventions of discourse.

Certain characters in Tolstoy's novels serve a metonymic function in relation to segments of society. One of these characters is the old Countess Vronskaya. Her appearance early in the novel alerts the reader to the presence of a society tale "overlay" on the beginnings of a family novel. Her wizened face, false ringlets, and little black eyes barely recall her career as a society belle decades back, who, both as wife and as widow, had had many love affairs known to society at large. She is tyrannical and without morals, but her sons and other younger members of society treat her with extreme respect. Her first appearance in the novel coincides with the first appearance of Mme Karenina. Together they emerge from a railway compartment they have shared on the trip from St. Petersburg to Moscow. Their conversation in this socially neutral setting allowed each of them to remain what she is: Anna the devoted mother of a small son, and the countess a scheming society matriarch. However, the countess has performed the dubious service of infecting Anna with curiosity about Aleksei Vronsky. She reappears physically only near the novel's end, but her spiritual presence remains. For all purposes the direct descendant of Countess Anna Fedotovna, Pushkin's Queen of Spades, Countess Vronskaya provides a literary lineage for the Petersburg society that will populate the drawing room of Princess Betsy Tverskaya.

In the present generation Princess Betsy is the counterpart of Countess Vronskaya. The personification of the beau monde, she is the center of the sophisticated set that Anna frequents increasingly after her return from Moscow and her fateful meeting with Vronsky. As Vronsky's cousin and Anna's relative by marriage,

Princess Betsy considers herself the logical intermediary in their growing intimacy. Betsy's values and rules of conduct are those of a group of people who live only for their own pleasure. Their satisfaction is spiced by the game of maintaining exterior decorum while flouting moral standards in private. They also eagerly occupy themselves with penetrating and exposing the pretenses of their friends. A new intrigue in this milieu is meat and drink so long as the players obey the rules that safeguard the arrangements of everyone in the group. Betsy is a guardian of these rules as well as one of the chief players.

The conventional settings for the society tale are, naturally, the salon, the ballroom, the boxes and foyers of opera house and theater, and the occasional modish boudoir. The reader first meets Princess Betsy in her opera box, where Aleksei Vronsky delights her with an improper story also drawn from the milieu of high society. Almost immediately thereafter, Tolstoy initiates the first of two sequences of scenes in which he employs the conventions of the minor genre with striking effect. The first of these occurs before Anna's surrender to Vronsky; the second follows it. In the first, Princess Betsy's soirée provides the occasion and background for an encounter that moves Anna and Vronsky decisively closer to their ultimate union. In this scene Tolstoy contrasts Anna with her setting. At the same time he hints at the alterations about to occur within her as with increasing ease she adapts herself, at least outwardly, to society's manners and moral behavior. The chief vehicle of his revelations is dialogue, seen both as social behavior and as communication.

In her illuminating study *On Psychological Prose* Lidia Ginzburg commented on Tolstoy's "conscious interest in the process of conversation" and on the variety of social conversational patterns in his repertoire.[5] As Ginzburg observed, Tolstoy found particular interest in those purely social situations where conversation was demanded without its content being fully determined.[6] As part 2, chapter 6, of *Anna Karenina* opens, Princess Betsy Tverskaya prepares quickly for the arrival of guests whom she has just left at the opera. Tolstoy's satiric intent is detected in the description of Betsy's cosmetic repairs—the art that conceals art—and of her "massive hall porter, who in the mornings read a newspaper behind the glass panes of the front door for the edification of passers-by."[7] The ordinary world thus decisively barred from the house on Great Morskaya, the author turns to describe the elegant arrangements of Betsy's drawing room. Here he submerges his intent and blends his language with that of the hostess, who surely observes with satisfaction her "large, dark-walled, drawing-room with its thick carpets and brightly-lit table, shining in the candle-light with white tablecloth, silver samovar and translucent china" (140/120). As the guests begin to converse, the salient feature of this group's speech emerges, namely, its self-conscious artificiality. Initially the object is to prevent any fresh, sincere observation on any topic of substance. There is a counterforce in the person of Princess Myagkaya, the only named member of the group. Her habit of speaking the truth bluntly as she sees it has won her the nickname "enfant terrible." On this occasion she enlivens the company with an account of a pretentious dinner given by a banker and his wife. " 'I was told that the sauce alone at that dinner cost a thousand roubles. . . . And a very nasty sauce it was too, something green! We had to invite them, and I gave them a sauce that cost eighty-five kopeks, and satisfied every one. I can't afford thousand-rouble sauces.' 'She is unique!' said the hostess" (142/122). Princess Myagkaya does not understand the effect she creates, but "her words were simple and had a meaning." In this milieu that is enough to earn her the epithet.

However, the conversation is dominated by the ambassador's wife, "a great adept at that kind of elegant conversation which the English call 'small-talk.' " When, in the manner of bored society lionesses, she charges a fellow guest, " 'Tell us something amusing but not malicious,' " the attaché finds himself at a total loss and offers instead a short disquisition on the art of conversation: " 'The theme is everything. Once one has a theme, it is easy to embroider on it.' " The ambassador's wife laughingly cuts him short: " 'That was said long ago' " (141/121). Underlying the apparent aimlessness of these exchanges is a hidden control that prevents the conversation from lingering too long on preliminary gambits and directs it toward a definite goal: slander of close friends. Part of the perennial appeal of this game is its dangers, since the polished surface on which it is played is thin and brittle, and the player may at any second become the object of sport. This type of conversational game was a familiar device in society tales, not to say "society," for decades. Tolstoy's use of it is distinguished by his stress on its "metaconversational" character. He thus is able to contrast the strictness of the game's rules with the looseness of the moral rules observed by this group.

Not infrequently one function of such scenes was to show a protagonist as an outsider to society's game and therefore, by implication, morally superior: such are Griboedov's Chatsky, Odoevsky's Princess Zizi, Pushkin's Tatyana. The manner of Anna's entrance into this group suggests some such intent. Preceded by Vronsky, who falls into the game with the ease of a regular player, she, on the contrary, brings with her the interests of another circle which, for the time, at least, passes as more elevated. No one in Betsy's circle is interested in Anna's account of "Sir John," the Indian missionary, but all are exceedingly interested in the prospect of a scandal involving Anna and Vronsky. When the ambassador's wife directs the conversation to love and marriage, double meanings abound. Vronsky seizes the opportunity to say, without change of tone, something that is clearly directed to Anna: "'Yes, but how often the happiness of marriages founded on reason crumbles to dust because the very passion that was disregarded makes itself felt later'" (145/125). When Anna's opinion is solicited, her answer is at once ambiguous enough to satisfy the game's rules and honest enough to satisfy Vronsky: "'I think . . . if it is true that there are as many minds as there are heads, then there are as many kinds of love as there are hearts'" (146/125).

The next moment brings a significant positional change among the players. Anna and Vronsky, having stepped outside the circle of play, will now become the game's objects. Yet more important, without the rules that both constrict and insulate they find themselves suddenly near the level of genuine self-revelation. On this level there are no rules except sensitivity to the signals given, consciously or otherwise, by the other party. Both speakers become acutely aware of the inadequacy of words either to communicate or to conceal what they really think and feel. Anna has seized on the news of Kitty Shcherbatskaya's illness as the chance to set things right with her conscience. "'I came on purpose, knowing I should meet you here. I have come to tell you that this must stop!'" (147/126). Vronsky realizes, of course, that she has come for nothing of the sort. Yet her moral seriousness affects him. "Struck by the new, spiritual beauty of her face," he asks, "'What do you want of me?'" By speaking thus "simply and seriously" Vronsky takes a giant step away from his previous fashionable position of adoring pursuer of a reluctant quarry. He now attempts to establish a new, more genuine discourse between them. Anna, still in her former posture, answers as her conscience demands. But her verbal response—that Vronsky should go to Moscow to ask Kitty's forgiveness—does not ring true. Vronsky perceives this immediately and uses his advantage to break through her fragile facade of righteousness. Sensing danger, Anna clings to the words she thinks will save her. She tries with "all the powers of her mind to say what she ought." Instead, her eyes, "filled with love," give her true answer (147/127).

Aleksei Karenin's entrance and Princess Betsy's intervention cut short the tête-à-tête. However, a few more words are exchanged as Anna departs. This exchange, even more than their earlier one, focuses on the problematic nature of communication, rendered no simpler by her tacit admission of love. "'Granted that you have not said anything! I don't demand anything, but you know that it is not friendship I want!'" Vronsky is far more sanguine about the possibility of clarifying their relations than is Anna: "'Love. . . . The reason I dislike that word is that it means too much for me, far more than you can understand'" (149/128).

The artificial language of Princess Betsy's drawing room is superbly fashioned to deal with unreal feelings. "'The theme is everything,'" says the attaché, quite correctly. He might have added, "Let it be as sterile as possible." Once the theme is found, it is easy to embroider on it. The game can then move to the next stage, where meanings are concealed in hints and allusions. The concealment capacity of verbal discourse obviously is one of the delights of such a game of hide-and-seek. As an experienced player Vronsky is better able than Anna to make use of this feature. But he also realizes that verbal gamesmanship has its limits; when individuals must cope with emotions having more than two dimensions, another system is needed. In the private scene between them, Anna tries to use words defensively to conceal her feelings. Vronsky steadily penetrates her defenses and brings her to admit that which she has hidden even from herself. But Vronsky's fluency, presumably gained in many society love affairs, betrays him as well. He tells her, in phrases becoming a romantic seducer, "'Whether we shall be the happiest or the most miserable of human beings . . . rests with you'" (148/127). The irony of his persuasive words will emerge only much later in the novel.

Meanwhile, as his novel unfolded, experiment with methods of rendering intimate human discourse continued to engage Tolstoy. So did the problem of human communication itself. These facts are more than suggested by his reliance on metadiscourse in the passages here discussed. The elegant discourse of Princess Betsy Tverskaya's circle, however useless to Anna and Vronsky for intimate communication, is eminently useful to Tolstoy in examining their situation and their characters. By closely juxtaposing scenes where his chief actors are a part of the social setting with scenes where they are withdrawn from it, he makes some interesting discoveries. Once Anna and Vronsky move beyond the pale of prescribed decorum, they find themselves in uncharted territory. Language is forced to function without guiding conventions, with consequences both for communication and for the inner flow of their relationship. Tolstoy pursues his exploration of this process in a second sequence that in certain key respects closely parallels the one just discussed.

The second sequence occurs in part 3, chapters 17, 18, and 22. Once again fashionable repartee with its brittle protective surface is juxtaposed to Anna's and Vronsky's efforts to communicate on a deeper level. More than before, their efforts are handicapped by inner interference from society's "voices." And once again Tolstoy's concerns are reflected in the metadiscourse of his characters.

The relations of Anna and Vronsky have changed decisively:

she is now his mistress and is pregnant. Her open declaration of this fact to Karenin after Vronsky's racing accident has not, as she had hoped, clarified her position. Karenin's letter delivered the morning after these events shows his inability to put facts ahead of appearances. It also shows his desperate faith in the efficacy of words: "'our life must go on as heretofore'" (299/258). Appalled, Anna resolves to do what Vronsky has repeatedly asked: to discuss with him their situation and, as she now frantically hopes, to find some kind of solution.

The day following the race Anna accepts Princess Betsy's invitation to an afternoon of croquet, expecting to meet Vronsky there. Only on arrival does she recall that he will not be present. However, having found a way to arrange a meeting with him later in the afternoon, Anna settles herself for a "cosy chat" with Betsy before the other guests arrive. That Anna has progressed a good deal in the ways of social deception appears in her swift concealment of chagrin at Vronsky's absence. Her hostess is not deceived, but both play out the scene gracefully. At this point Tolstoy makes a telling observation: "This play on words, this concealment of a secret, had a great charm for Anna, as it has for all women. It was not the necessity for secrecy, not its purpose, but the process itself that was fascinating" (313/270). However this remark bears on his view of women, Tolstoy seems to hint here at his artistic intention. Like many authors and critics, he apparently regarded the society tale as a ladies' genre. Its female protagonists were formed by, but were also sometimes in revolt against, society's values and conventions. Its plots frequently centered on love intrigues. Drawing room discourse, dominated by feminine tastes and requirements, was an important means for revealing conflict, satirizing mores, and generally for moving action forward. As has been seen, Tolstoy made use of all these features. His heroine, after all, must work out her destiny in a society whose arbiters of behavior, in the last analysis, are other women. Part of her nature is ill at ease in this milieu, but at times she retreats into its deceptively safe confines. Thus in the seductive setting of Betsy's small drawing room, Anna is led to hope that her problems are not, after all, insoluble. Luxurious surroundings, amiable manners, and above all the smooth flow of words make it possible for a while to believe herself other than she is. Only upon emerging from that mesmeric atmosphere does she face again the basic contradictions of her situation. Following Anna through one crucial afternoon, Tolstoy uses discourse, metadiscourse, and generic splicing to explore both his heroine's psyche and the narrative resources of his art.

Over a cup of fragrant tea Anna and Betsy discuss Betsy's expected guest, Liza Merkalova. With a husband and two admirers, Liza is one of those who "manage" these matters comfortably. Betsy, of course, is another. Moreover, even in intimate chat, Princess Tverskaya is mistress of all the nuances of social discourse. She shifts easily between Russian, English, and French in the course of a few moments, at the same time assisting Anna, without seeming to do so, in the delicate task of writing to Vronsky. The art with which she does all this is as invisible as the tensile web of words used to insulate the social space in which she moves. In this space manners are relatively free, but speech is not. In fact, to speak seriously and honestly of genuine concerns is nearly impossible here where only one tone of voice resonates. When, during their chat, Anna puts an indiscreet question, Betsy laughingly reminds her that "'in good Society no one talks or even thinks about certain details'" (314/271). When she persists in speaking too gravely about these matters, her friend gently admonishes her, "'Perhaps you are inclined to take things too seriously.'" The earlier scene is recalled as Betsy merrily compares Anna to Princess Myagkaya: "'Enfant terrible! enfant terrible!'" (315/272).

With this social reminder Princess Betsy has temporarily subdued Anna's troublesome instinct for truthfulness in human relations. She has also prepared the entrance of representatives of a yet higher—and, as Tolstoy makes clear, even more immoral—social set. Liza Merkalova and Sappho Stolz with their admirers are paraded before Anna as models of the new fashion known as "kicking over the traces."[8] Of these two Anna finds Liza the more attractive. She has already heard from Betsy that her public show of distress at Vronsky's racing accident the day before prompted Liza to call her "a real heroine for a novel" (314/271). Now Anna is beguiled by this "perverted but . . . sweet and irre-

sponsible woman" (316/273). Despite Betsy's hint that Liza's in-
genuous manner is a pose, Anna accepts her sympathy as sincere.
Liza's naive-seeming questions and open admiration are perfectly balanced by the suave geniality of her elderly admirer
Stremov. Because he is Karenin's public foe, Stremov tries to be
especially gracious to Anna. "As he rarely met Anna, he could
not say anything to her except trivialities, but he said these trivialities . . . in a way that expressed his whole-hearted desire to be
agreeable to her, and to show her his respect and even more"
(318/275). His smooth flattery and Liza's pleas very nearly per-
suade Anna to remain. With her critical faculties lulled, all of this
carefully tuned discourse sounds spontaneous to her ears. When
she rises to depart, claiming that she must visit Countess Vrede,
Stremov's pleasantly specious argument causes her to hesitate:
" 'Your visit will give her an opportunity to backbite, while here,
on the contrary, you arouse the best feelings' " (318/275). For a
moment she longs to remain.

Anna goes to her rendezvous with Vronsky full of dread. She
feels that her present situation is false and yearns to have
Vronsky resolve it. However, her failure to tell him at their previous night's meeting of her confession to Karenin has com-
pounded her sense of falseness and awakened a feeling of shame.
Moreover, the afternoon's lessons have left their impression. In
her heart she now believes no change can occur. Vronsky, on the
other hand, though superbly happy in their present love, has realized that change is occurring and must occur, whatever their
wishes. "Latterly new inner relations had sprung up between
himself and her, which frightened him by their indefiniteness"
(322/278). He has begun to doubt the adequacy of the behav-
ioral code that has served him so far, but he has found no new
guiding principle. This is all too evident in the dialogue that
follows.

When Anna and Vronsky meet in the Vrede garden, there are
no rules to guide their discourse any more than their future behavior. Moreover, their love has not yielded the intimate access
to each other's feelings that Vronsky, at least, expected. Catching
sight of Anna's figure from a distance, he experiences a surge of
joyful recognition. The fact that her face is veiled offers no hin-

drance. Yet in Tolstoy's system, that veil is an early sign of lessened mutual perception. Infected by her agitation, Vronsky cries, "'What is it? What?'" (332/286). Silent at first, Anna then brokenly recounts her confession to Karenin. At certain stressful moments Anna seems to place an excessive burden of meaning on certain words. Here her extreme affliction over her failure to tell Vronsky earlier of her confession shows itself in repetition of a key word. The word "tell/told" (*skazala*) occurs three times in one sentence: "'I did not tell you . . . I told him . . . I told him'" (332/287). Vronsky, on his side, has not broken his habit of reliance on social formulas. However much he desires to find a new pattern of behavior, his response to this development is dictated chiefly by formula: he envisions a duel that will settle everything. "'Yes, yes, that is better! A thousand times better!'" And then he adds, "'I understand how hard it must have been for you'" (333/287). Yet "understand" is what he has failed to do—or, rather, he has understood the wrong thing. Realizing that his words are of no consequence, Anna does not listen. Instead she tries to read his expression and in her turn misunderstands. While Vronsky thinks of formal honor and its demands, Anna silently begs for the only words that she thinks could save her: "Give up everything and fly with me!" When these words do not come, she thrusts her husband's letter at him. "'I understand, I understand,' he interrupted, taking the note but not reading it" (333/287). Karenin's words are meaningless enough, but Vronsky does not attend to them. When he does read the letter at last, his thoughts are on that other note that he expects, the challenge from the abused husband, and how he will meet it. At the same time he recalls his talk earlier that day with his old comrade Serpukhovskoy, about his career and the folly of binding himself to a woman. Though he tells himself he has rejected society's formula for success, ambivalence remains. All of this prevents him from understanding Anna's state or responding as she expects. But now, ironically, when he most wishes to hide his thoughts, communication is instant: "After he had read the letter he looked up at her, but his look was not firm. She understood at once that he had already considered this by himself, knew that whatever he might say he would not tell her all that he was thinking, and knew that her last hopes had been deceived" (333/288). In their remaining minutes together matters go from bad to worse. Vronsky begs Anna to let him explain his words, but she has ceased to attach any importance to them. He tries to assure her that after the inevitable duel a change will take place, "but he said something else." When at last he is driven to express in so many words the choice she faces—to give up her son or " 'to continue in this degrading situation' "—she fixes on the word that seems to encapsulate all her shame: " 'You call it degrading! do not call it that; such words have no meaning for me' " (334/288). But when she tries to elaborate, to speak of her pride in his love, her words falter and she bursts into tears. And Vronsky, too, "for the first time in his life . . . felt ready to cry" (334/289).

These several scenes, whatever else their purpose, clearly focus attention on the function of dialogue in character dynamics and their depiction. This was hardly a new concern for a novelist, and mid-nineteenth-century realism especially demanded a keen ear for language and for social intonation. Tolstoy's own art in this regard had reached a high degree of perfection. However, he here seems particularly struck by what happens when discourse conventions break down.[9]

The scenes in Betsy's drawing room are necessary counterweights to the passages where Anna and Vronsky face each other alone. In the first sequence, the contrast is only sketched. Even à deux they do not depart decisively from their initial roles as society seducer and reluctant quarry. But in the second sequence, where all is focused on Anna's situation, contrasting elements are sharpened. The lesson of Betsy's drawing room is that skillful handling of a situation on the level of social discourse and behavior by that very fact prevents its becoming socially troublesome. No other level of concern is recognized. But when Anna meets Vronsky in the Vrede garden, Betsy's lessons are of no help. There is no counterpoint, either of clever conversation or of literary scenario. Tolstoy now lets his characters fend for themselves. And when most needed, their resources in the matter of communication are pitifully thin. They fall back, in Vronsky's case, on inbred social patterns—how a gentleman responds to an outraged husband's challenge—and in Anna's on fantasy from high romance: "Give up everything and fly with me!" Each hears only his or her own thoughts, and the rustle of emotions prevents them from hearing even these clearly. Each is inarticulate in his or her own way. Their failure to establish a coherent dialogue reflects the inability to address each other's real concerns and expectations and, at the same time, to listen deeply to themselves. Here revealed, then, are the basic contradictions in character and conditioning that will shape their behavior from now to the catastrophe.

We now know that *Anna Karenina* stood near the watershed of Tolstoy's artistic career. His debt to Pushkin's prose, as we have seen, lay partly in the impetus to adapt existing narrative modes to solve artistic problems. For both authors, though in different ways, the society tale served in this process. Without entering into the continuities and discontinuities in Tolstoy's later art, we may ask toward what future developments the explorations of social discourse in *Anna Karenina* pointed: the dialogue of Chekhov's plays? Bely's fiction? the lyrics of Anna Akhmatova? [10] Tolstoy had little sympathy with modernist literary trends, so far as he saw them develop. However, it may not be farfetched to link him with them in certain respects. As Chekhov once said, in *Anna Karenina* (as in Pushkin's *Eugene Onegin*) not a single question is answered, but the reader is completely satisfied because "all questions are posed correctly." [11] Perhaps Tolstoy's probing questions regarding methods of verbalizing inner experience contributed not a little to the drastic revision of literary conventions in the period that separated *Anna Karenina* from *The Sea Gull* and *Petersburg*.

NOTES

1. Boris Ejkhenbaum, *Lev Tolstoj v semidesjatye gody* (Leningrad, 1974; first published in 1960), pp. 147ff. Pushkin's fragment "Gosti s"ezžalis' na daču" apparently suggested to Tolstoy the first version of

his novel's opening. Another fragment, "Na uglu malen'koj ploščadi," sketching a plot of a married woman giving her lover the unwelcome news that she has left her husband for his sake, provided Tolstoy, as Eikhenbaum said (p. 149), with a conspectus for *Anna Karenina*. See "Gosti s"ezžalis' na daču" and "Na uglu malen'koj ploščadi," in A. S. Puškin, *Polnoe sobranie sočinenij*, 10 vols. (Moscow, 1956–1958), 6:560–69, 571–75.

2. Ejkhenbaum, *Lev Tolstoj*, p. 156.

3. R. V. Iezuitova, "Svetskaja povest'," in *Russkaja povest' XIX veka: Istorija i problematika žanra*, ed. B. S. Mejlakh (Leningrad, 1973), p. 173.

4. Given the great popularity of the genre in the years of Tolstoy's youth, he was presumably well acquainted with both Russian examples and their French and English prototypes and counterparts. It is perhaps only a matter of curiosity that the names of both Levin and Vronsky occur in tales concerning love triangles involving a married woman (Iezuitova, "Svetskaja povest'," p. 180; Elizabeth C. Shepard, "The Society Tale and the Innovative Argument in Russian Prose Fiction of the 1830s," *Russian Literature*, no. 10 [1981]: 134).

5. Lidija Ginzburg, *O psikhologičeskoj proze* (Leningrad, 1971), p. 378.

6. Ibid., p. 381.

7. *PSS* 18:140. Leo Tolstoy, *Anna Karenina*, trans. Louise Maude and Aylmer Maude, ed. George Gibian (New York, 1970), p. 120. Page citations to both editions will be given hereafter in the text, Russian followed by English (e.g., 140/120).

8. Literally, "Oni zabrosili čepcy za mel'nicy," "They've thrown their caps over the windmill," a literal translation of the French idiom "jeter son bonnet pardessus les moulins," "to throw caution to the winds." Tolstoy very likely intended the phrase to be recognized as a gallicism, in keeping with the artificial style of Princess Betsy and her milieu.

9. Words failed the characters of other authors, of course. Turgenev, for example, specialized in heroines who were less than articulate. However, Tolstoy seems to have taken matters a step further to suggest that, in crucial matters of communication, the spoken word is either counterproductive or irrelevant.

10. I am indebted for this suggestion to Ruth Rischin. Our "metadiscourse" was most helpful to me in defining the argument of this essay.

11. Čekhov to A. S. Suvorin, 27 October 1888, in A. P. Čekhov, *Polnoe sobranie sočinenij i pisem*, 30 vols. (Moscow, 1974–1983), *Pis'ma* 3:46.

Truth in Dying

Hugh McLean

It has long been a commonplace of Tolstoy scholarship, duly noted in every commentary on *Anna Karenina*, that Nikolai Levin is an artistic reincarnation of Tolstoy's own brother Dmitry, who died of tuberculosis in 1856, nearly twenty years before that novel was written. It would seem, therefore, that a comparison of the fictional character Nikolai Levin with what is known about the real Dmitry Tolstoy should provide some means, however meager and inadequate, for exploring the mysterious relationship between life and art, for measuring the distance between them and studying the processes by which the one is metamorphosed into the other. In short, it should help us understand how Tolstoy's artistic machinery worked. What happens when a real blood-brother Tolstoy is transformed into a Tolstoyan character?

The metaphor "artistic machinery" is misleading, however. It implies a mechanical process: you feed reality in at one end and out comes art at the other. Yet the "whys" behind an author's varied operations in transmuting real experience into fictional representation, his innumerable decisions, great and small, of what to include and what to exclude, what to duplicate faithfully and what to alter—such decisions are anything but mechanical. They emerge from a murky region in which the author's real emotions, aroused by his real experiences, confront and tangle with the aesthetic and structural requirements these reincarnated experiences must serve in their new environment. The present study is an effort to examine one particular instance of the art-life relationship. To what extent were Tolstoy's decisions con-

cerning the character of Nikolai Levin artistic decisions, or at
least justifiable in artistic terms; and, conversely, to what extent
(if any) did Tolstoy use his art not only as a means of recapturing
the past but of reshaping it into a form more comfortable and
agreeable to him?

To judge from the surviving drafts, Konstantin Levin enters
Anna Karenina complete with two brothers. He also has a sister,
but Tolstoy keeps this shadowy lady hidden away in some foreign abode. Perhaps rather implausibly, she is not stirred to return to Russia even for the marriage of one brother or the death
of another, nor, as far as we know, does she even come to visit
the dying Nikolai during his stay at Soden, where he is seen by
Kitty Shcherbatskaya. (She is recuperating there from being jilted
by Vronsky, and he arouses her animosity both by his unpleasant
habit of jerking his head and by reminding her of the brother
whom she in turn had jilted.) Tolstoy clearly did not want the
Levin sister physically present in his novel; her sole function, it
would appear, is to own estates which Konstantin can manage
for her, thus displaying both his generosity and his managerial
talents. These duties also conveniently oblige him to move about
in his rural neighborhood, and it is on a journey to his sister's
estate at Pokrovskoe that he catches the providential early-
morning glimpse of Kitty driving by in a carriage—a glimpse
that fortunately restores his sexual aspirations, which had temporarily been deflected into fantasies of melting by marriage into
the peasantry, to ones more appropriate to his station, that is,
marriage to a lovely and virginal gentlewoman. In any event, the
Levin sister is a less than vital presence in the novel. Konstantin's
two male siblings, however, are both important, though secondary, characters, each with an important part in the life of their
brother.

Sergei Ivanovich Koznyshev is a subject in himself, to be
treated here only in the most summary fashion, as the occupant
of the right-hand side of the symmetry that has Konstantin Levin
looming large in the center, whole and complete, with a flawed
and one-sided brother at either hand. Though in early drafts Sergei is a full-blooded Levin, Tolstoy soon demotes him to the
status of a half-brother, and notably a half-brother on the

mother's side, *edinoutrobnyj*, which gives him a different surname, rather than on the father's, *edinokrovnyj*, which was apparently regarded as a closer bond. This dilution of the relationship doubtless is needed to signal the fact that the respectable Sergei Koznyshev is emotionally more distant from Konstantin than the disreputable full brother, Nikolai Levin. It may also incidentally tell us that Koznyshev does not have a Tolstoy prototype: certainly neither of Tolstoy's other two brothers bears the slightest resemblance to him.

Koznyshev's principal function in the novel is to serve as a foil for his younger brother, who, though at first overawed and overshadowed by this famous writer and thinker, "known to all Russia," is ultimately shown to surpass him on every count (except, perhaps, in such ironic notoriety). At the same time, Koznyshev serves as a target for Tolstoy's own social and ideological satire. In this latter capacity he represents that hateful creature, the academic intellectual, deracinated, city-dwelling, and excessively cerebral. He is rich in book-learning but poor in spirit, a man for whom ideas are only playthings and chess problems are as absorbing as the question of the immortality of the soul. Tolstoy is really very hard on poor Sergei Ivanovich; he seems to miss no opportunity to ridicule and humiliate him. Though he expatiates on agricultural economics, Koznyshev has no roots in the soil and no farmer's feeling for how agriculture actually works. He lies abed while Levin displays both his muscular prowess and his democratic spirit in the great mowing scene. Koznyshev prates about the beauties of nature—something true country people never do; and worse still, he goes fishing, destructively driving a carriage through a meadow to reach a stream. Despite their passion for hunting—which to some of us seems a much uglier, more bloodthirsty sport than fishing—both Tolstoy and Levin for some reason consider fishing a foolish waste of time. And, as the ultimate humiliation, Tolstoy never lets Koznyshev catch a single fish!

More seriously, Koznyshev's magnum opus, a book ponderously entitled *An Experimental Survey of the Bases and Forms of Statehood in Europe and in Russia*, the fruit of six years' toil, proves a flop. To divert himself from this disappointment Koznyshev begins to beat the dubious drums of pan-Slavism, rallying Russian support for the oppressed Balkan Slavs groaning under the Turkish yoke. For this misplaced enthusiasm Koznyshev has to bear the brunt of all Tolstoy's anger against the journalistic fakery and manipulation he perceived among the promoters of that questionable cause. Perhaps the bitterest blow of all, Koznyshev is a flop with the fair sex: his Rudin-like failure to propose to Varenka, despite his intentions and all his well-considered reasons for doing so, is one of Tolstoy's great scenes, demonstrating his marvelous awareness of the frequently vast gulf between conscious purpose and unconscious wish (or fear). And just to rub in the insult, Tolstoy has Kitty and Levin demonstrate immediately afterwards, as far as they decently could within the confines of a Victorian novel, that *their* relationship, by contrast, has in it plenty of physical passion. Becoming progressively disillusioned with his brother as the novel develops, Levin sums up for us the author's (and presumably our) judgment of him: Koznyshev is lacking in "life force, what is called heart." Thus he not only has wrong ideas; he is something short of being a complete man. And by comparison Levin looks all the better.

Now what about Nikolai? First of all, Nikolai Levin obviously serves at least one of the same functions for which Tolstoy has used Sergei Koznyshev: he lights up his brother Konstantin from the other side. By the time we meet him in the novel, Nikolai is already a derelict, physically, socially, economically, emotionally. He has squandered his share of their mother's estate (whereas Konstantin has carefully husbanded his); several attempts at a career have ended in failure; he has never married, but lives with a former prostitute, Marya Nikolaevna or Masha, whom—in that romantic gesture so popular in nineteenth-century fiction—he has rescued from a brothel. But in its quotidian aftermath even this noble gesture proves flawed: Nikolai treats Masha badly, despite her meekness and devotion, and at one stage of his illness drives her away, as if to prove to himself that he needs no nurse.

Nikolai is hostile to both his brothers, who, he claims, have cheated him in the division of their mother's property; but his antagonism toward Koznyshev is stronger. Koznyshev shows toward Nikolai his characteristic dryness and lack of "heart," whereas Konstantin, though troubled and uncomfortable with his difficult brother, retains with him a deep, unbreakable bond of fraternal love, trust, and acceptance, a bond that Nikolai also recognizes, though he may appear to deny it or strain it to the limit.

Finally, Nikolai represents, as does Koznyshev, an ideology of which Tolstoy disapproves: in this case, socialism. To be sure, he is never given much chance to expound his ideas. He makes a beginning of explaining the theory of surplus value, but his brother Konstantin, through whose eyes and ears we receive our impression of this encounter, tunes out Nikolai's lecture, absorbed as Konstantin is in thoughts about his brother's tragic state of health. Nikolai's ideas are made to seem almost a by-product of his illness and thus discredited. We do learn, however, that their most concrete manifestation is a scheme for a workers' *artel'*, or cooperative guild, to be organized in a provincial village. The reader is evidently expected to dismiss this project as illusory, not so much, perhaps, because it is inherently impracticable as because Nikolai obviously has neither the resources nor the stamina to implement it.

Besides the economic and ideological contrast with Nikolai, which are both highly advantageous to Konstantin, Konstantin Levin has two other important areas of superiority to his brother: sexuality and health. Whereas Nikolai's sexual partner is a low-class ex-prostitute, Konstantin, after a temporary setback, acquires a pure and beautiful young bride, a princess or *kniazhna;* and he is clearly destined to sire a large brood of Konstantinovichi and Konstantinovny. To be sure, Tolstoy carefully avoids any impression of aristocratic or moral snobbery in his depiction of Marya Nikolaevna and of Levin's behavior toward her. Levin politely addresses her with the formal pronoun *vy*—something rare in her experience and even disconcerting—and, despite some initial qualms, he allows his wife to remain in the room with her at Nikolai's deathbed (though in her latter-day capacity as respectable matron Kitty is reluctant, despite their in-law relationship, to meet that other besmirched woman in the novel, Anna Karenina). Nevertheless, Marya Nikolaevna cannot begin to match Kitty's charms: she is pockmarked, wears tasteless clothes, and can barely read and write. And in the deathbed scene it is Kitty, not Masha, who displays so impressively that marvelous feminine sickroom know-how, utterly inaccessible to Tolstoyan males. Within a few hours she transforms a drab and smelly hotel *nomer* into a clean and cheery hospital room, ministering with unfailing tact and efficiency to all Nikolai's needs. Konstantin's superiority is thus vicariously reinforced, as it were, by his wonderful wife.

Of all the events in Nikolai Levin's life, however, the most central in the novel are his illness and death: one might almost say that his function there is to be ill and die. By so doing he confronts his brother Konstantin, emotionally as well as intellectually, with the reality of death—that supreme existential fact which his creator, Lev Tolstoy, found such an unacceptable feature of God's arrangements for us. Besides providing a stimulus for Konstantin's philosophical ruminations on mortality, the representation of Nikolai's illness and death enables Tolstoy greatly to deepen the characterization of Konstantin Levin himself, showing him struggling with the tangle of conflicting feelings evoked by this troublesome and moribund brother. In the early encounters the fraternal blood-bond, with its warm associations from childhood, plus a sense of duty, contend with shock and revulsion at Nikolai's antisocial behavior and exasperation with his constant aggressiveness; later, pity for the dying man's plight clashes with irritation at his refusal to face his predicament honestly; and in the deathbed scene, impatience with the long-drawn-out process of dying triggers a reaction of guilt and horror at discovering such an unworthy feeling in himself. (After all, to be impatient with your brother for taking so long to die seems despicable in the extreme; yet Levin cannot deny that the feeling is there.) With their searingly honest presentation of all these conflicting emotions, the chapters describing the death of Nikolai Levin, including the climactic one entitled "Death"—the only titled chapter in the novel—are among the most powerful and moving in world literature. To use Tolstoy's term, the reader's "infection" with Levin's emotions—pity, love, irritation, frustration, terror, and guilt—is complete. We too find it almost too much to bear when Levin, needed to help turn the dying man in bed, is forced to reach under the bedclothes and feel that emaciated body in all its physical reality, and when Nikolai takes Levin's hand and in a final gesture of reconciliation, gratitude, and forgiveness presses it to his lips.

Yet despite all the truthfulness in Tolstoy's portrayal of Konstantin Levin's feelings about his brother—about both his brothers, in fact—there is one familiar emotion that seems all too obviously inherent in the material as presented but is never explicitly articulated. That emotion is *rivalry,* sibling rivalry, in twentieth-century psychological jargon. Tolstoy seems to see and identify for us all Levin's emotions but this one. And yet, if we dig to the bottom of Konstantin Levin's heart as he stands by his brother's deathbed, we can hardly fail to discover there what is perhaps the most powerful and certainly the guiltiest emotion of all: *triumph.* We do not know who won the pillow fight Konstantin remembers from their childhood, but he has certainly come off the victor in all life's other contests. Where Nikolai's scorecard has nothing but black marks—poverty, a flawed and failed cause, a flawed and sullied mistress, and, finally, illness and death—Kostya's is studded with stars: relative (though not unseemly) affluence; deep roots in and efficient management of ancestral lands; sound, responsible, independent ideas about social problems; a beautiful, capable, loving young wife, whose revelation of her first pregnancy is perfectly—perhaps a little too perfectly—timed to follow Nikolai's death; and perhaps most of all, the simple triumph of remaining alive when someone else dies, that guilty triumph later to be experienced so vividly by all the associates of Ivan Ilyich. How could Levin help feeling triumphant?

Yet to feel triumphant over a brother's corpse, a brother pitied and loved despite all his failings—such a feeling, however understandable, would inevitably be followed by a rush of shame and guilt. This guilt would be a larger edition of the guilt already experienced over the feeling of impatience at death's delay. The latter feeling, however, is directly articulated by the author and recognized by the character, whereas the former must be deduced by the reader. Since Tolstoy's art places so much stress on whole-truth, dig-to-the-bottom psychological revelations, this failure to identify Konstantin Levin's feelings of fraternal rivalry and aggression might be considered an artistic flaw. If so, it might be suggested that Tolstoy's usually unerring intuition may have been inhibited here by emotional resistances stemming from his own life. He could not quite perceive *this* truth even about a somewhat distanced, fictional alter ego.

To pursue this hypothesis from literature into life one obviously has to look to the prototype of Nikolai Levin, Dmitry Tolstoy, and his relations with his celebrated sibling. To be sure, the difficulties are considerable: our data are limited and their objectivity questionable. Except for the barest facts of his curriculum vitae, what we know about Dmitry Tolstoy is almost entirely limited to what his brother Lev chose to record about him, either in his letters and diaries written during Dmitry's lifetime or in autobiographical writings of a later date. But we must make do with what we have.

The two principal autobiographical documents in which Dmitry plays a significant part are *A Confession (Ispoved')*, written immediately after *Anna Karenina,* and the unfinished *Reminiscences (Vospominanija),* written in 1902–1906.[1] Both these sources inform us, as we are told about Nikolai Levin, that as a young man Dmitry Tolstoy went through a period of intense religious involvement during which he punctiliously carried out all the required observances—fasts, vigils, and ceremonies—of the Orthodox Church. He also "led a pure and moral life," avoiding alcohol, tobacco, and sexual relations. For this excess of puritanical zeal, according to *A Confession,* Dmitry's friends and relations, including both his elders and his brothers, made fun of him and christened him Noah. Even in the most confessionally truthful of autobiographies, however, there are problems of *Dichtung* and *Wahrheit,* questions involving the uses made of a given episode and the coloration given it. In *A Confession* Tolstoy presents the "Noah" incident simply as an illustration of the hypocrisy endemic in this nominally Christian society: its upper-class representatives, at least, do not expect any of their number to take religion too seriously, and the passionate commitment of this earnest young man is treated with cruel mockery. In the *Reminiscences,* however, where the same memory is revived more for its own sake than as an illustration, it is presented quite differently. There the "Noah" taunt is attributed, not to friends and relations in general, but to one disagreeable fellow student in Kazan, S., who came into Dmitry's room, messed up his mineral collection, and teased him about his religiosity, adding "Noah" as the final sting. Dmitry's response, notably omitted from *A Confession,* was a burst of uncontrolled fury. He struck his tormentor in the face and menaced him further with a broom handle. The threat from this weapon was so convincing that S. took refuge in the adjoining room, which Lev Tolstoy shared with his second brother, Sergei; from there S. had to crawl out through a dusty attic to avoid mayhem at the hands of the still raging "Noah." [2]

Dmitry Tolstoy makes only this one appearance in *A Confession;* but in the *Reminiscences* he gets the most extended treatment of any of Tolstoy's brothers. From his physical description there we can easily recognize Nikolai Levin's double: "with thoughtful, stern, large brown eyes, he was tall, thin, rather, but not very strong, with large, long arms and a rather bent back." [3] Most of all, we instantly spot Nikolai Levin's physical trademark, his habit of "jerking his head as if trying to free himself from a necktie that was too tight." [4] This tic is also attested in a contemporary document, a letter to Tolstoy from his brother Sergei of 14 July 1852: "Mitenka . . . looked at me very fixedly, made with his head and neck the motion you are familiar with, and gave a shout." [5] We also recognize the same difficult character: explosive on occasion, but otherwise withdrawn and self-absorbed, perhaps a bit self-righteous in his moral rigors, and something of a loner among the four brothers. In Kazan Dmitry, unlike the other brothers, refused to learn to dance; had a threadbare plebeian friend symbolically named Poluboyarinov, whom the brothers called Polubezobedov (half-minus-dinner); and faithfully spent hours at the bedside of a poor ward of their aunt's, a woman suffering from a disease that caused her face to swell horribly, her hair to fall out, and her body to stink. This St. Julian—like display of nonsqueamishness, much stressed in the *Reminiscences*, is notably missing from the moral exploits of Nikolai Levin. We can only guess at the reasons, of course. It would seem that in the self-accusing, look-how-terrible-I-was spirit of his later years, Tolstoy's strategy in the *Reminiscences* is to elevate his brother at the expense of his own earlier self, emphasizing Dmitry's moral courage and denouncing himself as one of the mockers and denigrators. In *Anna Karenina*, however, to canonize Nikolai Levin or even to represent him temporarily as Konstantin's moral superior would have upset the balance of the novel. Moreover, to celebrate Dmitry's austere Christian asceticism would have undercut the ideal of family happiness and biological fecundity that Tolstoy presents in *Anna Karenina*, via Konstantin Levin, as the solution to the ever-troublesome problem of sexuality. Later on, as John Kopper's essay in this volume demonstrates, Tolstoy's ideals gravitated back to those of "Noah."

In the *Reminiscences* Tolstoy says that he loved his brother Dmitry with a "simple, even, natural love," a love he did not notice and does not remember, adding that such love is natural toward everyone unless offset by fear or intensified by some special attachment. For his two older brothers, Nikolai and Sergei, however, he, Lev, felt just this "special" love, and for Nikolai there was respect and admiration as well. "Special" love for Nikolenka and Seryozha, but only "natural" and forgotten love for Mitenka, the nearest to him in age: one is tempted to translate such subtleties into cruder language and conclude that Tolstoy liked Dmitry the least of all his brothers and perhaps did not like him much at all.

Evidence of hostility between the two brothers dating back to Dmitry's lifetime is scanty, but there are a few clues. On 13 February 1854, for instance, after passing through Moscow on his way from Bucharest to the Crimea, Tolstoy wrote in his diary that he had seen all three of his brothers, with two emotional reactions strikingly opposed: "Mitinka hurt [*ogorčil*] me, but Seryozha gave me joy [*obradoval*]."[6] Unfortunately, he gives no particulars. And a clue even more revealing, at least for those with Freudian oneiric inclinations, is found from three years earlier. In 1851, living in the Caucasus, Tolstoy wrote in his diary: "Today, December 22, I awoke from a terrible dream—the corpse of Mitinka. This was one of those dreams you don't forget. Can it mean something? I cried a lot afterwards. Feelings are truer in dreams than awake."[7] The next day he wrote Seryozha about this dream, afraid that it might be prophetic or telepathic: "What's with Mitinka? I had a very bad dream about him on December 22. Has anything happened to him?"[8] Even in this letter we can perceive a suspicious bit of censorship: to Sergei, Tolstoy writes only of a "bad dream," not a dream of Dmitry dead.

It would be wrong to maintain that Tolstoy was consistently hostile toward his brother Dmitry. Rather, his feelings were a complex mixture of the positive and negative, very much as were Konstantin Levin's toward his brother Nikolai. If irritation and antagonism, not to mention unconscious death wishes, were indeed a strong component of Tolstoy's feelings about Dmitry, however, the recollection of them would in turn evoke a reaction of guilt after Dmitry's sickness and death. And the pain of the guilt might then produce an effort to deny or mitigate the offense.

In the *Reminiscences*, written in his old age, Tolstoy professes to admire his brother Dmitry for his religious fervor and especially for his indifference to what other people thought of him, a trait he is said to have shared with the oldest brother, Nikolai; it is one that Lev Tolstoy admits he himself entirely lacked. (Indeed, acknowledging by implication that it was the thirst for fame that energized his own literary career, Tolstoy cites with approval Turgenev's observation that *Nikolai* Tolstoy had all the prerequisites—Tolstoy calls them defects—needed for becoming a writer except this one, vanity.)[9] In general, in the *Reminiscences* Tolstoy is clearly trying to give Dmitry every credit he can. One feels his finger on the scale in the sequence of adjectives he applies to him there: "serious, thoughtful, chaste, decisive, ardent, courageous." And to cap it all, he even as it were seeks to erase the ultimate injustice of Dmitry's early death: "How clear it is to me now that Mitenka's death did not annihilate him, that he existed before I knew him, before he was born, and that he exists now, after he has died."[10]

Tolstoy espoused this Platonic or Hindu-like conception of immortality, of course, too late to bestow it on Nikolai Levin. But in the 1870s, in creating the character out of his memories of his brother, Tolstoy had to make countless decisions about what to include, what to omit, and what to change.

First of all, in the novel's time sequence, the *syuzhet,* Nikolai Levin appears only toward the end of his life; there is little for him to do from that point on but to sicken and die, in the process displaying his prickly personality and thus testing his brothers' charity and forbearance. But if we include all the events that precede the main action of the novel, its *Vorgeschichte,* we can compile a fairly extensive biography of Nikolai which can then be compared, item by item, with events in the real life of Dmitry Tolstoy.

After a happy childhood at Pokrovskoe, Nikolai went on to study at and graduate from the university, as Dmitry Tolstoy did at Kazan. (One might at this point cattily note in parenthesis that Tolstoy has Konstantin Levin *graduate* from the university, something he himself never did.) After the division of their parents' property, the youthful Dmitry Tolstoy attempted to follow the principles set forth in Gogol's much-ridiculed instructions to Russian landowners (from *Selected Passages*). Not questioning the institution of serfdom as such, he wanted to do his moral duty to his peasants, sitting in judgment on them and trying to raise their standards of behavior. This display of earnest *krepostnichestvo* is, of course, excluded from the characterization of Nikolai Levin, though it may remind us of the autobiographical hero of Tolstoy's much earlier "Landlord's Morning" or even of Dmitry Nekhlyudov in *Resurrection.* This exclusion, however, could be accounted for simply by the difference in time. By making his alter-ego character Konstantin Levin more than ten years younger than himself, Tolstoy moves the entire action of *Anna Karenina,* including the *Vorgeschichte,* past the Emancipation. Thus none of his characters has to confront the moral ambiguities of serf-owning, though Tolstoy has his Levin perversely sympathize, in one of the arguments at Sviyazhsky's house, with the unregenerate *krepostnik* whose hardheaded realism contrasts refreshingly with the wishy-washy liberalism of Sviyazhsky himself.

In any event, Dmitry Tolstoy, like his brother Lev, did not persist very long in his efforts at benevolent serf-management. He next decided that his gentry privileges morally required service to the state. Again very much like Gogol, he bought himself a directory listing all the government departments, decided that legislation was the most important activity of government, and set out for St. Petersburg to present himself for legislative service. The reality of the bureaucracy he found there was as distant from Dmitry's idealistic dreams as it had been from Gogol's, and his bureaucratic career proved even briefer: he departed from St. Petersburg without ever serving at all. In an early draft of *Anna Karenina*, Tolstoy ascribed this same naive behavior to Nikolai Levin, having him also choose his area of service from a government directory, for which his brother Koznyshev, who through his connections could have helped Nikolai obtain a post, disparaged him as an infant and an eccentric.[11] The episode was later eliminated, however; perhaps this quixotic, humorous ingredient seemed out of place in the characterization of Nikolai Levin, the prevailing tones of which are irritability and gloom. Even more out of keeping would have been another episode told of Dmitry Tolstoy in the *Reminiscences*. At one point in his search for the ideal position in St. Petersburg, Dmitry had sought advice and aid from an old acquaintance from Kazan, one Dmitry Obolensky. Dmitry Tolstoy arrived uninvited at a garden party at Obolensky's house, wearing a nankeen overcoat. Obolensky introduced him to his guests and invited him to take off his coat. This proved impossible, since Dmitry had to admit that he had nothing on underneath it![12] He always dressed, Tolstoy tells us, "merely to cover his body" and was totally indifferent not only to fashion but even to convention.

The sex lives of Dmitry Tolstoy and Nikolai Levin appear to coincide quite closely. Both, in their character as "Noah," lead pure, undefiled lives until their mid-twenties. At that age they both undergo a sudden transformation. Dmitry Tolstoy "began to drink, smoke, squander money, and frequent women."[13] Nikolai Levin does the same, his associates in these diverting activities, as his brother recalls, being "the most disgusting people." In the *Reminiscences* Tolstoy puts the blame for Dmitry's downfall on a single "disgusting" individual, a family friend named Konstantin Islavin, whom he goes on to describe as an "externally very attractive, but profoundly immoral person."[14] (It is ironic, however, that Tolstoy himself preserved for decades a warm friendship with this "profoundly immoral person," who often visited at Yasnaya Polyana. To be sure, perhaps Tolstoy had little choice: Islavin was the countess's uncle.)[15]

Though not by the old Tolstoy, for most of us the youthful dissipations of Dmitry Tolstoy and Nikolai Levin could be written off as fairly harmless wild oats. To be sure, at times they went rather far: Nikolai is said to have been arrested for rowdyism (*bujstvo*) and spent a night in a police station. (I have no evidence that Dmitry Tolstoy had a comparable police record.) But certain other actions are harder to forgive. According to the final text of *Anna Karenina*, Nikolai Levin is guilty of several more serious misdeeds. He took a peasant boy from a village to educate him but in a fit of rage beat the boy so badly that charges of battery were brought against him. (In the drafts it is the boy's mother who brings charges.)[16] In the *Reminiscences* the parallel incident concerning Dmitry Tolstoy is somewhat modified. There it is said that by order of their aunt and guardian, Pelageya Yushkova, when the four orphaned Tolstoy boys moved to Kazan each was assigned a serf boy as a personal servant. Dmitry's boy was called Vanyusha, and Tolstoy reports that "Mitenka treated him badly and I think even beat him. I say 'I think' because I don't remember it, I only remember his remorse for something he did to Vanyusha and his humiliating pleas for forgiveness."[17] There is no mention in the *Reminiscences* of any legal case against Dmitry, and no mention in *Anna Karenina* of any remorse. Here we may perhaps stifle our psychiatric suspicions and attribute the changes to purely artistic motives. It would seem that Tolstoy, to enhance the contrast with Konstantin, wanted to make Nikolai Levin look worse than Dmitry

Tolstoy. For the sake of greater simplicity and consistency Nikolai's life after the "Noah" episode is made a steady downhill slide.

To propel poor Nikolai further and faster down this slope, Tolstoy has him commit some other crimes not attested for Dmitry. During his service in the Western borderlands he beats up a foreman (*staršina*), and in a similar episode from the drafts he is said to have taken some tickets from a lady to exchange them and then simply stolen them.[18]

Although prototype and character seem roughly similar in their overall economic behavior, Tolstoy again seems to have "heightened the colors" in his depiction of Nikolai Levin's financial dealings. At the time of his last illness, Nikolai is reduced to virtual destitution, from which he is rescued temporarily by his brothers and permanently by death. Nothing so dire seems to have been true of Dmitry Tolstoy. The financial arrangements among the four Tolstoy brothers (and one sister) are too complex to describe here in detail. After the original division of their parents' property, there were many subsequent transactions among them: they borrowed money from one another, bought and sold property, and administered one another's estates during absences, just as Konstantin Levin does for his brother and sister. It seems that *all* the Tolstoy brothers, very much including Lev, squandered a good deal of money, mostly by gambling; but at the time of his death Dmitry was by no means destitute, though he was short of cash. Furthermore, his general financial behavior was much less irresponsible than Nikolai Levin's. In a letter to Tolstoy of 20 October 1854, for example, he outlines his financial condition: debts amounting to 6,800 rubles, but 4,000 rubles owed to him, leaving a cash deficit of 2,800 rubles. Of the 6,800-ruble indebtedness, 4,500 rubles were owed to one Fedor Dokhturov; by the time of his death in 1856 Dmitry had repaid 1,400 rubles of this sum.[19] Thus Dmitry seems to have been making a serious effort to straighten out his affairs during his last years.

None of this effort, however, is credited to Nikolai Levin. Another, less creditable episode in Dmitry's financial history has, however, been faithfully transferred to the novel. In his summary history of his brother's misdeeds, Konstantin Levin recalls that after losing a large sum at cards Nikolai Levin had signed a promissory note for the money, but later claimed that he had been cheated and refused to pay. Such behavior violated the gentlemen's code outlined for us by Vronsky: gambling debts among gentlemen always take precedence over debts to tailors and such middle-class scum. Even the usually unresponsive Koznyshev is shocked by this impropriety and pays Nikolai's debt of honor for him, receiving a rude letter for his pains. Something very much like this seems to have happened with Dmitry Tolstoy, judging from a letter to Lev Tolstoy from his brother Sergei of 12 April 1853. Dmitry, Sergei writes, "keeps committing frightful stupidities. . . . He gambled away quite a lot and in a stupid way gave promissory notes to various persons. . . ." Later he said that "he had been forced to give the notes and doesn't want to pay. In a word, it's *disgusting*. He's now living in Moscow, organizing some sort of druggist's shop [*apteka*]."[20] Tolstoy's reply to this letter does not refer to the gambling, but only to the commercial activities, which he apparently regards either as unbecoming a gentleman or simply unpromising: "I got a letter from Mitinka in which he asks me to recommend [apparently to the army] some sort of chemical supplies from his shop. Very sad."[21] In *Anna Karenina*, Konstantin Levin applies to his brother Nikolai's behavior the same epithet, "disgusting" (*gadko*), that Sergei Tolstoy had used to characterize Dmitry's, though, to be sure, Konstantin quickly qualifies it, reflecting that Nikolai's misdeeds seem worse to those who do not know his history and his heart as he, Konstantin, knows them.

Dmitry Tolstoy's druggist shop too almost found its way into literature, though in a poetically enlarged form. In a canceled draft for *Anna Karenina* Tolstoy has Nikolai Levin angry at his brother Koznyshev because the latter refuses to sell an estate they own in common so that he, Nikolai, can use his share to start a chemical factory (*khimičeskaja fabrika*) "which would bring happiness and riches to a whole province."[22] This Midas-like chemical factory was eliminated from the final version, perhaps because it lacked the ingredient of *moral* degeneration Tolstoy needed for Nikolai's prehistory.

As for the main action of the novel, the most notable change from Dmitry Tolstoy to Nikolai Levin is ideological. In the final version, as noted earlier, Nikolai is a socialist, contrasting with the academic liberalism (and, later, pan-Slavism) of Koznyshev and also with Konstantin Levin's Tolstoy-brand anarchistic, anti-urban peasantophilia. Nikolai's transformation into a socialist, however, comes rather late in the novel's genesis. It emerges as part of the novel's engagement with various social issues of the 1870s, issues with which Dmitry Tolstoy, of course, could have had no connection. In the earlier drafts Nikolai Levin's intellectual preoccupations are less up-to-date. In one version he is found translating the Bible, which he discusses animatedly, though drunkenly, with his brother.[23] The views he expresses on social questions are then more generally cynical and pessimistic—perhaps "social Darwinist"—than socialist. He applauds Konstantin's disillusionment with the zemstvos, calling such artificial institutions nothing but "lies, toys, and reshufflings of the same stupid old cards. . . . One law," he maintains, "governs the whole world and all people as long as there will be people. If you are stronger than someone else, kill him, rob him, cover your tracks, and you are right; but if they catch you, he is right. It is not permitted to rob one man, but to rob a whole people, as the Germans have robbed the French [after the Franco-Prussian war], is allowed. The man who sees this and takes advantage of it and laughs is a sage, and I am a sage."[24]

Likewise, in earlier drafts the visitor whom Konstantin encounters in Nikolai Levin's room in Moscow is not the radical ex-student Kritsky we know from the final version, expelled from the university for founding a society to help poor students and for teaching in workers' Sunday schools. Instead, the other man is simply an unsavory lawyer whom Nikolai has hired to help him collect a huge, if dubious, gambling debt.

Nikolai's socialist convictions in the final version of the novel thus appear to conflict with the general pattern observed so far, whereby Tolstoy works to make Nikolai's errors and misdeeds seem more consistently reprehensible and misguided than those of which Dmitry Tolstoy was guilty. At least most of us, surely, would regard socialism as an improvement over the social Dar-

winism Nikolai expounds in the earlier drafts, and one assumes
that Tolstoy thought so too, even though he disapproved of the
socialists for their materialism, their lack of interest in spiritual
and moral values, and their assumption that society's ills were all
of economic origin. One can only speculate about the reasons for
this change. Perhaps social Darwinism, with its justification of
unlimited mutual aggression of individuals, classes, and nations
in the name of the survival of the fittest, seemed too malevolent a
philosophy for Nikolai, whom Tolstoy wants us to regard as fun-
damentally good-hearted, however erratic and irrational his behavior may be.

It remains to compare Nikolai Levin's most important "action"
in the novel, his death from tuberculosis, with the death of his
prototype. Dmitry Tolstoy died in Orel on 21 January 1856, at-
tended only by his faithful Masha and an unidentified "T.L." [25]
Not only was there no Kitty to brighten his room and his last
days; Lev Tolstoy was not there either. Lev Tolstoy was at that
time still technically in the army, stationed in Petersburg. Two
weeks earlier, on 9 January, he had taken a brief leave and come
to Orel to visit his dying brother, staying only one day. His diary
entry for that day is laconic, but revealing. "I am in Orel. Brother
Dmitry is at death's door. How the bad thoughts that used to
come to me on his account have turned to dust. . . . I feel terrible. I can't do anything, but I am composing a drama." [26] Back
in Petersburg, Tolstoy did not learn of Dmitry's death until 2 February. His diary for that date simply records the bare fact: "I am
in Petersburg. Brother Dmitry died. I learned about it today.
[And continuing without a break] From tomorrow on I want to
spend my days so that it will be pleasant to recollect them. Tomorrow I will put my papers in order, write letters to [Aunt] P[el-
ageya] I[l'inishna] and to the bailiff and will make a fair copy of
'The Snowstorm,' and in the evening, I'll drop in on Turgenev, in
the morning take an hour's walk." [27] The impression is not of
overwhelming grief.

There are, to be sure, expressions of grief in the letter Tolstoy
duly wrote (in French) to his aunt the next day, but they seem
routine and conventional:

You probably already know the sad news of Dmitry's death. When I saw him, it was something I was already prepared for, and I would even say that it was impossible not to wish for it. I have never seen a man suffer so much as he and suffer patiently, praying to God to forgive him his sins. He died as a good Christian, and that is a great consolation for all of us; but in spite of everything you could hardly believe how painful a loss it is for me.

He added in Russian, "imenno dlja menja" (particularly for me), as if in an effort to give some aura of sincerity to this very artificial letter.[28] Note that this passage comes *after* an extended discussion of where his aunt plans to live and, in that connection, of his own marriage prospects (presumably since she might think of making her home with him): "I confess to you frankly that for some time I have been thinking seriously of marriage, that involuntarily I consider all the young ladies I meet from the point of view of marriage, and that I think about it so often that if it doesn't happen to me this winter, it will never happen to me at all."[29] This proved a poor prophecy, needless to say; but the point here is that only from the topic of his dreams of marriage did Tolstoy pass on to that of Dmitry's death.

Fifty years later, looking back on this seemingly unfeeling response to the loss of his brother, Tolstoy judges himself severely:

> I was especially repulsive at that time. I came to Orel from Petersburg, where I had been going into society and was all filled with vanity. I was sorry for Mitenka, but not very. I turned around in Orel and went back, and he died a few days later. Truly, I think the worst thing about his death for me was that it prevented me from taking part in a court spectacle which was being organized at that time and to which I had been invited.[30]

This self-accusing memory is partly confirmed, partly contradicted by the earlier reminiscences of Tolstoy's relation and confidante, Countess Aleksandra Andreevna Tolstaya. The very day Tolstoy got the news of his brother's death, she recalls, there was a party at her sister's house (not a "court spectacle") to which Tolstoy had been invited. In the morning she got a note from him to the effect that he could not come because of the news he had received. To her surprise, that evening he appeared after all. When she disapprovingly asked why, he replied, "Why? Because what I wrote you this morning was not true. You see—I came, therefore I was able to come." Moreover, according to Tolstaya, a few days later Tolstoy admitted to her that he had gone to the theater afterwards. " 'And you probably had a very good time,' I said to him with even greater indignation. 'Well, no, I wouldn't say that. When I came home from the theater, there was real hell in my heart. If I had had a pistol, I would certainly have shot myself.' " Tolstaya attributes this behavior not so much to indifference or callousness on Tolstoy's part as to his fondness for conducting psychological experiments on himself. He liked, as it were, to press certain levers in his heart and then stand back and observe the results. " 'I want to test myself down to the fine points,' he used to say."[31]

In any event, the picture Tolstoy draws in the *Reminiscences* of his brother Dmitry as he looked two weeks before his death is undeniably close to the image we know so well from *Anna Karenina:*

> [Dmitry] looked terrible. His huge wrist was connected to his elbow by two bones, his face was nothing but eyes, and they were splendid—serious and now inquisitive. He coughed continually and spat and did not want to die, did not want to believe that he was dying. Pockmarked Masha, whom he had brought from a brothel, with a kerchief on her head, looked after him. In my presence a thaumaturgic icon was brought at his wish. I remember the expression on his face as he prayed to it.[32]

In his portrayal of the death of Nikolai Levin, Tolstoy may have added to his own memories of his brother's appearance and behavior some further details from the letter that brought him the news, written by the "profoundly immoral" Konstantin Islavin. It was Masha, Islavin wrote him, who came from Orel to Moscow with the news of Dmitry's death. She reported that a few hours before he died, Dmitry had at last recognized the hopelessness of his condition. He asked first for a priest, then a doctor. He wanted the doctor to make it possible for him to move to Yasnaya Polyana to die there in peace. If that were impossible, he asked to have his life prolonged by just two hours so that he could make a will. He was very restless before death, and the doctor gave him some drops that calmed him down. He went to sleep and never woke up again. Not long before his death he asked to be buried at Yasnaya Polyana, and this was done.[33]

From these accounts it would seem that in many respects the picture of Nikolai Levin's death in *Anna Karenina* reproduces quite accurately not only the external circumstances of Dmitry Tolstoy's death, but also the dying man's behavior during his final illness. The provincial hotel, Masha, the long refusal to face the inevitability of death, the clutching at false hopes, the impassioned prayers before an icon, the demands for more doctors and more medicines, with the struggle for life subsiding into resignation only just before the end—in all this literature has faithfully reproduced life. However, precisely the most moving parts of the death scene in *Anna Karenina* are *not* taken from real memories: the deft and loving care given Nikolai Levin by his wonderful sister-in-law, Kitty, and the anguish of her husband, whose deep tenderness and pity contend with his irritation and impatience, while the stark reality of his brother's death forces him to reflect on the meaning of life itself.

In accounting for these additions, we could hypothesize that in his reconstruction of his brother's death in the novel Tolstoy was engaging in a form of retroactive wish-fulfillment. Still feeling guilty over his own callous and unsympathetic behavior at the time of Dmitry's death, he was taking the opportunity through fiction not only to relive these events but to correct them. No more would he rush back to St. Petersburg after only one day; he would sit there to the bitter end, meekly bearing all his brother's petulance and irritability, and there would be heartwarming breakthroughs of tenderness and mutual love. Such a hypothesis may well be correct, though it in no way invalidates the artistic appropriateness of these added elements in the novel.

However, these imaginary self-compensations may have been reinforced by another set of recollections from real experience. Dmitry Tolstoy's was only the first of two fraternal deaths from tuberculosis that Tolstoy had experienced long before the writing of *Anna Karenina*. The second, a far more poignant experience and more grievous loss for him, was the death of his eldest brother, Nikolai Tolstoy, some four years later, on 20 September 1860. Nikolai was the especially beloved and admired brother, a worshipped model all through the years of childhood, companion during the adventures in the Caucasus, literary consultant, and even fellow writer, author in their childhood of the celebrated myth of the green stick on which was written the secret of how to do away with all human hostility and strife.[34]

Tolstoy did not run from the dying Nikolenka after a two-day visit; he faithfully kept a bedside vigil throughout the many long weeks that Nikolai took to expire. True, it was only in the very last phase of Nikolai's illness that Tolstoy assumed this responsibility. Earlier, Nikolai had gone abroad with Sergei to take the waters at Soden. Tolstoy himself went abroad a month later, but did not immediately join his brothers. He accompanied their sister Marya Tolstaya and her children to Berlin, sent them on to Soden, and occupied himself with his researches into educational theory, later combining these with treatments at a different spa, Kissingen in Bavaria, for illnesses of his own. (He was suffering, as he informed his "auntie" Tatyana Yorgolskaya, from a terrible toothache, migraine headaches, and hemorrhoids.)[35] But when Sergei returned to Russia in late July, the responsibility for Nikolai, Marya, and her children fell upon Lev. In mid-August they all moved from Germany to Hyères, near Toulon, on the Mediterranean coast. A month later Nikolai died there. Tolstoy remained with him the whole time, and Nikolai expired literally in Lev's arms.

Though this experience must have been much more vivid and poignant for Tolstoy than the death of Dmitry, it left comparatively little trace in his autobiographical *Nachlass*. Though a month later he called it "the strongest impression of [his] life," it was evidently too strong for words.[36] He made no entries in his diary at all from the twenty-ninth of August until the thirteenth of October, some three weeks after Nikolai's death. His fullest immediate response to the event is found in his letter to Sergei of 24–25 September/6–7 October 1860:

> You must already have gotten the news of Nikolinka's death. I am
> sorry that you weren't here. No matter how painful it is, I am glad
> that it took place in my presence and that its effect on me was as it
> should be. It was not like the death of Mitinka, which I learned
> about in Petersburg when I was not thinking about him at all.

This was quite another matter. With Mitinka I was bound by memories of childhood and by familial ties, while this one was a genuine man for you and for me, one we loved and *respected* more than anyone on earth. You know the selfish feeling that came the last time, that the sooner the better, but now it's terrible to write that and to remember that you thought that. Until the last day he, with his extraordinary strength of character and concentration, did everything he could so as not to be a burden to me. . . . As for suffering, he did suffer, but only once, a day or two before his death he said that the sleepless nights were terrible. . . . On the day of his death he asked to be dressed; and when I said that if he weren't better, Mashinka [Marya Tolstaya] and I wouldn't go to Switzerland, he said, 'Do you really think I'll get better?' in such a voice that it was clear what he felt but didn't say for my sake, and for his sake I didn't let on; however, from that morning on I seemed to know what would happen and stayed with him. He died quite without sufferings, external ones, that is. His breathing became less and less frequent, and it was over. . . . I now feel what I have often heard, that when you lose such a person as he was for us, it becomes much easier to think about death.[37]

A later letter to Aleksandra Tolstaya is also revealing:

For two months I followed his fading hour by hour, and he died literally in my arms. Not only was he one of the best people I have met in my life, not only was he a brother with whom are connected the best memories of my life—he was my best friend. . . . It's not only that half my life has been torn out, all my vital energy has been buried with him.[38]

And finally, one to Fet, written the same day:

I think you already know what happened. He died on our September 20, literally in my arms. Nothing in my life has made such an impression on me. He told the truth when he used to say that there is nothing worse than death. And if you really believe that it is the end of everything, then there is nothing worse than life. Why take trouble and make an effort when from what was N. N. Tolstoy nothing remains for him. He didn't say that he felt the approach of death, but I know that he followed its every step and knew for sure what was left. Several minutes before death he dozed off and suddenly awoke and whispered with horror, "What is that?" He had seen it, that swallowing up of oneself into nothingness. And if he didn't find anything to cling to, what will I find? Still less. . . . Until the last minute he didn't give in to it, he kept doing things for himself, kept trying to occupy himself, wrote, asked me about my writings, gave advice. But it seemed to me that he did this not from inner inclination, but from principle. . . . All those who knew him and saw his last moments say how amazingly peacefully and quietly he died, but I know how terrible and agonizing it was, because not a single feeling escaped me. . . . What's the use of anything, when tomorrow the torments of death may begin with all the base vileness of lies and self-deception and will end in nothingness, in a reduction of the self to zero. What a funny joke! Be useful, be virtuous, be happy while you live, we and other people have been saying to one another for centuries; and happiness and virtue and usefulness lie in truth, and the truth which I have extracted from my 32 years is that the situation in which someone has placed us is the most terrible deception and crime, one for which we (we liberals) would not find words if a human being had placed another in such a situation. Praise Allah, God, and Brahma. What a benefactor![39]

Konstantin Levin, at the end of *Anna Karenina,* is doubtless filled with similar anger at the Creator for so cruelly condemning us all to death and extinction, though the censors (or Tolstoy's anticipation of the censors) would hardly have allowed him to express these rebellious feelings quite so bluntly. Nevertheless, the parallels are striking:

And [Levin] repeated to himself in brief the whole course of his thinking during those past two years, the beginning of which had been the clear, obvious thought of death at the sight of his hopelessly ill, beloved brother. Clearly understanding then for the first time that for him, as for every man, there was nothing ahead but suffering, death, and eternal oblivion, he had decided that one could not live like that, that one must either explain one's life in such a way that it no longer seemed the malicious mockery of some devil or else shoot onself. But he had done neither the one nor the other.[40]

Thus is it clear that the death of his brother Nikolai in 1860 was an overwhelming experience for Tolstoy, hurling him once more up against the question that had plagued him since childhood, of the finiteness of human life, most of all his own, and the apparent futility of all human endeavor in the face of that inexorable fact. It seems more than likely that he drew on this experience in his representation of the death of Nikolai Levin, not so much in the behavior of the dying man—for Nikolai Tolstoy was evidently much more courageous and less petulant in the face of death than Nikolai Levin (or Dmitry Tolstoy)—as in the reactions of the witnessing brother, Lev Tolstoy himself. For the death of his brother Nikolai was for Tolstoy not at all an occasion for conducting a psychological experiment in self-degradation, as he had done at the time of his brother Dmitry's death; it was the real thing.

What conclusions can we draw from this lengthy demonstration of the novel's genetic ties to the novelist's life? To be sure, the existence of these ties has long been known, but it may be of some use to have viewed their many strands in detail. Certainly, in portraying the death of Nikolai Levin in *Anna Karenina* and the response of Konstantin Levin to this death, Tolstoy did draw heavily on his own experiences at the death of his brother Dmitry, perhaps with some considerable admixture from the death of Nikolai Tolstoy. Without these experiences it seems unlikely that he could have represented Nikolai Levin's death with the consummate power he did. Tolstoy's art is introspective; his extraordinary intuitive capacities were the product of years of fascinated self-scrutiny.

However, substantial changes occur in the transition from life into art. Some of these changes seem to be externally, as it were mechanically, motivated, by the change in date and historical circumstances, since the action of the novel takes place more than a decade later than the deaths of the author's two brothers. Other changes can be viewed as necessary to produce greater symmetry, consistency, or intensity in the characterization of Nikolai Levin; at least he seems to be more consistently disagreeble and difficult than Dmitry Tolstoy was in life. Finally, some of the changes seem to originate in the author's emotional needs—in those wish-fulfillment fantasies he needed to assuage the guilt he felt over his relationship with Dmitry, over his attitude toward Dmitry's death, and perhaps over the simple fact that he had remained alive while these two blood brothers had, through no fault of their own, perished.

There is undoubtedly artistic danger when a novel, especially a novel whose strength depends so heavily on the representation of psychological truth (or what the reader accepts as psychological truth), becomes a vehicle for the author's imaginary wish-fulfillments: it runs the risk of foundering in emotional spuriousness, sentimentality. Art becomes cover-up, not revelation. If Tolstoy avoids this pitfall, it is because in the crossfire of relentless self-directed aggression he maintained toward himself, and even toward such a favored alter-ego character as Konstantin Levin, it was almost impossible for sentimentality to survive. Even if Tolstoy could not quite bring himself to name the intense fraternal rivalry that fueled his own powerful drive to overtake and surpass (*dognat' i peregnat'*) his brothers, he actually did *represent* it forthrightly in the person of Konstantin Levin, even to the point of triumph at his brother's deathbed. And even if Tolstoy, via Konstantin Levin, gratifyingly represented his behavior at his brother Dmitry's deathbed as having been more devoted and sympathetic than it actually was, he was in fact only substituting his own truly devoted and sympathetic behavior at the bedside of his brother Nikolai. And if he, by the power of imagination, made his wife, Sofya Andreevna, care for a dying brother-in-law she never met, he had by the time of *Anna Karenina* seen her display comparable solicitude at countless sickbeds, including his own, and at least two deathbeds, those of their baby sons Petr, who died in 1873, and Nikolai, who died in 1875.

It would appear, therefore, that our scrutiny of the case of Nikolai Levin has succeeded only in demonstrating once more that fundamental paradox of art, especially realistic art: "truth" in art and "truth" in life are not to be equated. Fiction inevitably incorporates elements from both experience and imagination. Some experiences are reproduced intact, others are altered or recombined, and both may be interlarded with wholly imaginary events and personalities. The motives for these manipulations may sometimes be influenced by extra-literary emotions stemming from the author's own life, including wish-fulfillment, denial, and cover-up; but it must be remembered that even alterations of literal, biographical truths so influenced may prove altogether appropriate in an artistic setting, conveying deep and universal truths about human life.

NOTES

1. I have excluded any consideration here of Dmitry Tolstoy's possible role as the model for Dmitry Nekhlyudov in *Youth*.
2. *"Vospominanija," SS* 14:460.
3. *SS* 14:458.
4. *SS* 14:459.
5. *PSS* 59:187–88.
6. *PSS* 46:236.
7. *PSS* 46:240.
8. *PSS* 59:132.
9. *SS* 14:465.
10. *SS* 14:461.
11. *PSS* 20:175.
12. *SS* 14:463.
13. *SS* 14:464.
14. *SS* 14:464.
15. Konstantin Aleksandrovich Islavin (1827–1903) was the son of Aleksandr Mikhailovich Islenev and Sofya Petrovna, née Countess Zavadovskaya, Princess Kozlovskaya by marriage. Princess Kozlovskaya spent most of her life with Islenev and bore him six children, but since her marriage to Prince Kozlovsky had never been legally dissolved, the children were considered illegitimate and bore the surname Islavin. Konstantin was a childhood friend of Tolstoy's. Later, Konstantin's sister Lyubov (1826–1886) married Dr. Andrei Evstafevich Bers (1808–1868) and became the mother of Sofya Andreevna Bers, later Countess Tolstaya. This "profoundly immoral" person, whom Tolstoy's children called "Uncle Kostya," thus had a double connection with the Tolstoy family.
16. *PSS* 20:174.
17. *SS* 14:458.
18. N. K. Gudzy's note in *PSS* 20:612.
19. M. Tsiavlovsky's note in *PSS* 59:269.
20. *PSS* 59:228.
21. L. N. Tolstoy to S. N. Tolstoy, 20 July 1853. *PSS* 59:242.
22. *PSS* 20:174.
23. *PSS* 20:174.
24. *PSS* 20:171.
25. *PSS* 47:65, 301.
26. *PSS* 47:65.

27. *PSS* 47:65.

28. *PSS* 60:50.

29. *PSS* 60:50.

30. *SS* 14:464–65.

31. "Vospominanija gr. A. A. Tolstoj," in *Perepiska L. N. Tolstogo s gr. A. A. Tolstoj, 1857–1903*, ed. B. L. Modzalevskij (St. Petersburg, 1911), p. 14.

32. *SS* 14:464.

33. Nikolaj Gusev, *Lev Nikolaevič Tolstoj: Materialy k biograffii s 1855 po 1869 god* (Moscow, 1957), p. 20.

34. Nikolai Tolstoy's sketch "Okhota na Kavkaze" (Hunting in the Caucasus) was published in *Sovremennik* (no. 2, 1857), and two other works by him were discovered in his papers and published in the 1920s. (See M. A. Tsiavlovsky's note in *PSS* 59:122.) Tolstoy's diary entry for 19 January 1858 (*PSS* 48:4) testifies that Tolstoy consulted Nikolai concerning whether to leave in or exclude the tree's death from "Three Deaths." Nikolai advised him to leave it in, which he did.

35. Tolstoy to T. A. Yorgolskaya, 24 July/5 August 1860. *PSS* 60:346.

36. Diary entry of 13/25 October 1860. *PSS* 48:30.

37. Tolstoy to S. N. Tolstoy, 24–25 September/6–7 October 1860. *PSS* 60:353–54.

38. Tolstoy to A. A. Tolstaya, 17/29 October 1860. *PSS* 60:356.

39. Tolstoy to A. A. Fet, 17/29 October 1860. *PSS* 60:357–58.

40. *SS* 9:421.

Tolstoy and the Narrative of Sex
A Reading of "Father Sergius," "The Devil," and "The Kreutzer Sonata"

John M. Kopper

Like their confrères in France twenty years before, the generation of Russian writers who began their careers around midcentury— Turgenev, Goncharov, Tolstoy, and Pisemsky—found a stubborn problem of narrative lying across their path. The enterprise that they collectively pursued demanded the bodying forth of a fluid social world, filled with the motions of decay and resurgence, mobility and disruption. Railroads made travel easier and extended the possibilities of economic and social commerce both within the country and abroad. Capitalism was focusing the economic life of nations more and more in urban areas, and writers had to record not only the new importance of cities but the functions of new classes dwelling in those cities. Though change in nineteenth-century Russia moved at a slower pace than in Western Europe, her writers did begin to describe this new geographical and social mobility, the evolution of the class hierarchy, and the gradual redistribution of power. In the preceding decades Gogol in "The Overcoat" and Dostoevsky in *Poor Folk,* delving as low into the class structure as their European contemporaries Eugène Sue and Charles Dickens had done, defined the aspirations to bourgeois respectability of Russia's clerical proletariat. In *A Hunter's Notes,* Turgenev crowned the bottom man on the social ladder, the serf, as worthy and ready to bear the weight of serious fictional discourse.

These literary achievements were followed by two events which would quickly put Russia on a par with Europe in terms of political instability and social malaise. First, the Crimean War of 1853–1856 began a moral erosion of the autocracy that no ruler till Stalin absolutely succeeded in reversing. Shortly afterward followed the emancipation of the serfs, which threatened the wealthier classes, for the first time since Pugachev, with the existence of a majority of poor, who if not capable of a jacquerie could at least bankrupt the landowning class. Thus Russia experienced its French Revolution and its Revolution of 1848, though in considerably watered-down versions.

But in recording recent social changes, writers confronted a narrative paradox: an event can only be seen as an intelligible change in the given scene, and change can only be registered if it takes place against a (relatively) stable background. The Renaissance code of kingship in force at Elsinore helps make the dynastic and familial struggles that occur there distinguishable actions. Laurence Sterne's traveler can make an eventful "sentimental journey" across a landscape of social immutability. In the nineteenth century, writers, describing a world that was defined by change, were compelled to find a new reference point against which the motion of both hero and society could be measured.

One solution, available in an age when social transformation was still felt to be a novelty, was to make an event out of the conflict between a semantic field consisting of the old and inflexible and an impinging semantic field of the new and fluid. In Regency England, Jane Austen discovered this solution and applied it in many of her novels. Mary and Henry Crawford in *Mansfield Park* are infected and infecting foreign substances who invade the sanctity and torpor of English country living like germs attacking a host. Their entry into and expulsion from the aristocratic universe of the Bertrams can be seen as events. Forty years later, Russian writers would hit upon the same formula. Turgenev, Goncharov, and Pisemsky seem consciously to dramatize in their works the search for forces of flux and instability: there is a Rudin for every Pigasov, an Andrei Stolz for every Ilya Oblomov, a Kalinovich for every Flegont Godnev. In each case the agent for change transgresses a field of inertia. His very restlessness in a stagnant culture constitutes an event.

Writers found a second solution in the stratification of rates of change within the plot. As Yury Lotman has pointed out, in *War and Peace* Nikolai Rostov does not undergo the same extensive metamorphosis of person as do Prince Andrei and Pierre Bezukhov. Despite his geographic mobility, his participation in great historical events, and his evolving of a sense of family responsibility, Nikolai appears to be the unchanging member of the novel's trio of male heroes. Against him the development of the other two characters appears in bold relief. Making Nikolai a background figure entails selecting paradigms of progress (spiritual, political) according to which Nikolai will appear fixed and opposing them to others (geographical, social) that grant him mobility. The result, in Tolstoy, is a character who transverses many semantic fields but who, relative to some characters, appears fixed. Hence the usual conviction of a reader of *War and Peace* that Nikolai changes, but—crudely put—Pierre and Prince Andrei change "more." [1]

A third solution depended very much on the reading conventions we associate with realist writing. First, plots tended to proliferate within the text. One has only to compare *Anna Karenina* with *Dead Souls* to see how dense the weave of the fictional universe had become. At the same time, narrative passed increasingly under the influence of a voice marked by its stability, articulateness, erudition, intelligence, and profound seriousness. The novels of Tolstoy record this change, as will any novel of Turgenev's, weighed against *A Hero of Our Time* and *Evgeny Onegin;* Balzac against Stendhal; or Eliot, and Dickens after 1850, with the Dickens of the late 1830s and early 1840s. The multiplication of plots led to a pretense of fictional universality, to a saturation of the narrative medium and the seeming exhaustion of its resources in every conceivable way. Narrative fiction presented a world in which every action, however cryptic and apparently unmotivated on emergence, could be recovered, traced, and described and thus be perceived as determined. Furthermore, the narrative voice became the voice of legitimacy and reconciliation in a world of indeterminate values and shifting claims to authority. By encompassing an overwhelming heterogeneity of material, the narrative came to represent a homogeneous vessel, the solid jar within which the stormy dramas of alteration and experiences of alterity could be contained.[2] Thus nineteenth-century narrative on the one hand came to illuminate its own projected world with the light of textual determinism, and on the other hand itself became the symbol for the authoritative reconciliation of diversity.[3] It thereby organized two new static fields against which its action could take place. The universality of its determinism and the uniformity of its narrative voice both helped to create the stability needed to describe a world in constant erosion.

This constellation of newly found narrative strategies accounts for a brief but significant moment in the history of nineteenth-century European fiction. It can be found operating in most of Dickens's and Eliot's novels and with surprisingly little qualification fits Thackeray as well.[4] In France, it describes Balzac; and in Russia, Turgenev, Goncharov, Pisemsky, and Tolstoy up to the time of his religious crisis. For them, a narrative that can embrace everything cannot be surprised. Moreover, since it accounts for everything it narrates, its goal is to remove surprise. Finally, its reassuringly stable narrative point of view cannot *give* surprise.

Dissatisfaction and impatience with the conventions of this moment—the moment that has worn the protean label "realist" with least challenge from the critics—permeates the work of the American writers of the period and causes the curious cleavage through the middle of Flaubert's oeuvre. In Dostoevsky's novels it is reflected preeminently in the lapse of a consistently maintained narrative focus; the "gratuitous," random action; the replacement of action with dialogue, which is not necessarily eventful or event-producing; and the retreat of the narrative into micro-societies: the family, the political group, the individual. Dostoevsky gives such prominence to these in the organization of value hierarchies that the stable ground of larger social units fades from sight.

Tolstoy, though he reacted just as strongly as Dostoevsky to the inherited canons of writing, took his fiction down another road. In three works of the 1880s and 1890s, "The Kreutzer Sonata" (published in 1889), "The Devil" (written in 1889 and published posthumously), and "Father Sergius" (completed in 1898 and published posthumously), Tolstoy tries to redefine the idea of "event."[5] These stories are often gathered up in one critical net. Grouped together for their merciless indictment of relations between women and men, they are taken to be the collective outcome of a meditation on chastity that Tolstoy began in the mid-1880s.[6] In fact the three stories should be judged as much for their typically Tolstoyan—and equally merciless—scrutiny of narrative.

To produce the absorbent wall which would first set off, then finally blunt, the dissonances of storytelling, the author relies neither on the stability of a sententious narrator nor on the intricate density of plot connections. In fact he compounds his initial difficulty. All prose writers of the time faced the problem of establishing a notion of event in a milieu in which not only the hero but the society itself was mobile, but Tolstoy sets himself the task of describing an event in a society so permissive that it has few norms to be violated.

His conception of the permissive society has its roots in earlier works. In *War and Peace* Tolstoy appears, if not to embrace the social order, at least to identify healthy elements within it. The society of Tolstoy's construction is itself under too great a threat during the war episodes of the novel for it ever to acquire sinister force in peacetime. In *Anna Karenina,* however—the novel that only escapes to war near its conclusion, with Vronsky's departure for the Turkish war—the question of whether to belong to social groups becomes paramount. Nor does it appear that Tolstoy finds much of his culture worth participating in. Town life is rejected, and country life, unlike its manifestation in *War and Peace,* becomes in large measure the appendix of municipal cultures. Zemstvos form a rural bureaucracy that apes the St. Petersburg ministries. A city dandy like Veslovsky intrudes into the country. On Vronsky's estate, Anna and Vronsky, with their Anglophile fads, are a terrifying tableau of unsuccessful flight. It would seem that here the rural idyll of Tolstoy—perhaps in spite of the author's wish to make it otherwise—is itself a fiction; Levin must resist the fact that country estates have become moral suburbs of city life.

It is from the isolation of Anna and Vronsky that Tolstoy begins in his late stories. He has paradoxically found culture so corrupt as to be of little interest, so incapable of respect that it cannot resist, refract, or mirror the hero's ethical positions in any meaningful way. Each of the three stories is built upon a society's collective failure to understand that anything of significance is happening. Thus Tolstoy applies to fiction-making the complications inherent in a Karamazovian universe, where "all is permitted." Tolstoy's three heroes must first define what event is, and each is constrained to find a private solution, since his culture does not provide a distinct moral field within which to operate. By describing permissive societies Tolstoy infinitely stretches the elastic domain of value networks in his stories and jeopardizes the very idea of event. When the hero seems to move toward a frontier, the moral horizon retreats, leaving him still helpless to define his event. Of the three stories, only "Father Sergius" records any violation of the social code before the denouement. At the very beginning of the story, Kasatsky astonishes St. Petersburg's beau monde by taking holy orders. But the narrator quickly moves to redefine this surprise and shifts the story's focus to Kasatsky's "inner motives." By the end of its first section, the story successfully resolves the enigma of Kasatsky's renunciation, as if Tolstoy were deliberately writing "through" a conventional plot to see what lay beyond.

More remarkable is the fact that the societies of the stories so quickly forgive the heroes' most violent behavior. In both of the endings that Tolstoy wrote for "The Devil," Irtenev's suicide and his murder of Stepanida are alike ascribed to his being "mentally ill." In "The Kreutzer Sonata," Pozdnyshev kills his wife and is acquitted as a "deceived husband" for defending "his besmirched honor." In "Father Sergius," Kasatsky cuts off his finger to save himself from a sexual fall, but the notoriety of his action only moves him more rapidly along the road to elder-hood. His action is ironic for being a cliché of hagiography.[7] Thus even his holy exploit becomes a conventional step. Like Irtenev and Pozdnyshev, Kasatsky finds himself in a world in which he has immense difficulty violating the norms of behavior.[8]

In these three stories, as in many of his late works, including "The Death of Ivan Ilyich" and "Hadji Murad," Tolstoy uses a conventional notion of event as a narrative threshold. Part of Tolstoy's solution to the problem of defining event, therefore, is to transgress the reigning codes of narrative and make violation of the notion of event itself eventful.

A closer look at the three stories shows how Tolstoy accomplishes this. Irtenev, the hero of "The Devil," exemplifies the protagonist whose actions threaten to remain uneventful. His search for a boundary to acceptable behavior reaches an absurd cul-de-sac in his colloquy with an alcoholic uncle:

—Но позволь, ты объясни мне . . .
—Ну, да вот. Когда я был холостым, я имел глупость войти в сношения с женщиной здесь, из нашей деревни. То есть, как я встречался с ней в лесу, в поле . . .
—И хорошенькая?—сказал дядюшка.
Евгений поморщился от этого вопроса, но ему так нужна была помощь внешняя, что он как будто не слышал его и продолжал:
—Ну, я думал, что это так, что я перерву и все кончится. Я и перервал еще до женитьбы и почти год и не видал и не думал о ней,—Евгению самому странно было себя слушать, слушать описанне своего состояния,—потом вдруг, уж я не знаю отчего,—право, иногда веришь в привороты,—я увидал ее, и червь залез мне в сердце—гложет меня. Я ругаю себя, понимая весь ужас своего поступка, то есть того, который я всякую минуту могу сделать, и сам иду на это, и если не сделал, то только Бог меня спасал. Вчера я шел к ней, когда Лиза позвала меня.
—Как, в дождь?

"But please, explain to me . . ."
"Well, it is like this. When I was a bachelor I was stupid enough to have relations with a woman here, one from our village. That is to say, I used to have meetings with her in the forest, in the field . . ."
"Was she pretty?" asked his uncle.
Evgeny frowned at this question, but he was in such need of external help that he seemed not to hear it, and continued, "Well, I thought it was the sort of thing I would break off, and everything would be over with. And I did break it off before my marriage. For nearly a year I didn't see her or think about her." It was

strange to Evgeny to listen to himself, to listen to a description of his own state. "Then suddenly—I really don't know why—it's true, sometimes you want to believe in witchcraft—I saw her, and a worm crept into my heart. It's been gnawing me. I curse myself, understanding the full horror of my act, that is, the horror of the act I may commit any minute. And yet I move toward it, and if I haven't done anything yet, it's only because God has preserved me. Yesterday I was on my way to her, when Liza called for me."
"What, in the rain?"⁹

Irtenev's other confidant, the watchman Danila, betrays a disturbing flexibility in his attitudes toward sex and prevents his master from establishing the limit he seeks:

Случилось ему раз зайти напиться в лесную караулку. Сторожем был бывший охотник отца. Евгений Иванович разговорился с ним, и сторож стал рассказывать старинные истории про кутежи на охоте. И Евгению Ивановичу пришло в голову, что хорошо бы было здесь, в караулке или в лесу, устроить это. Он только не знал как, и возьмется ли за это старый Данила, «Может быть, оп ужаснется от такого предложения, и я осрамлюсь, а может, очень просто согласится». Так он думал, слушая рассказы Данилы. Данила рассказывал, как они стояли в отъезжем поле у дьячихи и как Пряничникову он привел бабу.
«Можно», —подумал Евгений.
—Ваш батюшка, царство небесное, этими глупостями не занимался.
«Нельзя», —подумал Евгений, но, чтобы исследовать, сказал:
—Как же ты такими делами нехорошими занимался?
—А что же тут худого? И она рада и мой Федор Захарыч довольны-предовольны. Мне рубль. Ведь как же и быть ему-то? Тоже живая кость. Чай вино пьет.
«Да, можно сказать», —подумал Евгений и тотчас же приступил.

He happened once to go into a watchman's hut in the forest to get a drink of water. The watchman had been his father's huntsman. Evgeny Ivanovich chatted with him, and the watchman began telling some old tales of hunting carousals. It occurred to Evgeny Ivanovich that it would be convenient to arrange matters in this hut, or in the wood, only he did not know how to manage it and whether old Danila would undertake the arrangement. "Perhaps he will be horrified at such a proposal and I shall have

disgraced myself, but perhaps he will agree to it quite simply." So
he thought while listening to Danila's stories. Danila was telling
how once when they had been stopping at the deacon's widow's
house near an outlying field, he had brought a woman for Fyodor
Zakharych Pryanichnikov.

"It will be all right," thought Evgeny.

"Your father, may the kingdom of heaven be his, did not go in
for nonsense of that kind."

"It won't do," thought Evgeny. But to test the matter he said,
"How was it you engaged in such bad things?"

"But what was there bad about it? She was glad, and Fyodor
Zakharych was satisfied, very satisfied. I got a ruble. Why, what
was he to do? He too is a lively one. And he drinks."

"Yes, I may speak," thought Evgeny, and at once proceeded to
do so.[10]

Irtenev's interview with the steward Vasily Nikolaich also illustrates the morally undefined position in which he finds himself.
Vasily Nikolaich remonstrates with him regarding the banish-
ment of Stepanida and her family from the estate:

—Да как же удалишь? Куда оп пойдет с своего кореня?
Да и на что вам? Что она вам мешает?

—Ах, Василий Николаевич, вы поймите, что жене это
ужасно будет узнать.

—Да кто же ей скажет?

—Да как же жить под этим страхом? Да и вообще это
тяжело.

—И чего вы беспокоитесь, право? Кто старое помянет,
тому глаз вон. А кто Богу не грешен, царю не виноват?

—Все-таки лучше бы удалить. Вы не можете поговорить
с мужем?

—Да нечего говорить. Эх, Евгений Иванович, что вы
это? И все прошло и забылось. Чего не бывает? А кто же
теперь про вас скажет худое? Ведь вы в виду.

"But how can they be sent away? Where is he to go—torn up
from his roots? And why should you do it? What harm can she
do you?"

"Ah, Vasily Nikolaich, you must understand that it would be
dreadful for my wife to hear of it."

"But who will tell her?"

"How can I live with this dread? The whole thing is very painful to me."

"But really, why should you distress yourself? Whoever stirs up the past—out with his eye! Who is not a sinner before God and to blame before the tsar?"

"All the same, it would be better to get rid of them. Can't you speak to the husband?"

"But it is no use speaking! Eh, Evgeny Ivanovich, what is the matter with you? It is all past and forgotten. All sorts of things happen. Who is there that would now say anything bad of you? You're in plain view." [11]

While Vasily Nikolaich holds solid views about keeping Stepanida's family together, his sexual code could not be less firm. His question "Who will tell her?" evades judgment of Irtenev's actions. His use of the proverbial formula "Whoever stirs up the past—out with his eye!" shifts the blame from the culprit to the would-be judge (and ironically inverts, through misapplication, the horrible mutilation imperative from Matthew, which Tolstoy uses as epigraph to the story). "Who is there that would now say anything bad of you?" in turn becomes the fulcrum of two phrases, one of which implies that Irtenev has sinned ("It is all past and forgotten"), and the other that Irtenev is prominent and able to punish loose talkers ("You're in plain view"). The focus of Vasily Nikolaich's replies is lost in a potpourri of morally incongruent statements.

The peasant Danila has no sexual standards. He operates within a code of subservience, changing his position to fit his master's whim. Irtenev's uncle sees no conflict at all; his interest is circumstance, and circumstantial detail reflects his obedience to a circumstantial code of behavior. Irtenev lives in a universe in which the moral code appears almost infinitely pliant. The event he tries to forestall—adultery with Stepanida—would not be an event to his uncle. Danila is concerned only with getting some money. Similarly, while the steward Vasily Nikolaich considers the expulsion of Stepanida from the village to be unacceptable conduct, the fact that Irtenev has had an affair with her is not.

Irtenev is left with no obstacles to his descent. The story, in fact, is built around his effort to *create* impediments and around the fortuitous introduction of further hindrances that he had *not* sought. Irtenev buries himself in farming and then flees with his wife to the Crimea. And three times on the way to meetings with the peasant woman Stepanida, he is interrupted by chance and called away to other affairs. These near-misses are reflected in his wife Liza's early miscarriage, a figure for his early missteps with Stepanida, and her second near-miscarriage, which parallels the many episodes in which he comes close to renewing his affair with Stepanida. In the ironic end, Irtenev commits the greater crime of murder in order to escape his own lesser sin of concupiscence. Pozdnyshev, the protagonist of "Kreutzer Sonata," finds that every aspect of his married life revolts him. Repugnance suggests standards, and their violation would produce events. But in fact Pozdnyshev repeatedly emphasizes the absolute ordinariness of his particular marital experience.[12] By marrying, he has located himself within a certain code of behavior that permits what he only later will conclude to be impermissible: jealousy, sex, and deceit. Thus Tolstoy has his characters choose certain isolated micro-cultures: the monastery (Kasatsky), marriage (Irtenev and Pozdnyshev), and rural life (Irtenev), but then traces the heroes' gradual recognition that these subworlds, like Leibniz's monads, in fact reduplicate the codes of a larger universe, a society of wide-ranging permissiveness. The characters in search of an ethical landfall remain on open seas.

Tolstoy's formulation of the ethical dilemma is romantic in conception and antiromantic in conclusion. The Tolstoy subject is in fundamental conflict with a social totality and employs various strategies for removing himself from the diseased context. But precisely what the subject demands for his world is a code of discipline. In his fancied isolation, he seeks to create the law which his culture has failed to furnish. In all three stories, the protagonist ends by replacing a potential act of at most venial gravity—in "The Devil," sex with Stepanida; in "Father Sergius," sex with Makovkina; and in "The Kreutzer Sonata," flirting with Trukhachevsky—with murder, suicide, and dismemberment. Of the original sexual impetus only its violent component survives. Tolstoy's stories have traversed a great distance from Karamzin's "The Island of Bornholm," where the isolation of the island's micro-culture does *not* prove illusory and the sexual act, in opposition to its place in Tolstoy's stories, is perceived as criminal by both the social commonality and the outcast group.[13]

The discussion has not yet acknowledged the specific forces that Tolstoy attached to his chosen topic, sex. To understand the centrality of sex to his sense of self and to his attitude toward art, one can look to the various media through which Tolstoy expressed himself, such as published conversations and his polemical works. And above all one can trace the arc plotted by his fiction over a fifty-year period. Sex and writing were closely linked for Tolstoy, because sex is preeminently a form of passion, and Tolstoy, with increasing Platonic fervor, came to believe that art aroused the passions.[14] The remainder of this essay, however, will concentrate on sexuality not as a moral, philosophical, or biographical problem but as a semantic field possessing specific laws. In "Father Sergius," "The Kreutzer Sonata," and "The Devil," the lead character puts himself in a position in which sex becomes a significant issue and therefore can be eventful. In order to move his characters onto a potentially charged narrative ground, Tolstoy finds a literary correlative for their moral impasse, a narrative where the issue is not the predicaments of plot but the difficulty of *generating* plot predicaments. His solution lies with male sexuality.

As *Anna Karenina* begins by destroying the happy families left at the end of *War and Peace,* so in the 1880s and 1890s Tolstoy seems to begin with the end of *Anna Karenina.* Sexual passion, a potential source of criminality hitherto assigned to female heroines—Natasha Rostova and Anna Karenina—now spreads to the male world. In "The Devil," "The Kreutzer Sonata," and "Father Sergius," Tolstoy inspects the sexual component of male identity as if it were something new. Vronsky's sexual values hardly matter; he is faithful to Anna, and his earlier affairs are overlooked by his society and by the narrator who relates them. Levin's premarital liaisons, to his astonishment, shock and anger Kitty, but the problem remains Kitty's, and it is Kitty who must change, not Levin. In both *War and Peace* and *Anna Karenina,* male characters who violate the sexual codes of the society as a whole are not heroes (Dolokhov, for example). Male heroes at most run against the private standards of their loved ones.

In the eyes of the culture within which Tolstoy's male charac-

ters must function, there is little they can do that is absolutely
wrong. It is extremely difficult for the hero to change position
with respect to his moral environment. Levin, for example, faces
a conflict between the religious standard of sexual behavior, established by the church and embraced by Kitty, and the highest
practical ideal of his society, which endorses matrimonial fidelity
but permits men to have premarital affairs with lower-class
women. The religious ideal he must reach is *beyond* reach because he must restore his virginity to obtain it. However much
Levin defers to his wife's prescripts for behavior, there is nothing
he can do to alter his fallen condition and therefore no change or
struggle toward change to narrate. The only taboo that his class
at large would recognize is the stricture against his having affairs
with women of noble birth who have never married. This line
seems so fixed to Tolstoy that he rarely brings a character to
cross it. Even the debauched Anatole Kuragin in *War and Peace*
contemplates polygamy rather than think of running off with
Natasha Rostova without marrying her.

What he perceives to be an asymmetrical relation between the
sexes provides Tolstoy, from *Anna Karenina* onward, with an
important field in which to explore these narrative issues. That
which remains a subsidiary matter in *Anna Karenina* (the disparate receptions given Vronsky and Anna by Petersburg society
while they are having their affair) becomes a central concern in
some of the stories of the 1880s and 1890s: the sexuality of a
man has little inherent plot interest. Because his chastity is not
valued, it is more difficult for a man to create a sexual field with a
distinct "here" (approved conduct) and "there" (reprehensible
conduct). A woman's threatened chastity, on the other hand, will
always provide the stuff of narration.

In "The Devil," the problem for Irtenev is that he has no one
except himself to prevent his descent. More than in the other two
stories under consideration here, the hero is isolated from contact with other men. Surrounded by women of the lower class,
who can only tempt him, and the women of his family—his wife,
mother, and mother-in-law—who represent the standard against
which male society bridles, Irtenev can appeal only to the vague
moral creeds of Danila and his uncle. He is deprived by them of a

sexual code which he might violate, and he eventually replaces one physical act for which there is no penalty (sex) with another for which there is (murder). The story ends when his search for a transgression ends. If anything, Tolstoy's ambivalence about who should be murdered (in alternate versions of the story, Irtenev murders Stepanida, or commits suicide) supports the fact that transgression itself, rather than any particular transgression, has become the point of the story.

In "Father Sergius" the roles of men and women are reversed so that a man's sexual life can acquire narrative interest. The story begins atypically, with the fiancée confessing her sexual past to her future husband. Tolstoy thus makes the precursor of the story what would normally be the story itself. The hero, Kasatsky, then restores his fiancée's chastity by substituting his own. Only as a revered monk could his chastity be as interesting as a woman's, and "Father Sergius" can become a tale of his fall.

In "The Kreutzer Sonata" we see Tolstoy's most radical experiment with narrative. Pozdnyshev plays a frustrated author, as it were, trying to bring his heroine to fall. Tolstoy thus correctly identifies the potential narrative interest of the threatened yet faithful woman, but also manifests his interest in evading this traditional plot. By firmly, irrationally insisting that his wife has transgressed, that she is "there" when we know her to be "here," Pozdnyshev creates the narrative. Instead of the story being about something that has happened, it is about the effort to make something from nothing, that is, about fiction-making. The irony of the story is that Pozdnyshev's wife resists participating, and Pozdnyshev must replace her inertness with his own activity. Pozdnyshev substitutes a traditional plot, the exposure of a woman's body (realized in his typically Tolstoyan obsession with low-cut gowns and with male doctors examining a nude female patient) with his own discourse, the self-exposure of confession.

This is not to say that Tolstoy's characters intend such replacements but, rather, that they perform them. Indeed, once they have created a context of potential eventfulness, his characters struggle with all their might to forestall situations in which they would have to act. The construction of barriers and their subsequent avoidance are both actions that acquire eventful force and help to constitute the story.

From here a discussion of Tolstoy's stories forks. One can look in greater detail at the replacements that the characters effect, not in their unwilled pursuit of a narrative, but in their conscious choice to avoid transgression, that is, to contain or circumvent the diffuse energies of sex. Or one can inspect the characters' actions as performance, with a view to discovering the ways their behavior dramatizes the undramatic material in the stories. We will follow both paths a little distance, knowing that farther away they will inevitably meet. What especially intrigued Tolstoy the writer about sex was that it was in two senses public. First, it was a form of commerce, a transaction that involved the potentially promiscuous possession and rejection of an ever-replaceable object of desire. And because it could be performed with a succession of people, it led, in his world of writing, to a thematic of circulation. Second, sex was public because it was performed not only with someone but before someone.[15]

To turn first to the operations of substitution and exchange: in all three stories the protagonists alter the venue of their activities in order to defuse a sexual crisis. Irtenev journeys to the Crimea with his wife. Kasatsky enters a monastery, then changes monasteries, isolates himself in a hut, and finally takes to the road. Pozdnyshev and his wife busy themselves with the transit from city to country and back again.

Specific to each tale are other displacements. In "The Devil," sex and economy are closely bound together. Irtenev engages in sex "for health's sake" and makes it a corner of his life as landowner, to be managed in the same way as any business on the estate. His passion for sex with Stepanida alternates with this enthusiasm for farm management. In the final scene he sees Stepanida on a site associated with the estate's economy, the floor of the threshing barn. On two of his three abortive journeys to meetings with Stepanida he is recalled by estate matters. Furthermore, sex is not only woven into the economic fabric but has its own financial dimension. Irtenev hesitates to become indebted to his wife when he needs cash to salvage the estate; he pays off Stepanida, and is satisfied that "money for sex" adequately disposes of the sex. Finally, the story distantly hints that Irtenev's father may have had a liaison with the widow Esipova for which the family is still paying. Sexuality has its own economy, despite Irtenev's insistence to himself that it is otherwise, Stepanida, moreover, is interested in that economy.

Под Троицын день Лиза решила, что надо сделать хорошую очистку дома, которой не делали со Святой, и позвала в помощь прислуге двух поденных баб, чтоб вымыть полы, окна, и выбить мебель и ковры, и надеть чехлы. С раннего утра пришли бабы, поставили чугуны воды и принялись за работу. Одна из двух баб была Степанида, которая только что отняла своего мальчика и напросилась через конторщика, к которому она бегала теперь, в поломойки. Ей хотелось хорошенько рассмотреть новую барыню. . . . Об барине она вовсе и не думала. «У него теперь жена есть,— думала она.—А лестна посмотреть барыню, ее заведенье, хорошо, говорят, убрано.»

Just before Trinity, Liza decided that it was necessary to have a thorough house cleaning, which had not been done since Easter, and she sent for two women to work by the day and help the servants wash the floors and windows, beat the furniture and rugs, and put on the slipcovers. They came first thing in the morning, put the cast-iron kettles of water on the fire, and set to work. One of the two women was Stepanida, who had just weaned her boy and had asked through the office clerk, whom she was now chasing after, for the job of washing the floors. She wanted to have a good look at the new mistress. . . . About the master she didn't think at all. "Now he has a wife," she thought. "It would be nice to see the mistress and her establishment. They say things are arranged well."[16]

And just before the story ends, Irtenev reaches the economic success that the beginning had predicted for him, so that the moment of financial achievement coincides with a sexual catastrophe. At this point it becomes clear that sex has been in no way weakened through its dispersal into the economy Irtenev has instituted on his estate. Indeed, because sex has been invested in a system of circulations, it now appears everywhere. Irtenev sees Stepanida outside the church; she is transferred to the house staff; on Trinity Sunday she dances in front of the manor house. Ultimately, what both carries Irtenev near to Stepanida and recalls him from her is as much the life of the estate as it is his own passion.[17]

In "Father Sergius," Kasatsky, like Irtenev, sees woman as a means to an end. The goal, in Kasatsky's case, is not personal health but a successful career. He courts Countess Mèri Korotkova because marriage will bring advancement, but soon discovers that his place as lover has been anticipated by the tsar, whom he cannot kill. As we saw, rather than participate in circulating Mèri's body among men (which would have meant that Kasatsky, who wishes always to be first, would have had to accept second place, behind Nicholas), Kasatsky removes his own body from circulation. The irony of Kasatsky's position, of course, is that he fails to perceive the equation between his course and Mèri's: she was elevated through a sexual relationship, and he wishes the same for himself. Just as Irtenev's did, Kasatsky's effort to curtail sex results in its redistribution rather than its eradication. As confessor in a monastery, he is brought into private contact with women far more than he would have been in a worldly marriage. Or, to look at the paradox differently, while Kasatsky tries to remove himself from situations in which he could again be hurt by another's sexuality, in essence he does the opposite. By adopting chastity Kasatsky dooms himself to repeating the painful experience he had had with Mèri, that is to say, realizing that sex belongs to the "other" and excludes him. Self-exiled, as it were, beyond the pleasure principle, he rehearses his misfortune over and over again. When he succumbs to sexual temptation, it is with a near-Mèri named Marya.

Pozdnyshev differs from the other two heroes, in good measure because of the autobiographical form of "The Kreutzer Sonata." There is a schism between Pozdnyshev's narrating and narrated selves. The married, jealous Pozdnyshev reflects little; it is Pozdnyshev the narrator who is responsible for the long philippics against women, sex, marriage, and children. Thus Pozdnyshev comes to use language to replace his miserable experience. As unstoppable commentary, the narration flows over and surrounds the unhappy event of his marriage, reducing it, managing it, substituting for it a didactic and generalizing discourse. But just as Kasatsky fixed and institutionalized the experience of chastity through his choice of profession, so Pozdnyshev does not dissipate, but prolongs, his passion by describing it. The emotions of his marriage appear redivivi for recirculation in his discourse. The acts of containment that the protagonists of these stories prefer—economy, career choice, and language—simply provide alternate routes for the migration of sexuality. Confession is also used to displace sex, and just as unsuccessfully. Irtenev speaks to his uncle, Kasatsky to a novice and then to Praskovya Mikhailovna, his cousin. Pozdnyshev addresses the train audience. (Pozdnyshev's face is never distinctly visible to his interlocutors, since he delivers his tirade at night. This darkness is also suggestive of the confessional.) Kasatsky's case is the most interesting. His confession to the novice does not achieve its purpose. But although Praskovya Mikhailovna does not understand his confession, this time Kasatsky succeeds in releasing himself from sexual desire. It is as if sex were not damaged by discourse but carried by it, with the result that the communicativity of sex ceases when communication itself fails. While still in the monastery, furthermore, Kasatsky reverses roles and acts as confessor for others. To be the confessor is to possess private knowledge which one does not disclose—it is to become the object of desire. Through the confessional, then, Kasatsky tries to make himself into Countess Mèri, or perhaps any woman. If he is in her place as an object of multiple desires, he himself is secure. In fact, though, Kasatsky's meetings with female admirers have the reverse effect, threatening to become assignations.

The idea of confession provides a transition to the second object of Tolstoy's interest in sex: its performative aspect. Sex is not only a form of commerce but a kind of theater.[18] Similarly, while the confession substitutes for sex, it is also like it in being an exposure of self to another. Tolstoy suggests that in the moment of revelation the self divides, becoming simultaneously a perceiving and a perceived self. In all three stories involving sex/confession, one would expect to find this schism within the "actor" self. In "The Devil" the self's fissure is realized metaphorically at the moment of Stepanida's entry into the Irtenev mansion as a housegirl. Hitherto Irtenev had managed to keep his affair outside, or "there," and his marriage inside the home, or "here." But the liminality of the house entrance figures a threshold of the self, and Irtenev is forced to be two persons, husband and amorous seigneur, on the same figural territory.[19] In "Father Sergius," Kasatsky is faced with a novelistically conventional choice between the red and the black and chooses the latter. He succeeds famously for a while, then, following his sexual lapse with Marya, declines into poverty and vagrancy. The trajectory of his career can be followed in the successive names he bears: Kasatsky—Sergius—Father Sergius—Sergius—Kasatsky—until at the end he is anonymous. The names change, but the bearer remains the same, split between the outward appellation and a troubled self.[20] The story ends by leaving Kasatsky without a passport: if he possesses no name, there can be no discrepancy between the sense of a name and who he is.

Pozdnyshev's schizophrenia lies in the autobiographical split discussed above.[21] Tolstoy makes explicit reference to the theater of schizophrenia by having the protagonist echo his most famous ancestor in the line of jealous spouses, Othello.

> Я Позднышев, тот, с которым случился тот критический эпизод...

> I am that Pozdnyshev, who was involved in that critical episode.[22]

Or, as Shakespeare has it, "That's he that was Othello. Here I am" (*Othello*, Act 5, scene 2, line 284).

All three stories thus chronicle the avoidance of event through a series of displacements. They also describe a fissure of the self induced by sex, a split which cannot be escaped through the strategies of displacement but is in fact reconstituted through them. The very titles of the three stories reflect displacements: desire is caused by music, the careerist is a holy father, woman is the devil.[23]

In harmony with his emphasis on the theatricality of sex, Tolstoy assigns a certain dramatic rhetoric to each of his stories. These lend artistic unity to the works and deserve detailed treatment, but here can only be mentioned briefly. "The Kreutzer Sonata" is obviously built on the spoken word. "The Devil" borrows from another aspect of the theater: its visuality. The story is permeated with references to the glance, to gazes, to darkness and day, to what can and cannot be hidden from view, to Irtenev's shortsightedness and propensity for losing his glasses (that is, his vision), especially during his encounters with Stepanida.[24] "Father Sergius" reenacts the fluctuations of dramatic time: intense, pivotal scenes of short duration are narrated in elaborate detail, so that the time of storytelling approximates, as it does on the stage, the duration of the action. These moments are punctuated by frequent summaries that span enormous lapses of time.[25]

The rhythms of sight, speech, and time unify the stories, but also remind one of the ever-present sexual theme, since each serves to answer a question for the hero: how can the sexual crisis be done away with? Irtenev avoids the gaze of others; Pozdnyshev incorporates his crisis into language; Kasatsky hopes that with the passage of time his sexual humiliation will be forgotten, for others will not survive to remember. (Ironically enough, Nicholas does not survive to know how Kasatsky has avenged himself. Shortly before he sleeps with Marya, Kasatsky muses about his reputation as a miracle worker.

В газетах пишут, государь знает.

They are writing about [my healing powers] in the newspapers; the emperor knows of it.[26]

But the emperor of this passage is not Nicholas, as can readily be determined if one tallies up the years that have passed since the earliest possible opening date of the story.)

If there is an aspect of sex that unites the two features that drew Tolstoy's attention—commerce and performance, exchange and theatricality—it would be repetition. Tolstoy's stories emphasize the fact that desire has the rhythm of repetition; it comes, goes, and returns, and the condition of its departure is always the same sexual act. Sexual desire is like the repetition, night after night, of a stage performance, and simultaneously like the repetitive uses to which money or words are put. The substitutions initiated by characters, and by the narrative, are all essays in repetition, and the stories are founded on this principle. Kasatsky repeats his military career as a monk. He has merely substituted the clerical hierarchy for a lay one and progresses through the churchly *tabula rangov* as quickly as he would have moved up a worldly ladder. He also duplicates a woman's body with his own. He seeks in the repetitiousness of ritual an escape from sex. Finally, his moment of temptation with Makovkina repeats in his episode with Marya, and he repeats his search for an axe.[27] Pozdnyshev repeats his sexual misfortunes through storytelling; even the milieu is repeated. Pozdnyshev recounts to fellow train travelers the anguish he felt on his own train trip back to surprise his wife. His sense of isolation and lack of a sympathetic audience are repeated in the train ride of the story's outer frame. Pozdnyshev's audience is soon reduced to the narrator, who offers little comment on the tale he hears. Irtenev three times is on the verge of renewing his affair with Stepanida, and it is his failure each time to do so that allows the possibility of the incident repeating. Furthermore, each story underscores the repetitiveness of human life and the succession of generations. Kasatsky looks on the tsar as his father and tries to emulate him. Irtenev wants to manage the estate as his grandfather did, be as careful with his sexual activities as were both his grandfather and his father, and reproduce himself in a family (in fact his family repeats; he has two children by two women). Of all Tolstoy's characters, Pozdnyshev is concerned most with the reproductive side of sex; his speeches on bearing and raising children take up nearly half his discourse. Pozdnyshev's chief aversion to childbearing is that the repetition of a human being reminds him that the sexual act will be repeated by new generations.[28] Tolstoy's three stories await a reading as essays on patriarchy and repetition.

To conclude, in "Father Sergius," "The Kreutzer Sonata," and "The Devil" Tolstoy takes a narrative situation that presents a rather infertile semiological field. What can be said about a man's sexuality when the man can do what he wants? The author makes each story into an experimental answer to his narrative dilemma. In each, first, the central characters struggle to erect moral barriers that they can then knock down. That is, they attempt to create the condition for narrative. Second, the heroes try to *avoid* knocking down the barriers of their own making, through an elaborate strategy of replacements and containments.

And, third, the story itself comes to include and reduplicate many of the aspects of the sexual act which so disgusts the protagonists. It produces rituals of self-exposure and makes repetition a founding principle of the narrative.

These three "actions" become Tolstoy's subject in "Father Sergius," "The Kreutzer Sonata," and "The Devil." In a sense he has made narrative out of (1) the effort to make narrative, (2) the actions carried out in an effort to avoid action, and (3) the narrative's mimesis of the taboo subject.[29] The consequences of these moves are radical enough to shake the foundations of storytelling. Tolstoy left "The Devil" unfinished; like a Nabokovian plot, it has a dual ending. "The Kreutzer Sonata" borrows from the literature of confession, but the protagonist is indistinctly seen, and his audience leaves; revelation has become isolation and mystery. "Father Sergius" models itself on many of the conventions of the *zhitie,* but at the moment Kasatsky has sex the genre is abandoned, and the holy father's bodily disappearance from the monastery becomes a travesty of the Resurrection and the Assumption. All three stories refuse a traditional closure and define a narrative space as fresh and interesting as the sexual politics that permits it is morbidly narrow.

NOTES

This paper is based on a draft first presented at the annual meeting of the Philological Association of the Pacific Coast, which convened at the University of California, Santa Cruz, in November 1985. During January and February 1986, I read a longer draft before the faculty and graduate students of the Slavic departments at Columbia University and UCLA, and the Russian departments at Dartmouth College and Wesleyan University. The helpful comments of these discerning audiences have enriched this paper in countless ways.

1. "Nineteenth-century Realism may ascribe evolution to some personae [heroes] and immutability, once again, to others. . . . Thus in the text of *War and Peace,* Nikolai Rostov changes perhaps no less than Andrei Bolkonsky or Pierre Bezukhov. But these changes do not constitute evolution: the immobile structure of the persona on the level of the general artistic conception of the novel corresponds to the mobile text." (J. M. Lotman, *Struktura khudožestvennogo teksta* [Providence, 1971], p. 315; English trans., by Gail Lenhoff and Ronald Vroon, *The Struc-*

ture of the Artistic Text [Ann Arbor, 1977], p. 260. I have altered the orthography of the translated Russian names.)

2. Compare Bakhtin's theory that the novel is the genre that can absorb all genres. Erich Auerbach's chapters in *Mimesis* on nineteenth-century realism are influenced by a reader's response to the intuitive equation of textual complexity with determinism.

3. In these twin tendencies we see the origins of the novel tradition in Protestantism and the bourgeois ascendancy, respectively.

4. The conscious puppetry in which the narrator of *Vanity Fair* engages only reinforces the determinism of event. Though the narrator's playful and assertive voice harks back to the Enlightenment, he does not manipulate writing conventions the way a Diderot or Sterne does. Without the narrator's periodic references to the fictionality of his universe, *Vanity Fair* would fit snugly into its period. With the addition of the Thackerayan voice, the novel becomes a gloss on the works of such contemporaries as Dickens, whose fictional universes were closely held by the author to a determinist principle.

5. The edition used throughout this chapter is *SS*. Translations are my own unless otherwise noted.

6. As late as 1883, in "What I Believe," Tolstoy was still advocating marriage as the appropriate outlet for sexual drives, a position he refutes in these stories, begun five years later.

7. Kasatsky's attempt to rid himself of lust through a fiery purgatory recalls an image realized by the "lustful" in Dante's *Purgatorio*. It finds its more immediate echo in Avvakum, who "cools" his passion for a female parishioner through a similar oxymoronic self-punishment (burning his hand). Tolstoy's parody of the *zhitie* derives details and some certain aspects of generic identity from Avvakum's "anti-*zhitie*" confession.

8. Kasatsky's adopted name has its own ironic ring. His obvious namesake is Sergei of Radonezh, whose two chief achievements, paradoxically enough, were to lead the hesychastic reform, a contemplative movement, and to preside as tutelary spirit over the gathering of Dmitri Donskoi's liberation armies. Kasatsky finds himself in the same ambiguous position. Each stage of his retreat from society is a step toward it (a general comes to see him in the monastery). As the most public of hermits, he is unable to escape the world's standards of judgment.

9. *SS* 12:264–65. I have based the English translation on that of Aylmer Maude, published in *The Kreutzer Sonata, The Devil, and Other Tales by Leo Tolstoy* (Oxford, 1940).

10. *SS* 12:231. My translation is based on the Maude.

11. *SS* 12:255. My translation closely follows the Maude.

12. The tic in Pozdnyshev's speech is the "percentage," which he uses to convince listeners of the universality of his position before enlightenment. The percentages belong to the period of Pozdnyshev's self-labeled spiritual ignorance. His newfound belief that sex is wrong puts

him in a tiny minority—a place of distinct notoriety, as he fancies it. I have listed below fewer than half the percentages Pozdnyshev invokes.

Я мучался, как 0,99 наших мальчиков. (*SS* 12:144)
Дело в том, что со мной, да и с 0,9, если не больше, не только нашего сословия, но всех, даже крестьян . . . (*SS* 12:145)
Я еще не знал тогда, что 0,99 супружеств живут в таком же аду. (*SS* 12:175)
Все это не произвело на меня и 0,01 того впечатления, которое произвело первое. (*SS* 12:194)

I was in torment, like 99% of our youth.
The thing is that to me, as to nine-tenths, if not more, not only of our own class, but everyone, including the peasants . . .
I still did not know then that 99% of married couples live in the same hell.
All this failed to produce on me even one percent of the impression that the first piece had produced.

13. Goncharov's *Oblomov* is perhaps the model for Tolstoy. The novel turns received wisdom about narrative on its head. Oblomov the man chooses sloth over *sueta,* and for much of the book, including the entire first section, the narrative makes the same choice. Other identities between Oblomov's ethic and the manner of narration are detailed by Kenneth Harper in "Under the Influence of Oblomov," in *From Los Angeles to Kiev: Papers on the Occasion of the Ninth International Congress of Slavists, Kiev, September, 1983* (Columbus, 1983), pp. 105–18.

14. "The Devil" garbs in aesthetic clothes Tolstoy's tortured experience with the peasant Aksinya on his own estate. "Father Sergius," mutatis mutandis, would stand well as Tolstoy's own *zhitie*—his renunciation of "world" (writing), and his fame at Yasnaya Polyana from the 1880s onward, when he played the role of holy elder. The tale also possesses a disturbing predictive force. Tolstoy wrote of Kasatsky's flight from the monastery and search for anonymity long before attempting much the same in 1910.

If Gorky's reminiscences are faithful, Tolstoy talked incessantly of sex. He was also something of a social Darwinist and, like the narrator of "The Devil," expressed himself on the contrast between an aristocracy of delicate health (Liza's proneness to miscarriage) and a robust peasant stock (Stepanida's strong physique). Gorky records Tolstoy's musing about a peasant woman they observed:

Вот такими кариатидами и поддерживалось все это великолепие и сумасбродство. Не только работой мужиков и баб, не только оброком, а в чистом смысле кровью народа. Если бы дворянство время от времени не спаривалось с такими вот лошадями [*sic*], оно уже давно бы умерло.

It is with caryatids like these that all this magnificence and extravagant behavior has been sustained. Not only with the labor of peasant men and women, or the quitrent, but literally with the blood of the people. If the nobility had not from time to time mated with such horses, it would have perished long ago. (Maksim Gor'kij, "Lev Tolstoj," in *Polnoe sobranie sočinenij*, vol. 16 [Moscow, 1973], p. 270).

In "What Is Art?" Tolstoy noted a fact which seems to have been rediscovered within the last ten years in Anglo-American and French criticism:

От Боккаччио до Марселя Прево все романы, поэмы, стихотворения передают непременно чувства половой любви в разных ее видах. Прелюбодеяние есть не только любимая, но и единственная тема всех романов. Спектакль—не спектакль, если в нем под каким-нибудь предлогом не появляются оголенные сверху или снизу женщины. Романсы, песни—это все выражение похоти в разных степенях опоэтизирования.

From Boccaccio to Marcel Prévost, all novels and poems directly convey the feelings of sexual love in its various forms. Adultery is not only the favorite but the only theme of all novels. A theatrical performance is not a performance, unless under some pretext there appear in it women who are naked above or below. Romances, songs—these are all the expression of lust in various degrees of poeticization. ("Čto takoe iskusstvo?" *SS* 15:112)

15. One wonders too if the greater exposure Tolstoy acquired as a writer was not interpreted by him as a sexual exposure, given that his ambivalence about sex increased concomitantly with his fame. Tolstoy appears to have allowed literary renown and the necessary renown of sex to work as metaphors for each other. His desire to destroy his life's work in fiction and Pozdnyshev's wish that by refusing to procreate man would give himself the opportunity for "purification before extinction" may have been the same thing, and yet for all their equivalence they are no more fathomable taken together than taken separately.

16. *SS* 12:246. My translation is based on the Maude.

17. Michel Foucault's history of sexuality describes the development of a discourse about sex and the ends to which this discourse was put. The sections entitled "Scientia Sexualis" and "The Deployment of Sexuality" address precisely the issues that intrigued Tolstoy, particularly the relationship of sex to economy, exchange, and the discipline of the confession. Foucault, furthermore, sees the concerns of Tolstoy as a class-specific trait:

The most rigorous techniques were formed and, more particularly, applied first, with the greatest intensity, in the economically privileged and politically dominant classes. The direction of consciences, self-examination, the entire long elaboration of the transgressions of the flesh, and the scrupulous detection of concupiscence were all subtle procedures that could only have been accessible to small groups of people. (Michel Foucault, *The History of Sexuality.* Vol. 1: *An Introduction,* trans. Robert Hurley [New York, 1980], p. 120)

Foucault would have insisted that Tolstoy's initial supposition of a "permissive society" is itself symptomatic of the reverse: a class that patrols itself for promiscuity is not permissive. Tolstoy's three male heroes are all brought to half-madness in their relationships with women. They also reach a logical *aporia* in their search for a key to understanding: woman is "the devil." The irrationality of his men and the absurdity of their conclusions about women suggest that with a slight shrug of the shoulders Tolstoy might have shifted the burden of his thought toward feminism. As Mary Poovey writes, in an essay on Jane Austen: "The fundamental assumption of romantic love— and the reason it is so compatible with bourgeois society—is that the personal can be kept separate from the social, that one's 'self' can be fulfilled in spite of—and in isolation from—demands of the marketplace" (Mary Poovey, "*Persuasion* and the Promises of Love," in *The Representation of Women in Fiction,* ed. Carolyn Heilbrun and Margaret R. Higonnet [Baltimore, 1983], p. 172). It is this premise that Tolstoy refuses to accept.

18. See n. 14 above. In "What Is Art?" Tolstoy refers frequently to theatrical performances. Tolstoy especially loved the theater because it afforded him the opportunity to watch the audience. See chaps. 13 and 14 of "What Is Art?"

19. Compare Irtenev's contrast between the house and the soul:

Все было так хорошо, радостно, чисто в доме, а в душе его было грязно, мерзко, ужасно.

Everything was so good, joyful, and clear in the house, while in his soul it was dirty, despicable, and horrible. (*SS* 12:263)

20. Twice Kasatsky's names are used together by the same person, as if Tolstoy were suggesting that with sufficient invocation the real self could be coaxed to the surface. Makovkina, out to seduce him at any cost, uses a nonexistent name and fails:

«Отец Сергий! Отец Сергий! Так ведь вас звать?»
«—Отец Сергий! Отец Сергий! Сергей Дмитрич. Князь Касатский!»

"Father Sergius! Father Sergius! Is that what one should call you?"
"Father Sergius! Father Sergius! Sergey Dmitrich. Prince Kasatsky!"
(*SS* 12:387, 388).

Praskovya Mikhailovna is more successful.

«—Да не может быть! Степа! Сергий! Отец Сергий.»
«—Да, он самый,—тихо проговорил Сергий. —Только не Сергий, не отец Сергий, а великий грешник Степан Касатский, погибший, великий грешник.»

"It can't be! Styopa! Sergius! Father Sergius."
"Yes, it is I," Sergei said quietly. "Only not Sergius or Father Sergius, but the great sinner Stepan Kasatsky, a great and lost sinner." (*SS* 12:405)

She rejects all these names, however, and settles on Stiva, a childhood nickname whose use preceded the fissure in Kasatsky's self.

21. Like Kasatsky after the adoption of vows, Pozdnyshev seeks renown. Notoriety of any kind would be a sign that the hero had crossed some boundary. The search of Kasatsky and Pozdnyshev for renown is a narrative's search for transgression. But Pozdnyshev is unknown, the antipode of Kasatsky, who wins a certain fame. Pozdnyshev's speech *is* his career. Like Dostoevsky's Underground Man, Pozdnyshev uses an extended monologue to draw attention to himself.

22. *SS* 12:131.

23. Actually, in each story, woman becomes the devil.

«—Что ты?—сказал он. —Марья. Ты дьявол. («Отец Сергий»)
«Да нет никакого Бога. Есть дьявол. И это она. Он овладел мной . . . Дьявол, да, дьявол.» («Дьявол»)
«Тоже попалась такая женщина, что распутевая. И пошла чертить.» («Крейцерова соната»)

"What are you?" he asked. "Marya. You are a devil." ("Father Sergius")
"There is no God. There is the devil. And it is she. He has mastered me. . . . The devil, yes, the devil." ("The Devil")
"Again it was a case of such a woman. A dissolute sort. And she started playing the devil." ("The Kreutzer Sonata") (*SS* 12:401, 272, 137)

It is a mark of the difficulty the men have in staging a "fall" that they cease to find human agency at work in their own actions or the actions of women.

For a discussion of various substitute representations of women, see the section "Myths" in Simone de Beauvoir's *The Second Sex*, trans. H. M. Parshley (New York, 1968), pp. 139–203.

24. Compare Pierre Bezukhov's myopia, an emblem of his failure to see past either the superficial lures of the dissipated Hélène Kuragina or the arcane fatuities of Masonry. Some of the many references to eyes and glances follow. When Irtenev goes to his first rendezvous with Stepanida:

Он острекался и, потеряв с носу пенсне, вбежал на противоположный бугор.

He was stung by the nettles and, losing his pince-nez from his nose, ran up the slope opposite him. (*SS* 12:232)

When Irtenev first courts Liza:

Духовно же он ничего не знал про нее, а только видел эти глаза. И эти глаза, казалось, говорили ему все, что ему нужно было знать.

He knew nothing about her spiritually, but only saw those eyes. And those eyes, it seemed, were saying to him everything that he needed to know. (*SS* 12:239)

When Irtenev's mother tells him that Stepanida has a child:

Марья Павловна хотела рассказать это незаметно, но ей самой сделалось стыдно, когда она увидала краску на лице сына и его нервные снимание, пощелкивание и надевание пенсне и поспешное закуриванье папиросы.

Marya Pavlovna wanted to say this in an inconspicuous fashion, but she herself became embarrassed when she saw the color on her son's face and saw him nervously removing, tapping, and replacing his pince-nez and hurriedly lighting a cigarette. (*SS* 12:241)

When Irtenev meets Stepanida in the house:

«Да что же я смотрю,»—сказал он себе, опуская глаза, чтоб не видать ее . . . но он не успел пройти пяти шагов, как, сам не зная как и по чьему приказу, опять оглянулся, чтобы еще раз увидать ее. Она заходила за угол и в то же мгновение тоже оглянулась на него.

"What do I see?" he asked himself, lowering his eyes so that he would not see her . . . but he had not gone five steps when, without knowing himself how and at whose command, he again looked around so that he might see her again. She was disappearing around the corner and at that very instant glanced at him too. (*SS* 12:247)

When the steward Vasily Nikolaich reassures Irtenev that he need not send Stepanida's family away:

А кто же теперь про вас скажет худое? Ведь вы в виду.

So who is going to say anything bad about you now? You're in plain sight. (*SS* 12:255)

25. For example:

Отец Сергий жил шестой год в затворе.

Father Sergius was living his sixth year in isolation. (*SS* 12:382)

В затворе прожил отец Сергий еще семь лет.

Father Sergius spent another seven years in isolation. (*SS* 12:391)

26. *SS* 12:372–73.

27. Simone de Beauvoir's discussion of the endless frustration of sexual possession bears mention here, for it touches on the problem of repetition:

> He takes great pride in his sexuality only in so far as it is a means of appropriating the Other—and this dream of possession ends only in frustration. In authentic possession the other is abolished as such, it is consumed and destroyed: only the Sultan in *The Arabian Nights* has the power to cut off each mistress's head when dawn has come to take her from his couch. Woman survives man's embraces, and in that very fact she escapes him; as soon as he loosens his arms, his prey becomes again a stranger to him; there she lies, new, intact, ready to be possessed by a new lover in as ephemeral a manner. (*The Second Sex*, p. 163)

28. Pozdnyshev notes this vicious rhythm:

> Я не замечал тогда, что периоды злобы возникали во мне совершенно правильно и равномерно, соответственно периодам того, что мы называли любовью. Период любви—период злобы; энергический период любви—длинный период злобы, более слабое проявление любви—короткий период злобы.

> I didn't notice then that the intervals of animosity would rise up in me in a regular and uniform way, corresponding to the intervals of what we called "love." An interval of love, then one of animosity. An energetic interval of love, then a long interval of animosity; a weaker manifestation of love, then a shorter interval of animosity. (*SS* 12:174)

29. Foucault writes: "The 'economy' of discourses—their intrinsic technology, the necessities of their operation, the tactics they employ, the effects of power which underlie them and which they transmit—this, and not a system of representations, is what determines the essential features of what they have to say" (*The History of Sexuality*, 1:68–69).

Contributors

Joan Delaney Grossman is Professor of Russian Literature, University of California, Berkeley. Her most recent book is *Valery Bryusov and the Riddle of Russian Decadence* (1985).

Irina Gutkin studied Russian history at Moscow State University and holds an M.A. degree in Russian literature from Columbia University. She is currently writing a doctoral dissertation at the University of California, Berkeley, on the problem of literary evolution and literary consciousness in the revolutionary epoch, encompassing several phases of Russian modernism, from symbolism to socialist realism.

John Kopper is Assistant Professor of Russian and Comparative Literature, Dartmouth College. He is the author of articles on Nabokov, Belyi, Aleshkovsky, Kafka, and Shakespeare, and is currently writing a book on family structure in the modernist novel.

Hugh McLean is Professor of Russian Literature, University of California, Berkeley. He is the author of *Nikolai Leskov: The Man and His Art* (1977).

Ruth Rischin, Ph.D. candidate in Slavic, University of California, Berkeley, is writing her dissertation on the works of Semyon Yushkevich (1867–1927). She is also preparing for publication the complete poetry of Dovid Knout (1900–1955), as well as an annotated edition of his letters from Toulouse and Paris (1941–1943).

Andrew Wachtel received his graduate training in Slavic at the University of California, Berkeley. From 1985 to 1988 he was a

Junior Fellow, Society of Fellows, Harvard, and he is now Assistant Professor of Slavic Languages and Literatures, Stanford University.

John Weeks, Assistant Professor of Russian Language and Literature, Amherst College, is working on a study of the *yurodivye* or "holy fools" in Russian literature.

Index

Compositor: G & S Typesetters, Inc.
Text: 10/12 Sabon
Display: Sabon
Printer: Braun-Brumfield, Inc.
Binder: Braun-Brumfield, Inc.